WE, THE OPPRESSORS

WE, THE OPPRESSORS

Dr JACK DAVY

QUERCUS

First published in Great Britain in 2022 by

QUERCUS

Quercus Editions Ltd
Carmelite House
50 Victoria Embankment
London EC4Y 0DZ

An Hachette UK company

A CIP catalogue record for this book is available
from the British Library.

HB ISBN 978 1 52941 392 2
TPB ISBN 978 1 52941 393 9
Ebook ISBN 978 1 52941 394 6

10 9 8 7 6 5 4 3 2 1

Typeset by CC Book Production
Printed and bound in Great Britain by Clays Ltd, Elcograf S.p.A.

Papers used by Quercus are from well-managed forests and other responsible sources.

To Nat, good luck

A man must die; and whether he died of a miserable old age in his own country, or prematurely of damp in the bottom of a foreign mine, was surely of little consequence, provided that by a change in his mode of life he benefited the British Empire.

– John Galsworthy, *A Man of Property*

CONTENTS

INTRODUCTION

We do not think of ourselves as oppressive. Very few people are, at least deliberately. Of course, there are times when we lose our temper and snap; we might put pressure on people to do what we want, and we can be rude to family, friends, neighbours and service providers. We can say things behind someone's back or online that we'd never say to a person's face. And when we do there is a tendency, a desire, to excuse this behaviour – it's not us, it's our situation, our emotion, we are tired, or under pressure. It wasn't us. We didn't mean it. And time will pass. They'll get over it.

Those of us in Western Europe or North America, until recently for the most part insulated from catastrophic natural disaster or violent political upheaval, see news about tragedies far away and think that it doesn't apply to us, that we are not responsible for these things. We get up, we go to work, we drive our cars and eat our food and read our books. We rarely think too hard about the choices we've made in our lives, the systems which have granted these choices to us, nor about the reality that for literally billions of people in the world, the trappings of this lifestyle we so take for granted are precious, rare and too often out of reach. And we rarely think about how we, and our histories, nations and belief systems, have contributed to the world being unbalanced in this way, about the privilege of our lives compared with others, how we might choose to change things, or why we should. It's easier to turn the page, to change the channel, and to focus on anxieties closer to home and more immediate.

We think of oppressors as bad people: the people we read about or see on television; the violent and corrupt and racist and cruel people we learn about in histories of other countries and other people and places. Oppressors are cruel and deny people their rights; they imprison, torture and murder people, and they do it for their own gain. They steal and cheat and kill. Maybe they enjoy it. We are not like them. Our families are not like them. Except that, without meaning to or realizing it, we often are.

We are by and large not bad people – this book is not suggesting that we are. But we all, in complicated, historical ways, participate in systems which cause oppression and hurt, whether we recognize it or not. These systems are rooted in our histories, in our laws and in our behaviour, both the things we do and the things we tolerate. Even in developed democratic countries like Britain and the United States, with complex and long-established representative processes and codified legal systems, public education and social safety nets, our societies are designed, from top to bottom, to oppress some people for the benefit of others. And this has happened not, or at least not just, through the self-interest, corruption and cruelty of some – though that inevitably plays a part – but because we all want it to work that way. The reason we do so is that the alternative – what we fear will happen if we do not oppress, and accept oppression in turn – can be terrifying.

I have spent my career trying to understand oppression – the processes by which one set of people dominate and control others for their own benefit. My expertise is in the European colonization of the Americas, which took the form of a rolling genocide enacted by many tens of thousands of people, very few of whom thought of themselves as bad people, pursued over generations and stretching far beyond famous military encounters like the Battle of the Greasy Grass (known to its losers as Little Big Horn), as we will find out in Chapter Six. It reached into every aspect of life for the oppressed, disrupting their economic, social, medical, cultural and political lives beyond the point that they were able to resist or organize against the invading settlers. It stretched from those first violent encounters in the Caribbean when Columbus raped and slaved his way into the 'New' World, right up to modern media like the *Twilight* series, which co-opts serious and sacred traditional stories into fantasies of sparkly vampires and sexy wolf boys, all masking the reality of endemic social problems directly stemming from their violent history, none of which are more terrible than the frequency with which

Native women and girls die violently and disappear, to widespread official disinterest.*

I have worked with Native American communities throughout my academic career, and have seen the lasting effects that this ancestral experience of oppression has had and continues to have on their families, relationships and sense of identity. I have in the course of this work come to confront some of my own behaviour as oppressive and to more generally recognize the broader responsibility within nations and institutions for trajectories of oppression, historic and recent. To illustrate this acknowledgement, this book selects historical case studies, some drawn from my own research, and some from the work and experiences of others, to create a structured narrative which seeks to explain not only how oppression operates, but also the way it reverberates through history. These case studies come from around the world and across the last century and a half, but with a stronger focus on Europe and North America, whose vast economic, military and colonial power has shaped and continues to shape, and perhaps warp, world history.

Oppression itself isn't a process that is difficult to understand; it's a state in which one person or group uses any method at their disposal to restrict the freedom of another in order to extract something from them. Where it gets more nuanced is to

---

* For an example of how severe and widespread this problem is, a good resource is the Canadian National Inquiry into Missing and Murdered Indigenous Women and Girls: see Reclaiming Power and Place: The Final Report of the National Inquiry into Missing and Murdered Indigenous Woman and Girls. Accessed online at https://www.mmiwg-ffada.ca/final-report/.

recognize that most oppression happens within systems which continue, facilitate and justify it via the contributions of large numbers of well-meaning people, those who do not seem bad and do not think of themselves as bad or oppressive. Though these systems are directed by leaders and institutions who make individual decisions, they are established and maintained by networks of millions of ordinary people, working together to enforce the systems which oppress for their own gain, and however we might justify their existence, for the oppressed these systems are conspicuously and deliberately unjust, unfair and cruel.

In reading the histories this book contains, you must remember one thing above all others – these are people just like us. The Mexicans abandoned to horror on a desert island; the Venezuelan villagers burned in the streets below Fort Maracaibo; the Shuar who watched their children beheaded for profit; starving Chinese farmers dying on the roadsides; the Kenyans taken from their homes and tortured; the Native Americans forced to earn a living dancing in mockeries of their sacred regalia for tourists; the taxi driver beaten to death by the police in his Belfast home; African Americans dying uncared for in ghettos at the centres of the richest cities Earth has ever seen. All of them, every single one, was or is a person just like you: loving and loved, hoping and hoped for, connected to networks of care and affection, imperfect and determined to wish for a better world for their children.

Part of the historian's burden when writing of such things is to take centuries of horror, grief and cruelty and distil it into some format palatable to a reader, an account interesting enough to keep you on the page, but shorn of all but the blandest accounting for those overwhelming moments of loss, terror and betrayal which came for them at the hands of oppressive forces, against which there was little they could have done to resist. Narrative history loses so much of this emotion; it is a vast memory hole from which only flutters of information emerge, to be read and interpreted and reinterpreted by the generations which follow, and in which too often the individuals are submerged by the whole.

This book will discuss oppression by using these historical examples to illustrate the key components through which society creates and sustains oppressive systems, including economic, ecological, racial, gender-based and military oppression. Some of these stories are little known and even less well understood – they are the stories of people and places we do not think about very often, and rarely learn of in school. Others have played out right before our eyes over the last decade, stories we all know and on which we have opinions, and which are rooted in systems in which we all participate, and need to better understand. Together they illustrate the layers of systematic, often insidious oppression which make up the world today, and reflect the choices of people just like us to participate in them. Though oppression is as old as humanity itself, these historical examples are all relatively recent, designed to complement and build on one another to demonstrate how oppressive systems have developed. They focus on the complicity of societies in Britain and the United States which generally think of themselves as free, fair and good, and the effects that this complicity leads to.

Change can only occur when we are self-aware. It is only when we've learned about our own inherited and taught oppressions that we can try to take steps, small at first and growing in potency over time, to reduce the harmful impact that oppression has on others.

To do this requires fundamentally rethinking crucial aspects of our communities and ourselves – our own actions, both collective and individual, our own assumptions and our own histories – in ways that can be painful. It is tempting, when shown our complicity in things we did not comprehend, intend or understand, to look away, to pretend that those things are not happening, that they are not too bad, that we can minimize or justify the hurt and the pain which results, to say that it has nothing to do with us. But that is what we have done as a society for far too long – looking away is how those who exploit these systems of oppression for personal gain have been able to prosper and how those systems and the lies on which they are built have endured. Reading this book should teach you not to look away any more.

Chapter One

THE SAFETY OF OPPRESSION: THE KING OF CLIPPERTON ISLAND

The story begins at its end. On 18 July 1917, under a blazing sun, the American gunboat USS *Yorktown* came to anchor off Clipperton Island, a tiny speck of sand lost in a vast expanse of blue in the Pacific Ocean far to the west of Mexico. *Yorktown* was an armoured steel behemoth, an old, clumsy, coal-fired reserve warship pressed back into service with the United States Navy, nothing less than a brutalist statement of military power, the very name marking the moment of American independence from the old colonial authority. Her presence here demonstrated the reach of the technological and military strength of the United States, which had recently joined the First World War on the side of the Allies.

Yorktown was alert for enemy activity: German warships had crossed the Pacific during the war, and at the time of *Yorktown*'s arrival off Clipperton Island, the raider *Seeadler* was still active in the French colony of Tahiti, some 4,000 miles away, capturing and sinking American schooners. *Yorktown* therefore was tasked with patrolling this isolated corner of the war, protecting whalers and steamers and the pockets of imperial sovereignty which had come to dot the Pacific Ocean. As *Yorktown* approached the island, the lookout spotted a group on the beach, waving frantically. It comprised not the Mexican soldiers *Yorktown*'s captain expected to be stationed there, but four women and seven children. No one else was in sight.

These eleven people were all that had survived from the island's original population of more than forty, the remains of the brief and terrible reign of the King of Clipperton Island, and their story is the one with which this book starts, because it explains why society requires, even demands, oppression, and why we have shaped our world the way that it is, preferring strong leaders who can save us from those who would murder us at their own desires and whims.

To understand how oppression manifests in our societies, we have to think carefully about what that word means and how we use it. It comes from the Latin 'to be pressed against', but sometimes definitions have more value in how we use them than in where they come from. For a contemporary understanding of 'oppression', we need to explore another word: 'justice'. Justice requires that the outcome of a decision or event is fair. Oppression is a situation in which the outcome of a decision or event is unfair, and thus oppression is defined by justice – it is, we assume, the other side of the same coin. But this creates a problem: justice is subjective, and oppression personally felt. What one person defines as a just process or outcome is likely to be defined by someone else as unjust and oppressive.

To cope with this problem, academic interpretations of oppression are divided into subjective oppression – the personal oppression that we feel and internalize both in individual incidents of injustice and from widespread systematic processes of injustice, and objective oppression, which can be codified and understood by its specific relation to injustice as defined by law. The latter is easier to study as it can be bound within specific rules and interpreted by relation to the law, the codification of justice, which determines for us and by us what is just and unjust. A law, however, is only a reflection of the system which created it, not founded in any kind of universal constant, and our systems can be very unjust indeed. This book will focus on the liminal point at which subjective and objective oppression meet, and examine the ways in which oppression that seems objective and unjust in isolation can occur as part of systems within which we participate and from which we may profit, are by law subjective, and open to interpretation, debate and dismissal.

These compromises were brought into stark contrast for all of us in the spring of 2020, when the COVID-19 pandemic caused society to come to a screeching halt. All of those things which most of us had taken for granted for our whole lives – socializing, shopping, working and school – became impossible in the face of a threat we couldn't see and didn't know how to stop. It killed hundreds of thousands, severed family and friendship bonds, destroyed businesses and careers. Almost overnight the entire population, barring essential workers, found itself under a form of house arrest. Though most of us engaged in this process voluntarily, anxious to preserve life and stop the spread of the disease, emergency laws were passed which mandated these restrictions and closures for those less willing to accept them; laws which spread into almost all corners of public life, including – rather dramatically, and under significant protest in the UK – the British pub. The pub indeed was to become a touchstone of how bad the pandemic in Britain was. Whether and to what extent pubs were open became a method of directly measuring the severity of the government response and, consequently, of the pandemic itself.

We all felt *subjectively oppressed*. That is, we all felt the oppression of the situation bearing down on us individually, as we scrambled to manage our professional and personal relationships, attempted to shield elderly loved ones from the disease and watched weddings cancelled and birthdays pass largely unmarked. For many, mental health deteriorated as the social, personal and economic effects spiralled, leaving us all questioning when and whether life would return to some semblance of normal. But a more complicated question is to ask whether we were *objectively oppressed* – to ask ourselves whether these laws, so willingly obeyed by millions under the pandemic, constituted an injustice.

Some, particularly those of a libertarian bent, certainly thought so, and said as much on whatever platform would grant them a voice. Social media, as so often a bullhorn for our worst collective instincts as a society, amplified these anxieties. In some places, particularly the United States, these opinions found a ready audience and the lockdown conditions were broadly understood as unjust objective oppression, even by the president who was supposed to be enforcing them. This led to their incautious repeal in a way which resulted in subsequent waves of infections and death, until more than half a million Americans had lost their lives.

In Britain, despite an anti-lockdown campaign, these views were largely peripheral and generally ignored. Tens of millions of Britons willingly accepted this oppression, with all its subjective effects, in a collaborative effort to stave off the disease. This was actively encouraged by the government, who directly likened the restrictions to those suffered by Britain during the Second World War. This attitude wavered over time, but on the whole the British – like many other countries – collectively accepted unprecedented restrictions on their lives and livelihoods, believing that the long-term ramifications of doing nothing would be significantly more destructive. Most of us did not collectively think it objectively unjust, except in a cosmic sense for which there is never any appeal.

Whether the COVID-19 lockdown was subjectively a case of oppression is therefore a matter of personal opinion. One might, as some commentators did, think that it was an unfair and unreasonable restriction on our right to free movement, profit and speech. One might acknowledge its destruction and criticize its application while accepting its necessity. Or one might consider it a noble effort and sacrifice in the face of an intolerable and unprecedented threat. All these opinions might be accurate based on personal belief and circumstance – but as a whole we in Britain decided, at that time, that the COVID-19 lockdown was not objectively oppression.

At any other time, however, we would likely have been horrified by the imposition on our lives – by the loss we all suffered in time, stability and employment, the longer-term effects on the economy and the state of the country's finances, the trauma it inflicted on our families. We collectively made a decision to accept the oppression of lockdown in a specific set of circumstances, to be alleviated once they had passed, and that means that oppression is not absolute. Most people did not follow lockdown rules out of fear of authority, but willingly, from fear of something worse. What constitutes oppression therefore is a continuum of opinion, decided collectively, and prone to sudden shifts based on circumstance, both personal and more broadly in society.

That this is the case was brought starkly into focus in June 2020 with the sudden surge in activity around the Black Lives Matter movement, a largely organic protest based on the justified perception in the United States that the lives of Black Americans matter less – to politicians, police, the media and their fellow citizens – than the lives of White Americans. This belief was dramatically reinforced when on 25 May a police officer in

Minneapolis killed an unarmed African American man, George Floyd, by choking him with his knee as Floyd screamed for help. Floyd died in full view of a recording cameraphone, and his death was broadcast to the world: a needless, callous violent death at the hands of an agent of a system which was ostensibly created to protect citizens, but which through a long history of violent extrajudicial killings has appeared to be designed to facilitate the victimization of African Americans. They are proportionally far more likely to be arrested than White Americans, and far more likely to be incarcerated, in a nation that incarcerates more people than any other. The contemporary United States reflects an environment which for many of the African American population is one in which the police, and the governmental and social systems they protect, are not defenders of their community, but oppressors of it. American police forces lock up Black children, send armoured patrols through Black neighbourhoods and kill Black men and women in the streets and in their homes, all in hugely disproportionate numbers, and they have done so for generations. All across America the subjective oppression of the African American community clashes with the legal refusal to acknowledge this situation as objective oppression in that country.

The African American community came out to protest Floyd's death, just as they had protested before, after other killings. But this time was different. This time, COVID-19 had disproportionately destroyed African American livelihoods and was wreaking a terrible toll on their communities. More likely to be affected more severely by the disease than other ethnic groups, less likely to have access to quality healthcare, more likely to have lost precarious jobs and businesses, and lacking any meaningful social safety net, more and more African American people came onto the streets to protest in anger and desperation. This time, too, they were joined by large numbers of Americans of other ethnicities, also suffering, also dispossessed: students and young people without jobs or studies, not only furious at the brutality with which law enforcement treats Black Americans, but also fuelled by the increasingly obvious incompetence with the way their government was handling the pandemic and the litany of corruption, insult, racism and violence of the preceding three years of Donald Trump's reactionary right-wing presidency.

In response to these street protests, police forces across the United States responded not as mediators of the public trust, nor as peacekeepers, but as aggressive defenders of the status quo. Before the cameras of citizens and news organizations, and heedless of the public impact of their actions, the police used every weapon at their disposal to disperse crowds, including baton charges and beatings, rubber bullets deliberately fired at protestors' eyes, military-grade tear gas, widespread, indiscriminate arrests, and in places live fire. At least two people were killed. As police brutality spread from city to city, often deliberately targeting journalists and vocally supported by President Trump and the Republican Party, police officials, including Bob Kroll, head of the Police Officers Federation of Minneapolis, demanded obedience and subservience, insisting on military-grade riot

gear and the greater powers necessary to inflict it on the protestors, who Kroll described as a 'terrorist organization'.* By
July unmarked, heavily armed government militias of unknown
origin were patrolling cities such as Portland and Washington,
DC, in direct opposition to those cities' authorities. The militias
were under the direct control of Trump's Department of Justice
and Attorney General Bill Barr, as the president led calls to sus-
pend the upcoming elections he was predicted to lose.

Here, before the eyes of the world, was naked state violence
happening in the United States, the supposed land of the free,
and, with the rest of the world locked down and focused on television and internet news, people who had never before had to
think seriously about oppression began to ask questions; to ask
why they had accepted the unique repressions of the pandemic,
repressions they would never had accepted in other circumstances, and under what other conditions you might accept these
restrictions. People were forced to question what they might do if
they saw a man being killed by a police officer in front of them,
and had to come to terms with the reality that – via apps on
their phones – they had done precisely that. They had seen that
happen. And then they had seen the police response to protests,
and they needed to understand why that was happening, and
think about how they can, should, would respond, and why they
had tolerated it until now.

In Britain maybe it was enough to see these as events happening

---

* CBS, 2020. "Minneapolis Police Union Head Speaks Out". Accessed via YouTube
at https://www.youtube.com/watch?v=CF41UMUKitI

in a distant country – one with a history of racial violence that Britons all too often like to pretend, incorrectly, is nothing to do with us – and imagine that such things don't and can't happen here. That would be wrong. As this book will demonstrate, Britain has an uncomfortable history of exporting oppression around the world. It has manifested time and time again in racism and brutality, and that has often been comfortably distant from our shores that the public has been able to avoid confronting it.

Clipperton is a desolate place, exposed to Pacific storms, waves and winds which batter it for half the year, resulting in an annual rainfall three times that of the distant Mexican coast. No more than a ring of raised coral on the rim of an ancient submerged volcano, its beaches covered by sand and dotted with stubby palm trees, it covers less than two and a half square miles in area, almost all of which is taken up by a large central lagoon of brackish water filled with swarms of biting sea-lice and acidic pits. On its southwestern shore is a large rocky outcrop, carved by wind and spray into a maze of holes and caves in which countless generations of seabirds have nested. Over millennia their faeces built up into vast layers of compacted nitrates called guano, which was such a valuable fertilizer in the late nineteenth century that it prompted a scramble for Pacific empires which changed the fate of Clipperton Island.

There have never been Indigenous Clipperton Islanders, no native population for settlers to displace. The Pacific peoples who had spread across the ocean in ancient history, inhabiting islands from New Zealand to Hawaiʻi, never reached this wind-swept place, or least never settled there. It is too far from other land, too small and too lacking in the basic necessities of life to support a society for any length of time. But Clipperton had not escaped notice by the wider world. In addition to its value as a guano mine, its position meant that whichever empire controlled it could also lay claim to a sizeable portion of the western Pacific as territorial waters, and the potential resources within.

The first documented visitors were French sailors, who arrived in 1711. These men, as European sailors of that age did, imme-diately claimed it as a property of the French crown and dubbed it Île de la Passion, after the religious holiday on the day of discovery, Passiontide. Shortly afterwards, it became the base of operations for the English privateer John Clipperton, who preyed on Spanish Pacific merchant shipping during the War of the Quadruple Alliance (1718–20), and who gave the island its English name. French visitors periodically stopped by over the next century to reinforce French claims of sovereignty, but the island's political future only became seriously contested in the 1850s, when the US government passed the Guano Islands Act, which authorized American officials and companies to seize any unclaimed land anywhere in the world which might contain valuable deposits of fertilizer.[*]

This aggressive act of legislative colonial expansion set off a chain of disputes between the United States government on one

---

[*] Elliott, Thomas F., 2005. *Clipperton: The Island of Lost Toys and Other Treasures.* Trafford Publishing, Vancouver, p. 58

hand and independent nations and rival empires all over the world – uninhabited islands in the Pacific and Caribbean suddenly came under American claims of sovereignty, challenged by other imperial powers as well as smaller, poorer nations such as Haiti and Colombia and officially unrecognized independent Indigenous governments in the Pacific, in places such as Samoa and Hawai'i. Clipperton Island, as an uninhabited and only sporadically claimed atoll, was among those targeted for annexation by American guano mining companies, prompting furious responses from Mexico, which had already quietly begun mining operations, and France, reflecting the original claims made a century and a half earlier. Emperor Napoleon III of France consequently declared Clipperton to be part of the French Empire and annexed it to distant Tahiti.

The disputes about Clipperton dragged on for decades, and became partially subsumed into the broader conflict between France and Mexico. In 1861 the French Army invaded Mexico on the pretext of reclaiming unpaid debts, and installed a cousin of the French Emperor, Maximilian, as Emperor. The Mexicans resisted and for five years Mexican republican armies battled French, Mexican imperial and European mercenary armies across the country, eventually overthrowing and executing Maximilian. Napoleon III himself fell from power three years later, ousted after a massive Prussian invasion of France.

In the aftermath of the establishment of the new republic in France and the Mexican dictatorship of Porfirio Díaz, the nations continued to quietly dispute ownership of Clipperton

Island, which was still sporadically subject to unofficial Mexican mining operations. In 1897, though, an American mining team arrived to reassert the United States' claim, unsanctioned by the US government. When the miners were discovered there and removed by a French Navy ship, the news was reported in California and stimulated a Mexican response. A month later a Mexican warship arrived to formally assert sovereignty.

In 1906, after agreeing a deal with the British Pacific Island Company, the Mexican government established a mining colony, guarded by a detachment of Mexican soldiers. Command of the remote outpost was assumed by Captain Ramón Arnaud, a descendant of French settlers who had accompanied Maximilian to Mexico and stayed after his fall. Arnaud would remain on duty on Clipperton, known to the Mexican inhabitants as Isla de la Pasión, for the next decade, accompanied by a small garrison. Arnaud had a history with Mexico's own imperial ambitions: at one time censured for desertion, he had later been decorated for his part in crushing an Indigenous Mayan uprising in southern Mexico in 1901, and then served as part of the military mission to Japan. He was tough, effective and spoke several languages fluently, and was therefore considered the perfect man for a posting at the edge of the earth like Clipperton.

In the years that followed France did not press its claim militarily, but did launch a sustained diplomatic effort to assert sovereignty, recognizing that the position of the island in a swathe of the eastern Pacific would be strategically valuable, more so certainly than the island's dwindling guano deposits. The claim was subject in 1909 to a treaty between Mexico and France, the United States having withdrawn its demands, which appointed King Victor Emmanuel III of Italy, as an ostensibly neutral party, to make the determination as to whether France or Mexico had the right to claim ownership of the island. Both nations agreed to abide by Victor Emmanuel's decision, but in the meantime the Mexican settlement and garrison remained, mining guano and entirely dependent for food and water supplies on regular visits of the *Tampico*, a Mexican Navy gunboat sailing from Acapulco.

Thus entangled, seemingly intractably, in the global network of imperial claim and counter-claim which dominated international politics, diplomacy and government in the first decades of the twentieth century, Clipperton Island and the small garrison under Arnaud remained in a legal limbo, its inhabitants unable to sustain themselves with the island's resources, and at risk at any time of eviction by a hostile foreign power. In these circumstances their numbers began to dwindle: in 1910, after the global price of guano was undercut by cheaper and more accessible fertilizers, the British company closed its operations and removed all but one of the guano miners. Arnaud and the garrison remained on duty, though, accompanied by their families. The only other resident was the island's lighthouse keeper Victoriano Álvarez. Álvarez, the illegitimate descendant of a Mexican general killed in a brief civil war in 1857 and the island's only Black Mexican inhabitant, was not part of Arnaud's garrison, living instead in a shack separate from the rest of the island's forty or so inhabitants under the craggy outcrop.

In the same year that the British withdrew their mining operations, President Porfirio Díaz stepped down after forty-three
years as dictator of Mexico. In the vacancy he left behind, a
scramble for power followed which split the country into multiple battling factions. Coup followed counter-coup and by 1914
Mexico had dissolved into open civil warfare. In February 1914,
as revolutionary fervour spread across Mexico, the crew of the
Tampico rebelled against the government, abandoned their
scheduled supply runs to Clipperton and took refuge in the
rebel-held town of Topolobampo, where they were attacked by
government gunboats, and sunk. As his ship went down, the
commander shot himself, and with him apparently went the last
person in Mexico to remember that the garrison on Clipperton
Island was still there, and needed supplies.

Clipperton was not yet completely abandoned. An American
ship had been wrecked on the island's northern shore in the
early spring. Distrusting the newcomers and reluctant to share
supplies, Arnaud excluded the wrecked sailors from his community. Some of the sailors took a boat from the wreck and sailed to
Mexico where they contacted the American authorities, who sent
the cruiser USS *Cleveland* to rescue the remainder of the crew.
The commander of the *Cleveland* offered to repatriate Arnaud
and his small community, but Arnaud refused, perhaps still
suspicious of American motives and having been instructed to
stay at his post until ordered to withdraw. His men then settled
back into his command to await the return of the supply ship
Tampico which, unbeknown to Arnaud, lay on the bottom of the

Gulf of California. Forgotten in a vast ocean, the inhabitants of Clipperton were alone.

It's worth pausing here to discuss an important realization: the story of how the inhabitants of Clipperton Island came to be marooned there reveals that everything we do – the choices we make and who we are – is shaped and moulded by the world around us, over which we have little or no control, a theme that we'll come to again and again in this book. The inhabitants of Clipperton came to be landed on, and then abandoned on, a desolate and deadly desert island in part due to personal decisions they had made, but more specifically by the decisions of the governments they served, which were shaped in turn by competition between nations.

We have free will and the ability to make our own decisions, but our ability to do so is constrained by the world in which we have learned from birth to exist, and we operate safely only within the laws and customs that our societies deem acceptable. These laws and customs are by no means universal; societies the world over have drawn lines on morality and immorality in wildly different places, but in each one the inhabitants have adapted to the systems around them to live their lives with the freedoms they can achieve. Those who operate outside these laws, often within systems and customs and traditions of their own which might not be more widely shared – think no further than the intersection of secular government and the restrictions of devout faith – can find themselves subject to legal restrictions. It is through this mechanism that under oppressive regimes entire populations can be oppressed solely through their membership of racial, religious or ethnic groups, whether voluntary or not. The way in which laws are shaped is dictated by forces acting on politicians and populations which choose to define justice in certain ways to reflect their priorities, often at the expense of others.

An example of how this operates is the Declaration of Independence of the United States, issued in 1776, which formally laid out the terms under which the Thirteen Colonies of North America were seceding from Britain. The document lists three unalienable rights to which all 'men', and it is specifically men, are entitled: 'life, liberty and the pursuit of happiness'. It is upon this foundation that this nation, and the philosophical movements which supported and sustained it, are built. Yet this was a fallacy – the nation was built not on universal rights, but on ensuring the maintenance of those rights for a very small sliver of the population: White, property-owning citizens. The Declaration excluded women, it excluded the poor and it excluded people of colour, most of whom were not considered fully human, but rather property. It also excluded the entire Indigenous population of North America. Such people were somehow less human, and more deserving of oppression, than the people who wrote the Declaration, and the people who were allowed to vote for one or other of them.

The legal and political systems that this document conceived bore this injustice, this oppression, at their heart, and despite the multitude of amendments and judgements and legislation in the centuries since, its legacy remains: women, minorities and the poor are still disadvantaged by mainstream American systems, from the road networks which strangle poor neighbourhoods and exclude those unable to afford a car, to reproductive health initiatives which politicize and criminalize women's life choices, to the entertainment industry and its history of dehumanizing ethnic groups and entire genders. These oppressions are subjective to the people who experience them, but they are not illegal or universally recognized – they are hard to classify unproblematically as objective oppressions, supported as they are by state apparatus and imposed by armed law enforcement.

This matters all the more because the United States has long been the self-appointed 'leader of the free world', a nation constructed and reconstructed in opposition to the old empires of Europe, the 'Evil Empire' of the Soviet Union or the 'Axis of Evil' during the War on Terror. Couched in explicitly religious terms, this modern crusade has been used to justify the invasion of foreign countries, the overthrow of governments and the deaths of hundreds of thousands – a pattern graphically and unapologetically played out in the Iraq War of 2003 under President George W. Bush, which was predicated on a lie about Iraqi military capability for which there has never been any accountability. A nation founded on flawed justice has continued to pursue flawed justice, termed by others oppression, ever since, wrapped in the notion of freedom it has never properly fulfilled, still maintaining the foundational inequalities which marked its birth.

In Britain the foundation documents are even less equitable:

though the disadvantaged groups may not be the same or disadvantaged in the same way, the processes by which systemic oppression plays out are insidiously ingrained within society, rooted within education, class privilege and social hierarchies that label some as productive and valued and others as not, and unworthy of meaningful support. We thus have oppression at home through a system designed to preserve privilege, and we exported this tiered, exploitative, violent and often racist system all over the world.

The origins of this lie as far back as Magna Carta, the document drawn up in 1215 to settle a civil war between King John and his aristocracy. It is popularly supposed to have initiated British democracy, but in fact it did no more than reiterate that massive power imbalances lie embedded within the British establishment and help to better cement them – it did not issue rights for 'all men', but rather affirmed the king's inability to enforce his laws on his nobles, and entrenched the British feudal system in which the vast majority of the population were directly and legally oppressed, forced into a servitude which was only nominally free. The history of Britain since, and in particular its ruthless imperial expansion in the nineteenth century, are marked by this maintenance of elite rule, at the expense of, but generally with the willing consent of, the majority of the population. British exceptionalism demands that the British do not question this system, or the notion that Britain and British are paramount; such became explicit government policy in February 2021, when ministers threatened academics and institutions that question this national myth with financial sanctions. So we once ruled the world as exceptional free men, the canard insists; thus we must still, in some way, rule it now.

Both Britain and the United States, though, are democracies: they are not autocratic regimes operating through the oppression of naked military force, or attaining their power through raw and unconcealed corruption. This means that they take their legitimacy as exponents of freedom and justice from the consent of the population, operating a political system supposed in its roots to be just and fair, and intended to give the majority of the country a say in who leads it; the leaders are in position with the support of the majority of the people, whose rule is consequently assumed to be benevolent. The authority to create laws, to place potentially oppressive restrictions on people's lives, stems from that consent. And yet, as history shows and as I will demonstrate, populations are sometimes willing to throw away the freedoms and protections democratic governance brings, if enough can be persuaded that it no longer works for them (without thinking of others), and to participate directly in their own destruction if an oppressive system encourages them to do so. Moreover, democracy favours dominant groups over minorities, granting authority to the largest identities grouped within a state, be those racial, religious, political or social groupings, and calling it fair.

It is, though, still an infinitely preferable system to that of so many other countries ruled by unaccountable presidents for life, absolute hereditary monarchs or tightly controlled oligarchies of billionaires. In those countries there is not even a nominal outlet or pretence of equality. There, hierarchies of oppression are baked into the national fabric, enacted and preserved over generations and jealously guarded: the limited successes and myriad failures of the Arab Spring in the last decade are glaring examples of how difficult it is to enact meaningful democratic change in places where systematic government oppression runs deep, and from which there is often no means of escape other than flight to places ostensibly more free and fair.

But still, fairness has to be for all involved to be meaningful. The vast majority of us make choices based on evaluations of which outcome will profit us most, or cost us least – not necessarily selfish, but certainly based on self-preservation. These are the choices with which we are presented, and we call them free will, which is perhaps misleading – it's a freedom to willingly not consider others' needs or feelings.

This leads us to the second lesson of Clipperton Island – that if we do not choose certain types of oppression over others, particularly if we do not know, or choose not to know, what effect the outcome will have for others, we might suffer. And our suffering may not be anywhere as severe as it was for those who suffered and died on that remote Pacific atoll, but we know and fear that that dreadful outcome might lie at the end of the road if we do not make these choices. The rest of the story of the King of Clipperton Island is the story of why we oppress and why we accept repression.

On Clipperton Island, Arnaud was able to maintain command of his dwindling band of survivors for two years by drinking rain water collected in open boats and ekeing out food from the island's inadequate supplies and the crabs scuttling on the beaches. During this period the dwindling population largely remained subservient to his authority, even as it grew clear that Arnaud no longer derived that authority from any higher power – it became obvious over time that no help was coming. He was of course unaware of both the Mexican Revolution at home and that the rest of the world had dissolved into the First World War, with empires clashing and disrupting international shipping: France was partially occupied by German armies and in no position to reassert any claims on tiny Pacific atolls. There were no boats capable of reaching Mexico on the island and the population became riven with rivalries and jealousies, some forming a religious movement and whipping their flesh in the hope of appeasing whatever deity had abandoned them there, but without success. In early 1915, denied fresh fruit and vegetables, scurvy spread through the colony and one by one the inhabitants fell ill. Among the casualties was Álvarez, who retreated into his cabin, delirious and with his body covered in sores. Arnaud and the surviving garrison gave him up for dead, along with at least fifteen others who did not survive, more bodies dotting the island's shores to be devoured by crabs.

By late 1916, two years after *Cleveland* departed, just half of the inhabitants remained – five men, eight women and seven children. The stored food had long run out, and they were reduced to eating crabs and scrawny seabirds, while rationing a single coconut a week between them to try and fend off scurvy.

Desperation set in, and thus when a distant ship was sighted from the rock, no more than a shadow on the horizon, Arnaud and his three remaining soldiers boarded a raft in an attempt to reach the vessel and secure help. In their weakened state the soldiers were unable to catch up with the ship, and eventually turned back, but in the attempt their raft was overturned on the reef and the crew flung out and lost in the ocean.

With Arnaud drowned, the tenuous power structures which had held the island's society together were severed entirely. As the women and children watched their husbands and fathers drown from the beach, Álvarez, the lighthouse keeper, who had recovered from his near-death bout of illness but was left physically and mentally scarred, slipped into Arnaud's command post and destroyed all but one of the garrison's firearms, dumping the ruined weapons into the lagoon. He retained a single Mauser rifle for himself, all he now needed to become the king of his own private, terrible kingdom. Without the checks and balances of official structures which ensured that laws were followed and that people fulfilled their responsibilities on the island, the rule reverted to one of anarchy, in which the strongest could impose their will on weaker members of society with impunity, with only their own conscience to hold them in check. Álvarez clearly had none. At gunpoint, he hunted the women on the island. There was nowhere for them to hide and no way to run. He stalked them along the beaches and lurked among the rocks, attacking them with his rifle butt and knocking them unconscious. He then dragged his victims back to his hut by their hair, grown long under the Pacific sun, and brutally raped them.

Over the following months Álvarez became increasingly paranoid and violent, eventually proclaiming himself the King of Clipperton Island, an absolute monarch no longer beholden to the laws of normal citizens, his rule enforced by violence and force, symbolized by his rifle. Those who resisted were shot as a warning to others, including a mother and daughter killed in front of the island's other women as examples of what resistance to his oppression would mean. Alicia Rovira, Arnaud's widow, ordered the other women to shave their heads to prevent Álvarez using it to drag them to his cabin, but this small act of resistance did not prevent him emerging periodically to terrorize the starving survivors. Clipperton Island became a world in which the structured objective oppression of the wider world had condensed into a brutal regime dictated by the whims of one armed man, unchecked in his domination of those subject to his rule.

Witnesses to the fate of the women who had resisted, and understanding that Álvarez would eventually kill them all, some of the survivors determined to defend themselves. One night a woman named Tirza Rendon, a repeated victim of Álvarez's brutality, visited his shack. Surprising him, she attacked him with the mallet used to shell coconuts. Joined by Alicia Rovira, the women wrestled with Álvarez as Arnaud's son Pedro seized his gun, and together Rendon and Rovira were able to crush their tormentor's skull. The brief and violent reign of the King of Clipperton Island was over, and Álvarez was left for the crabs. For the islanders, though, there was another glimmer of hope – even as the women had struggled with Álvarez, a ship had appeared in the distance, the USS *Yorktown* on its lonely Pacific patrol. Coming ashore, startled to find people still living on the bare island, the commander took the survivors aboard, abandoning their ruined settlement and sailing back to Mexico. The wider world, whose systems had first planted and then abandoned the colony, now returned to reassert authority, and was gratefully received by the eleven survivors of the reign of the mad King of Clipperton Island.

When American newspapers reported on the story, reflecting on the suffering of the women on their lonely island, the most important feature of their reports was Álvarez's race – he was depicted in cartoons, a hideous caricature of a Black man in a straw hat chasing virtuous and modestly clad White women across a beach, with the caption that the women 'Lived in Terror of the Negro'. A year later the First World War ended, and in 1920 the Mexican Revolution drew to its bloody close. Clipperton was left to its birds, crabs and feral pigs, introduced by Arnaud and devastating to the local ecology. In 1931 the King of Italy, under pressure from Mussolini, who sought better relations with France, declared that Clipperton should be a French colony, and despite an outcry in the Mexican press, the Mexican government acquiesced in the decision. The island was formally transferred to the colony of French Polynesia, thousands of miles away.

Clipperton Island has remained empty almost ever since, though it is periodically visited by US and French warships.

President Franklin D. Roosevelt visited the island in 1935 and 1938 during fishing holidays on the cruiser USS *Houston*, during which an aeroplane took photographs of the atoll, in a secret but ultimately abandoned initiative to reassert US claims to the island and build a naval base there. Other islands seized under the Guano Islands Act, like Midway Island and Wake Island, were turned into military installations and were to play a prominent role in the Second World War, but Clipperton was too remote, too barren. After the war, it was mooted as a site for French atomic bomb testing, though rejected as impracticable, and as recently as 1986 there were plans to re-establish a French colony on the island and turn it into a Pacific fishing hub. None came to pass – Clipperton is probably too lacking in the necessities to sustain life ever to become a permanent site of human habitation.

Today Clipperton is an occasional destination for naturalists, marine biologists, shipwrecked fishermen and French military patrols, but mostly it stands empty day after day, year after year, a desolate dot on the map with a history that holds the key to understanding why the world is configured the way it is today, and why we allow it to be configured that way despite the suffering we witness and cause.

The self-appointed King of Clipperton Island was an unjust ruler, a man whose sole legitimacy and authority was asserted by force and fear rather than any meaningful consensus, and who treated his 'subjects' as no more than property, to be disposed of in accordance with his personal whims. The fear of this force, of unpredictable violence and cruelty coming to govern our lives without recourse to justice, drives much of our impulses towards oppression; we decide all the time to tolerate certain restrictions in our lives – oppressions to some – because of fear. Fear of a pandemic or an invasion or of a reign of terror such as that on Clipperton Island is ever present, and potentially lying just beyond the systems we have put in place to avoid it, systems we call justice, and from which we profit.

We rarely stop to think, though, about how these compromises have been reached, or to question who it was who decided that one rule is justice but another oppression, and in whose name these decisions are made. It is perhaps counter-intuitive to think of oppression as a necessity, and so we also do not often think about the ways in which oppression, a trait we conflate with cruel leadership, helps us in our everyday lives. The things we use, the things we do, are all parts of systems which oppress, whether ourselves or others, whether directly or indirectly, whether before our eyes or out of sight.

Following rules is hard. We don't set them, at least for the most part not directly, and though they provide protection, they often stop us from doing things which might be fun. Some rules seem self-evident – we don't kill others or steal things because we can recognize that to do so is damaging and hurtful, and those who do are arrested by paid protectors of the public and placed in cages so that they can't do it any more. But for others it is tempting to think that rules shouldn't apply to us – speeding restrictions feel constricting on a clear road, and even good, normally responsible drivers can be tempted to push things, to see if the car can go that little bit faster, to feel the speed underneath us and the trees whipping by. It's exhilarating, and you question why they have these rules you're supposed to follow – after all, you're a good driver, you don't crash.

Maybe you are lucky and nothing happens. Maybe you zip around a corner and find yourself looking down the barrel of a mobile speed camera and a few days later an infuriating envelope drops on the mat and you have a fine and speeding points and you curse the injustice of it. No one was hurt, after all. Or maybe there's a tractor or a broken-down car, or a kid on a bike just around the bend and you can't stop in time, and you learn, if you survive, why the speed limits are set where they are.

As a society we agree that there are limits on personal behaviour that are designed, we understand, to provide safety and security for the people who live there. Each society arranges these laws in different ways and none quite agree on what the right balance between personal liberty and legal restriction should be. In some countries these are established as foundational gospel, a set of inalienable rights which lay out at a minimum the freedoms citizens can expect. In other nations freedoms themselves are not set, only laws, with the freedoms comprising everything that is left.

When multiple oppressions collide, academics refer to the situation which results as intersectionality.

Intersectionality is an important aspect of the study of

oppression, because it recognizes that oppression isn't a binary between powerful and powerless, but a network of repressive actions between peoples – those who oppress can also be oppressors, and oppressions can work upon one another collectively – though it is by no means the whole picture. Society can in many ways be understood as a structure constructed and conceived of oppressions interacting with one another which generate hierarchies of power. We assume our roles in these hierarchies of power, often unconsciously, and make our decisions accordingly, believing we are acting from our free will, but all too often unconsciously re-enacting oppressions with which we have been raised and in which we still live.

Chapter Two

OPPRESSION AND IMPERIALISM: THE BURNING OF SAN CARLOS

In January 2014, Monica Spear, a former winner of the Miss Venezuela beauty contest, was travelling along a road near her childhood home in the coastal state of Carabobo with her British ex-husband Thomas Berry and their five-year-old daughter when their car broke down on a rural highway. Partially raised in Florida, Spear was a US citizen and was famous for having come fifth in the 2004 Miss Universe contest before a moderately successful career as an actress on Venezuelan television. She wasn't exactly a household name, but she was young, wealthy, beautiful, American and popular, all things which might have insulated her from the turmoil descending on her country had she not broken down in the wrong place at the wrong time. For that evening, as Spear and Berry waited inside their car for assistance, another vehicle pulled up and several men got out. Rather than help the stranded family, the new arrivals attempted to rob them at gunpoint. When Spear refused to open the doors to the robbers, the men opened fire on the vehicle. With the occupants incapacitated, the assailants rifled through the car, stealing valuables and electronics, and then left the family bleeding at the side of the road. Spear and Berry died; their daughter survived, shot in the leg.

The death of a celebrity in such a brutal manner marked something of a tipping point for Venezuelans after two decades of turmoil and political dysfunction. In 1998 Venezuela had elected Hugo Chávez as president, marking quite a turnaround for a man who had attempted and failed to violently overthrow the previous government just six years earlier. He was elected on a socialist platform and pledged to redistribute land and wealth from the country's elites and foreign corporations to the populace. This promised a truly vast redirection of economic power from rich to poor: Venezuela sits on some of the largest oil reserves in the world, its wealth traditionally the preserve of the social elite at the expense of the rest of the population.

Chávez's regime made some improvements to Venezuelan infrastructure, but most of the redistribution was from one set of elites to another, most conspicuously to Chávez's own family and his closest supporters. Through a mixture of genuine popularity, bribery, propaganda and intimidation, Chávez won four elections in a row, but his dominance of Venezuela was entirely buoyed by oil revenues, and when global oil prices began to fall in the late 2000s, the corruption and contradiction became unsustainable.

Chávez's social programmes began to collapse. Poverty and food shortages soared and protests and uprisings spread across the country, prompting aggressive government crackdowns. When Chávez died in 2013, his nation was less equal, less stable and more fractured than before his authoritarian regime began.

Chávez's presidency was inherited by Nicolás Maduro, Chávez's right-hand man, but noticeably less popular or competent than his former boss. Maduro deepened Chávez's propaganda efforts and strengthened his clampdown on dissent, despite which he almost lost the 2013 presidential elections, prompting fresh rounds of repression. Under his increasingly authoritarian rule, Venezuela spiralled further into poverty as presidential supporters siphoned ever greater wealth away from the people they had promised to support. The murder of Monica Spear, followed shortly after by the violent attempted rape of a student on a university campus in Caracas, prompted a sudden and furious public reaction against crime and the political corruption which was fuelling it, at the broken promises, food shortages and all the myriad indignities of living in a country whose leaders lied to their citizens about progress even as they lived the reality of their government's failures. Protestors gathered in the Venezuelan capital, demanding changes to reverse the breakdown in law and order, rising unemployment, and continual shortages of basic goods.

Maduro responded by sending in heavily armed police and armed pro-presidential militia to break up the protests, and on 12 February 2014 they opened fire on protesting students in Caracas, murdering student Bassil Da Costa. Seven days later,

Génesis Carmona, a Venezuelan fashion model, was murdered by paramilitary *colectivo* militiamen at a protest in Valencia, in Carabobo, not far from the site of the murder of Monica Spear. In the face of a growing outcry at home and internationally, Maduro responded by accusing the protestors of being paid agitators of the United States – that they were thus effectively not true Venezuelans but agents of a foreign power. This was a baseless accusation to try to obscure Maduro's direct culpability in grotesque human rights abuses: a UN report of September 2020 drily stated that he 'should have known about conditions of detention and that torture and/or ill-treatment was being practised and that [he] had the effective authority and control to prevent and repress such violations, but failed to do so'. In less diplomatic language, the killers were uniformed, and acting under orders.* However, Maduro's accusations had particular force in Venezuela because there is a long history of imperialist meddling in the country, and it is worth exploring in more detail why the claims of foreign interference made such an effective attack, as well as how Venezuela came to be in the parlous situation it now finds itself in.

The war between Germany and Venezuela in 1902–3 is a conflict forgotten by almost everyone nearly 120 years on, and after a brief flurry in the papers mostly forgotten outside Venezuela

---

* United Nations, 2020. "Detailed findings of the Independent International Fact-Finding Mission on the Bolivarian Republic of Venezuela". UN Human Rights Council. Accessed online at https://digitallibrary.un.org/record/3884107?ln=-fr#record-files-collapse-header

even at the time. It exemplifies the historical movement that may have done more to shape the human world than any other in the modern age: the rise of imperialism. Whether we recognize it or not, the myriad legacies of imperialism dominate contemporary political, economic, social, technological and cultural movements. Imperialism and the new world it shaped changed not only the political maps of the world, shaded in the empire of choice, but also how people thought of the world and their place in it, emotional responses which still play out directly in their descendants today. If you watched the statue of Edward Colston fall during the Black Lives Matter protests in Bristol in 2020 and wondered why a statue of a slave owner was standing in that city, or why statues of slave owners are so offensive to many Britons, especially those of colour, nearly two centuries after the end of slavery in the British Empire, or indeed why there was such a fervent counter-movement in the British government and parts of the British press condemning the removal of the statue commemorating a slaver, the answer lies in understanding imperialism.

The term imperialism refers to a political policy of the expansion of power into territory belonging to or occupied by other peoples. It is enacted more directly through colonialism, which is the process of military, economic and commercial domination of territory, and the exploitation of that territory's resources. This process, while often advertised at the time as benevolent or justified, has throughout history always been driven by one goal: the movement of wealth – whether in people, trade, raw materials or solid gold – by force if necessary and from all corners of the world, to the colonial centres of power, generally via complicated networks of trade and communication which laundered that wealth through colonies and other nations in ways which made it grow and grow. Imperialism was the extraction of that wealth and its transportation to new destinations, and for centuries these destinations were the capitals of Europe, and the later nations born from European empires, such as the United States.

Imperialism requires a system of exploitation and extortion, the forceful appropriation of resources and people for profit, and it is in aid of this that wars have been fought, genocides enacted and ancient political systems upended. It has caused famines, plagues and ecological disasters whose echoes carry down the centuries and which fundamentally reshaped the history of the world. While empires have been a staple of human political structures from the earliest recorded periods, spreading across the map as kings and emperors competed for power and wealth, it was technological advances in seafaring – in ship-building, navigation and sailing – that allowed empires to expand beyond regional dominance and become both global and sustainable by the sixteenth century, turning empires based on river systems, caravan routes or inland seas into empires which used the oceans as thoroughfares. Suddenly empires were no longer based on moving from one territory to the next over-land or across inland waterways like the Mediterranean, but could become global. It was this which allowed empires based in relatively small but technologically advanced and culturally rapacious countries in Western Europe to spread rapidly across the entire world.

These empires enabled small cliques of ruling aristocracy in imperial capitals to develop a political, economic and social system dedicated to oppressing millions to hoard wealth. The wealth transferred back to these imperial centres led to an explosion in scientific enquiry funded by imperial growth called the Enlightenment. Most of what we now consider the pillars of Western civilization – scientific enquiry, museums, universities and modern democracy itself – stems from this period and context. This scientific and educational movement brought dramatic advances in technology, medical care and logistics which today permit the almost continual expansion of the human population and have significantly improved human quality of life, but the cost of these advances is a legacy of violence, oppression and inequality which defines our world today.

On 21 January 1903 the German cruiser *Vineta* steamed back and forth off the entrance to the channel which led to the Venezuelan city of Maracaibo. Six thousand tonnes of steel built four years before in the imperial dockyards at Danzig on the Baltic, *Vineta* had crossed the Atlantic as part of an international coalition, with the mission to block shipping entering the principal port of the nation of Venezuela. Maracaibo is a city lying at the mouth of Lake Maracaibo, a huge estuary which forms almost an inland sea and dominates western Venezuela and its then-lucrative imports from inland coffee plantations.

The town lies on the narrow isthmus at its mouth, protected by the Spanish-built Fort San Carlos, a defensive castle built to deter French pirates from raiding Maracaibo 300 years before, whose maritime importance was marked by being the site of the last battle fought and lost by Spain in its vain effort to prevent Venezuelan independence, when a Spanish fleet attempted to enter the lake carrying an invading army, and was beaten back by the fort and the Venezuelan Navy. Fort San Carlos is a large star fort, built to the latest specifications in the eighteenth century, but by 1903 largely obsolete against properly prepared modern warships, its gun batteries pointing out more in hope than deterrence across the channel to protect the entrance, and manned by Venezuelan soldiers. Under its great walls was a village of clustered houses supporting the garrison and mostly occupied by fishermen plying the shoals where the lagoon meets the sea. Close to the equator, the weather is hot and the winters mild, but Lake Maracaibo is a strange, sometimes otherworldly place, its basin comprising fresh water layered over salt water, and its unique atmosphere riven by almost constant lightning storms known as *Catatumbo*.

Since declaring independence from Spain in 1811, and then separating from the federation of Gran Colombia in 1830, Venezuela had ostensibly controlled its own foreign and domestic policy and maintained its borders – as far as arbitrary lines traced across unmapped jungles by European bureaucrats can be considered borders. The *Vineta*, though, made the true nature of this freedom crushingly apparent. As the German warship

46

steamed, its eight-inch guns opened fire on Fort San Carlos. Shells crashed onto the fortifications, built to withstand nothing more than cannonballs, blasting the structure to rubble and igniting fires. Careless in their aim, shells whistled over the fort to plunge into the streets of the village of San Carlos below, where at least twenty-five Venezuelans were blown apart or burned alive in their homes.

Quite why German warships were, at the turn of the twentieth century, bombarding a Venezuelan fortress with careless abandon is a question which strikes to the very heart of the consideration of imperialism and its systems of oppression. For Venezuela, then as now an independent nation, has never really been free. It is enclosed by systems of influence, politics and economics which were designed to keep Venezuela and dozens of other nations, organizations and peoples all over the world in positions that allow others to exploit them, and, supported by corrupt local politicians and dictators, a system within which we all very much still live.

Venezuela, like much of the rest of South and Central America, was invaded and colonized by Spain in the sixteenth century. The local population was, as elsewhere, treated as no more than an exhaustible resource, taken as slaves and worked to death or driven into the jungled interior. Decimated by disease and dominated by Spanish armies raised from the wealth generated from the resources of their own lands, they were able to offer little determined resistance. Rebellions were crushed, the leaders tortured and executed. Their depleted labour was replaced by vast influxes of enslaved Africans, who died in their millions to keep agriculture and industry moving and silver flowing back to Spain. Venezuela, though, reportedly named for the stilt houses of the Indigenous inhabitants built along the coastal waterways of the region which reminded the invaders of Venice (hence Venezuela – Little Venice), was always a colonial backwater. It lacked the vast wealth in gold or silver found in New Spain (Mexico) to the north or Peru to the south, and sat within the Viceroyalty of New Granada, most famous perhaps for the legends of El Dorado, the city of gold, lost somewhere in the interior and subject to hundreds of expeditions over the centuries, many of which never returned.

By the late eighteenth century New Granada, like the other Spanish colonies in America, was becoming isolated from a Spain whose wealth and power were increasingly squandered on failed wars with other European powers. The toppling of the Spanish monarchy by Napoleon in 1808 led to quasi-independence for the colonies, including Venezuela, as Spain itself became a de facto colony of France and the nation dissolved into a bloody internal conflict between the French Empire and an alliance of Spain, Portugal and the armies of Great Britain, a war which killed up to a million people. Spanish efforts to reassert dominion after the Napoleonic Wars came to a close in 1815 and led to a series of protracted and vicious conflicts across the Spanish Americas. The colonies, one by one, defeated the Spanish armies, broke away from Spain and established their independence.

For the first time in a long time a well-established,

continent-spanning global empire was splintering into its component pieces. Philosophically it could perhaps have been an opportunity for rethinking what nations meant and how they could develop, if only there hadn't been such strong vested interests in preventing that kind of reconsideration from happening effectively. For the world into which the new countries of the Americas were born was one still dominated by empire. As the Spanish Empire tumbled, other nations were growing, particularly the British, whose dominance of ocean trade in the aftermath of the Napoleonic Wars allowed them to build the largest, most populous empire the world has ever seen, one which daily affected hundreds of millions of lives as swathes of Africa, Asia, North America and Oceania turned pink.

Like the Spanish Empire before it, the British Empire was intended solely to provide vast wealth for a tiny sliver of the population of a small nation in a corner of Europe by exploiting the labour and resources of a third of the world. The British Empire shaped global systems of diplomacy and trade more than any other of the last 500 years. It was an institution which fundamentally remade much of the world, and which despite its advertised demise, continues to influence the lives of hundreds of millions in complicated and intersecting ways. As Sathnam Sanghera has noted, we have in Britain a selective amnesia about the British Empire and its lasting effects on us as a nation and society which interprets examination as disloyalty,* an inability

---

* Sanghera, Sathnam, 2021. *Empireland: How Imperialism Has Shaped Modern Britain.* Viking, London, p. 188

to correctly understand the nature of empire which is easily exploited by those who see it as a national memory of which we should be proud, or are scared that too close an examination might start to unpick the noble myths which underpin so much of British nationalism.

The distorting effect of such a vast concentration of wealth and power on politics and economics all over the world directly shaped the fate of nations and billions of people. Even those places to which the British Empire did not officially stretch were not immune from its impact. It is likely for example that the garrison of Clipperton Island might never have been sent to die on their deserted atoll had not the British Pacific Mining Company secured the guano concession on the island. So it was with Venezuela; the presence of the British Empire across its borders, and the British interplay with its European rivals, dominated Venezuela for most of its first century.

In the decades following independence as a province of the nation of Gran Colombia in 1823 and then as an independent country seven years later, Venezuela struggled to maintain political stability. Coups and civil wars followed one another with depressing regularity, and control of the country passed, often violently, between an authoritarian upper class of military officers and politicians known as caudillos. Most came from the relatively wealthy coastal regions of eastern Venezuela, while the west, including Maracaibo, remained largely undeveloped. The reason for this was simple: the economy, reliant on agricultural exports, was propped up by foreign investment. Successive presidents took out large loans from foreign companies and nations, ostensibly to build railways and develop social programmes, but in reality to hoard money for themselves and their families. Large companies, principally German, began to intervene in the governance of Venezuela, leveraging the country's debt to influence policy-making in their favour, using the power their wealth brought in a comparatively poor nation to further extend substantial loans at excessive interest to autocratic governments unable to do more than keep up with interest payments.

Empires distort human history. Their expansion erases and erodes the nations they subsume, and they extract capital. Raw materials, wealth, human beings and human culture are com-modified and processed and removed from colonies for the benefit of colonial centres. The Spanish came to the Americas seeking wealth, crudely at first in the raw pursuit of gold, and in doing so instigated one of the worst genocides the world has ever seen, spreading diseases and starting wars that collapsed civilizations and killed tens of millions. Such an outcome was not accidental, but a recognized and systematic part of their approach: by devastating existing populations and upending their economic and political systems, it enabled relatively small numbers of invaders, working with local allies, to destroy large Indigenous empires and replace them with new borders, cut arbitrarily through the remains of those of the Indigenous popu-lations they had overwhelmed.

In 1895 those colonially imposed, highly theoretical borders became a contentious issue once more as Britain, whose small colonial holdings on the Caribbean coast in British Guiana sat alongside independent Venezuela, challenged Venezuelan sovereignty over the Essequibo River basin. Disputes over this undeveloped rainforest territory stretched back to the days when Guiana was a Dutch colony, and was rooted in an historic disinterest in the interior – it was too remote and too dangerous for exploitation, and so it was never adequately defined by colonial governments. The European colonists had settled along the coasts and larger rivers, establishing plantations and mines, but leaving the vast and uncharted forests of the interior largely untouched except for a few expeditions, many of which never returned. The British seized control of the region from the Dutch in 1796 during the French Revolutionary Wars and did not return it when the Napoleonic Wars drew to a close. In an effort to firmly establish where the nebulous inland boundaries lay, a British-commissioned German expedition led by Robert Hermann Schomburgk was sent to map the borders in 1840, producing a supposedly definitive border through the previously unmapped forests. Schomburgk's line was generous to the British, and provoked a response from Venezuela disputing the findings of the investigation – the attempt to define the boundary had worsened the dispute rather than resolving it.

British Guiana, now Guyana, also went through extensive social upheaval in the nineteenth century: a slave rebellion in 1823 severely disrupted the plantation systems, which collapsed almost entirely on the emancipation of the colony's African slaves in 1838. Unwilling to continue the dirty, dangerous and poorly paid work of harvesting and refining sugar for absentee plantation owners, and taking advantage of the vast acreage of unclaimed land, the former slaves set up farming communities along the territory's rivers and became a class of successful co-operative smallholders and traders. The planters responded by shipping in indentured labourers from across the British Empire and its trading networks, first Portuguese immigrants from Madeira, then Chinese labourers and finally large numbers of workers from India, many of whom were brought halfway around the world without any real notion of where they were going or why. Though by contract these communities were supposed to be returned to their countries of origin when their terms of service were up, many did not do so, and they too settled into a diverse multi-cultural community, ruled, as in neighbouring independent Venezuela, by a wealthy class of landowners, who sought constantly to wring wealth out of their corner of the British Empire.

Thus it was that in the 1870s, gold mines were established in the Cuyuni River basin in the jungles of the western Guianan interior, lying within the poorly defined, disputed region on the vague border between Guiana and Venezuela territory. The miners and the money were British, but the mine lay on the Venezuelan side of the putative border, and so the British Empire simply annexed the territory – claim and counter-claim overlapping across unreliable maps depicting land mostly occupied by communities of the Indigenous Kalina people, whose societies had been badly damaged by European-introduced diseases and rapacious exploratory expeditions. As miners intruded on their homelands, their claims to thousands of years of occupancy were once more blithely ignored equally by the British colonial government and independent Venezuela. For twenty years British settlers and Venezuelan soldiers participated in a hostile stand-off in the region, the Venezuelans unwilling to challenge the might of the British Empire and the settlers unwilling to test the Venezuelan resolve. In 1894, however, unsatisfied with the territory already obtained, British settlers began to illegally spread beyond the undrawn lines, and in consequence were expelled by the Venezuelan Army.

It was at this stage that the United States, hitherto neutral in the dispute, began to look more closely at what was happening. In early 1895, British forces had raided the coast of Nicaragua in a similar territorial dispute, and President Cleveland became concerned that American hegemony in the Caribbean might be under threat. The Monroe Doctrine, declared in 1823, asserted that the United States, and not the empires of Europe, would exercise hegemony over the independent former colonial states of the Americas. It guaranteed their independence, but only under the protection of the American government, and said nothing of debt colonialism as practised in Venezuela. As a doctrine it failed at times when directly challenged – the French invasion of Mexico being a case in point – but it granted successive US presidents the excuse they required to intervene directly in the affairs of South and Central American nations. British incursions into Venezuelan territory clearly violated the Monroe Doctrine, and Cleveland was concerned by British expansion in the Cuyuni Basin. His fears were amplified by a man named William Scruggs, a Washington lobbyist engaged by the Venezuelan government to appeal to Congress and the president in the hope that the favour of the burgeoning financial and military power of the United States might force the British to withdraw their expansion across Venezuelan borders.

This, though, was how the British Empire grew, spreading across the map as merchant explorers, colonial governors and ambitious military officers continually probed the borders of British hegemony. The British Empire was not the monolith its propaganda pretended, but, like the Spanish Empire before it, a largely unplanned and sporadically organized institution, expanded and sustained only by continual exploitation: trampling the rights of the peoples who lived there in search of profit. All along the Cuyuni River, miners, many drawn from the immigrant waves Britain had imported into Guiana, felled virgin rainforest, dammed rivers and tore up the earth in search of gold, wreaking ecological damage and causing further havoc to the Kalina communities. Venezuela set up border posts to try to deter the mining expeditions, but British-led militias attacked them, sparking a back-and-forth border war – too small to draw in the military forces of the British Empire, unconcerned with yet another scuffle at the edge of a colonial backwater which had never turned a noticeable profit, but significant enough to raise alarm in Washington.

In an effort to resolve the dispute raging on the Venezuelan border, to disrupt British expansion deeper into South America and prompted by Scruggs's urging, President Cleveland ultimately insisted on, and the British reluctantly acquiesced to, the establishment of a border panel to conduct an inquiry and rule on the matter. Two members of the panel were to be British and two Venezuelan, with a neutral Russian member to provide the casting vote. If this set-up, requiring only a single member to be compromised by bribery, blackmail or diplomatic considerations in order for one side or another to take control of the wealth of the disputed region, was not sufficiently prone to corruption, the so-called 'Venezuelan' delegates to the panel were both Americans, selected by Cleveland. After three years of leisurely and less than dedicated research and deliberations, the panel, without detailed explanation or excuse, awarded almost all the disputed territory to Britain, without the right of appeal. The Venezuelan government was furious, accusing the British delegates, quite probably with cause, of leaning on the Russian, the representatives of three empires conspiring to ensure that the wealthiest resources of Venezuela were withheld from that country and added to the British Empire. Thus it was that the imperial giants of the Old and New Worlds carved up the richest parts of Venezuela for themselves.

The loss of the territory and ongoing political disorganization was economically crippling for Venezuela. Successive caudillo presidents, unable to fund their constant internal conflicts and rampant corruption from the country's limited financial resources, had taken out huge loans against future economic development, including the promise of the gold wealth of the Guinean border region. These debts were incurred to bankers and merchant houses from several countries, including Britain and Italy, but most particularly in Germany. German companies had used their outstanding leverage to gradually seize control of Venezuelan assets. Banks, ports and especially railways had been turned over to German operators, their infrastructure and maintenance paid for through regular payments from the Venezuelan government. But the loss of the gold mines, followed by a civil war as the government changed hands once more by placing Cipriano Castro, a cattle baron commanding a private army raised in Colombia, in control, meant that Venezuela was leveraged far beyond its assets. Castro exacerbated the situation, looting the Venezuelan treasury and distributing the spoils of his war to his followers.

This had happened because the empires of Europe couldn't simply invade or overrun the independent countries of South and Central America; the French invasion of Mexico (while the United States was distracted by its own civil war) had ended in disaster. The looming threat of the Monroe Doctrine dissuaded further adventurism. Overt intervention promised war, or – perhaps worse – a trade embargo by the huge market of the United States, should a European country launch a war of conquest in the Americas. This problem led to alternative approaches which ensured that there was no point in invasion and annexation anyway, since companies could do the job of colonization and extraction just as well without the risk of losing soldiers, public opinion and public money in lengthy campaigns of the kind which constantly flared at the edges of empire, as seen by the French in Morocco, or the British in Afghanistan. From every border the empires of Europe expanded their hegemony ever further through the economic clout of almost entirely unregulated private enterprise.

Debt management was an essential part of this approach, exemplified in Venezuela, by pushing smaller nations into unsustainable loans which allowed companies leverage over government decisions. When those debts went unfulfilled, the leaders of these companies had direct access to their national governments for redress. Able to pay lawyers and lobbyists to approach kings and tsars and parliaments – just as Scruggs had in Washington in the run-up to the 1895 crisis – they could demand, loudly and insistently, that governments step in to make good their losses. This was a combination of capitalism and imperialism not far removed from racketeering. Companies entered poorer nations, stripped their most valuable assets and demanded payments for the privilege, taking advantage of and actively stoking political instability in order to ensure that they were never faced with investigation, restriction or restraint. Gradually the Venezuelan caudillos came to be entirely dependent on these companies, reliant on them for financing, for military support and for the regular operation of critical national infrastructure. They were now no longer independent nations, but puppet states for semi-national corporations that could, if their investments were threatened, call in the vast military might of their imperial governments to enforce collection.

Thus it was that the Venezuelan government, owing five times its annual national income to its creditors and unable to pay its huge debts to the German companies, found itself under pressure from the imperial German government, responding itself to pressure in Berlin from the German commercial interests whose investments in Venezuela were at risk. These demands were compounded by other European powers, particularly Britain and Italy, demanding recompense for their own loans, as well as for damage and injury suffered by European settlers and companies during the continual civil wars. In 1902, his resources empty and facing a renewed civil war from a European-backed banking baron named Manuel Antonio Matos, President Castro defaulted on Venezuelan debt, refusing to pay any more crippling interest to foreign powers and diverting money to his army to stave off Matos's forces – in July Matos was defeated in a battle at Ciudad Bolívar and fled to France.

This refusal to pay Venezuelan loans provoked fury in Europe and undermined the vast networks of imperial trade. If Venezuela was allowed to abandon its debt obligations, then other nations that owed money to the European empires might feel emboldened to default on their own, and loosen the imperial grip on their governments and resources. Thus it was that British, Italian and German ships, joined by a Dutch squadron from Curaçao, spent the winter of 1902 sitting off the Venezuelan coast as a threatening presence. The flotilla was commanded by British

Rear-Admiral Robert Montgomerie, supported by the extravagantly moustachioed German Kapitän-Leutnant Titus Türk.

Montgomerie was under very strict instructions to limit the violence of his interventions in Venezuela. The alliance with Germany was unpopular in Britain and neither the European powers nor Castro were sure how the American President Theodore Roosevelt would interpret the actions of the imperial powers should they actually attack Venezuela, rather than just menace its coast. Cleveland's concerns in the previous decade had been reinterpreted by the new president, who had a long history of supporting imperial ambitions: he had been a key player in the Spanish-American war of 1898 which had seen the American seizure of the remnants of the Spanish Empire, building a new American Empire in the Philippines and Puerto Rico. He thus had a vested interest in maintaining American hegemony in Latin America, but had also expressed strong support for the maintenance of debt payments to imperial powers, and the right of those powers to ensure payment of those debts by force.

The blockade began by seizing or destroying the obsolete and hopelessly outmatched Venezuelan Navy and then shelling Venezuelan forts at Puerto Cabello. Castro responded by arresting more than 200 British, German and Italian citizens in Venezuela, but they were released on the intervention of the US ambassador, following Roosevelt's instructions to de-escalate the crisis. The blockade then prevented shipping from entering or leaving Venezuelan ports, particularly targeting merchant vessels, but a dispute between the allies had arisen; Germany wanted

Venezuelan merchant shipping seized in partial payment of the debt, while Britain refused, and, via Montgomerie in overall command, insisted. Regardless, the blockade was crippling to the Venezuelan economy, preventing engagement in the global networks of trade dominated by the empires whose ships sat off the Venezuelan coast.

Castro refused to back down and agree to the European debt demands, relying on Roosevelt's tacit neutrality and encouraged by anti-European sentiment in the American press. Britain, unwilling to launch a war in South America on behalf of largely German debts, agreed to American arbitration, followed by Germany, and negotiations began in Washington with German, British, Italian and American diplomats. Venezuela was once more represented, at Roosevelt's insistence, by an American, the United States' ambassador to Castro's government, Herbert Bowen.

The blockade remained in force as negotiations began. Montgomerie had, under instructions from London, withdrawn to a distant position offshore, avoiding exacerbating the situation further, but Türk was determined to make an impression on the Venezuelans of the martial prowess of the German Navy. He ordered the gunboat *Panther* to enter Lake Maracaibo as a direct act of intimidation ahead of the talks, but *Panther* was fired on by Fort San Carlos – ironically the fort had recently been supplied with modern German-made artillery – and *Panther* was damaged by heavy shellfire, unable to respond to the bombardment as the channel was too shallow to permit it to draw within range.

Smarting from this perceived defeat, Türk ordered his flagship *Vineta* to punish the fort for its resistance.

On 21 January, Türk led his ship into the mouth of Lake Maracaibo and opened fire, bombarding the fort with heavy artillery until it was a blazing wreck. High shells looped over the fort and fell among the streets and alleyways of the fishing village beneath it, and by nightfall the fort and community burned. At least twenty-five Venezuelan civilians were killed in the fires. His pride satisfied, Türk sailed out of the bay.

Türk's impulsive actions were completely unsanctioned by either the British or German governments, and in direct opposition to the orders given to Montgomerie, though the British admiral had declined to pass these instructions onto Türk on the grounds that as he was the senior officer, Türk would in the normal course of matters defer to him before undertaking operations. The German government subsequently justified the attack as retaliation for the 'unprovoked' Venezuelan attack on *Panther*, an account to which Britain reluctantly agreed while privately criticizing Türk's actions. In America, however, an outpouring of public anger at the bombardment pressured Roosevelt to quietly inform the allies that should any further offensive actions be taken against Venezuela, the US Atlantic fleet, currently at sea off Puerto Rico, would be ordered to steam south and interpose itself between the allied squadron and the Venezuelan coast, an escalation in the conflict far beyond the reclamation of debts and one which none of the Imperial powers wanted to risk.

Türk's actions had handed the initiative to the Americans, who had already effectively suborned the Venezuelan supreme court: on the day *Panther* was turned away at Maracaibo, the court awarded the enormous sum of $711,307 in damages to the American businessman Henry Rudloff, who ten years earlier had briefly been under contract to manage a market in Caracas. The contract had collapsed due to the endemic corruption of 1890s Venezuela, but now that the nation was on the back foot, Rudloff and dozens of other creditors emerged clutching violated contracts and unpaid invoices. Rudloff got paid an exorbitant sum for eighteen years of work he never completed, as well as a full refund of his costs and compensation for damage to his credit rating. A news report drily notes that 'the United States Legation watched the case closely, sending representatives who attended all the sittings of the court',* neatly obfuscating their role in ensuring the verdict was little more than a calculated insult and embezzlement, a great power protection racket designed to continue to transfer wealth from nominally independent Venezuela to the imperial capitals of Europe and North America via merchant adventurers like Rudloff.

Thus it was, with Venezuelan law and government creaking and the fort still smouldering, that Roosevelt used his new-found

---

* *Globe*, 1903. "'Panther' Forbidden to Enter Lake Maracaibo". 19 February 1903. Accessed online via the British Newspaper Archive at https://www.britishnewspaper archive.co.uk/viewer/bl/0001652/19030219/055/0006; *United Nations*, 1905 [2006]. "Rudloff case (on merits)". Reports of International Arbitral Awards, Vol IX, pp. 255–261. Accessed online at https://legal.un.org/riaa/cases/vol_IX/255-261.pdf

initiative to force the government to the negotiating table. On 13 February an agreement on Venezuelan debt was signed in Washington by Bowen, acting ostensibly on behalf of the Venezuelans, but really for Roosevelt. The terms were harsh. The treaty cost Venezuela 30 per cent of its export duties, and forced them to pay an indemnity of nearly half a million dollars. Individual panels were set up to renegotiate the myriad network of debt contracts for which the Venezuelan government was now once more responsible. Castro and Venezuela were subsequently sued at the International Court in The Hague by Germany and Britain and they lost, the judges awarding preferential repayment to the imperial powers, further crippling the economic position of independent Venezuela. Having used the massacre at Maracaibo to full advantage in forcing the allies into a negotiated withdrawal, Roosevelt found American debtors sidelined by the judgement, and responded with a doctrine of his own. Called the Roosevelt Corollary, it amended the Monroe Doctrine to state that the United States now had the absolute right to intervene, militarily if necessary, to secure the economic and political stability of South and Central American countries, and consequently to exert total hegemony over external influence. It was now US policy to prevent foreign powers from building the kind of economic and political dominance the Germans had managed in Venezuela, and to use US military force to ensure preferential debt repayment.

Nearly six years later, with his country crippled economically by its enforced debt repayments, Castro, who was suffering the effects of syphilis and kidney disease, became embroiled in another international incident, this time with the Dutch. Roosevelt, then in his last months as president, took the opportunity to overthrow the Castro government, using the US fleet to install another caudillo, Juan Vicente Gómez. In December Castro fled to, of all places, Berlin. He sought medical treatment in Europe, living for a time in Spain, until attempting to enter the United States in 1913. Refused entry, he took up residency in Puerto Rico, railing increasingly erratically against the Gómez government and the powers who had betrayed him. He died in 1924, by which time the alliance that had come together to attack Venezuela in 1902 had long been in tatters.

The most important effect of the forgotten Venezuela Crisis of 1902–3 was the Roosevelt Corollary – it authorized and indeed mandated American involvement in the Americas when American interests were threatened. Roosevelt stated that

> If a nation shows that it knows how to act with reasonable efficiency and decency in social and political matters, if it keeps order and pays its obligations, it need fear no interference from the United States. Chronic wrongdoing, or an impotence which results in a general loosening of the ties of civilized society, may in America, as elsewhere, ultimately require intervention by some civilized nation.

The implication was clear – the United States was a civilized democracy, former colonies in Latin America, run by caudillos and dictators, were not, and the United States must take the burden of their protection for their own good – while ensuring that American interests and businesses, such as the fortunate Rudloff, received all the preferential treatment they could desire. This implied political and cultural supremacy, deliberately placing the United States, newly possessing its own overseas empire taken from the Spanish, on the same level as the empires of Europe. This was all the authority American presidents needed to intervene in any way they saw fit in the governments and economies of nations in the Americas. In one fell swoop it drastically limited the nature of the independence these nations held; their leaders now had to maintain good relations with the US government and the corporations which lobbied it to ensure political stability and American support. If they failed to do either, the United States had the self-proclaimed right to topple their governments and install new ones, enforced by the military power of its armed forces. To go alongside the seized Spanish empire and the burgeoning American imperial expansion in the Pacific, Roosevelt had ensured that the Americas, at least those parts not currently controlled by a European empire, were now American, North American, in all but name.

Over the next century American troops enforced this doctrine again and again; American soldiers landed in Cuba, Nicaragua, Haiti, Mexico and the Dominican Republic, all before 1920. Though the Corollary was subsequently amended several times, it remained in force and in practice – in 1954 it was directly cited in a CIA operation against the government of Guatemala.* Though no longer official policy of the American government, it underpinned additional interventions in Mexico, Cuba, Nicaragua, the Dominican Republic and Venezuela again, and later during the Cold War period in Haiti, Panama, Grenada, Brazil, Peru, Chile and Colombia. Officially the legislation and explanation differed each time, but the reality remained the protection of US economic interests over those of the other imperial powers or the nations in which the operations took place.

What the British-provoked miners' disputes on the Essequibo and the German bombardment of Maracaibo enabled was nothing less than the establishment of an imperial economic and military domination of the nominally independent countries of Latin American and the Caribbean by the coming superpower of the United States. To this day the inland colonial borders between Venezuela and now-independent Guyana are subject to international dispute. Venezuela, the most oil-rich nation on earth, is crippled by international debt and constant internal political instability and authoritarianism, and the United States continues to use its wealth and strength to interfere in the political, economic and social structures of its near neighbours for its own profit and protection. As recently as 2019 the Trump administration forced the Guatemalan government to sign a restrictive asylum law designed to make it harder for immigrants from Central America to reach the US border. When the

---

* Ganzert, Frederic W., 1954. "The Caracas Conference". *World Affairs* 117(2) (Summer 1954). Accessed online via jstor at https://www.jstor.org/stable/20668889

Guatemalan courts blocked the law, the Trump administration threatened punitive taxation on Guatemalan goods unless the law was ratified. The threats worked, and though it was never directly cited, the justification for this action was unchanged from that of the Roosevelt Corollary.*

The massacre of San Carlos in 1903 is a small but significant step in understanding the structures of imperialism which surround and enmesh smaller nations, peoples and societies within vast multinational conspiracies of economic and political exploitation. It was the international structure of great power relations which repeatedly stymied any attempts at meaningful self-expression of political stability in Venezuela, which snuffed efforts at true independence and political stability at every opportunity. It was the carefully constructed capitalist structures of international trade and business which enabled Venezuela to be held hostage financially and militarily by powers thousands of miles away, and it was the colonially imposed social structures which ensured that internal political cohesion was and remains near impossible to the present day. Venezuela's recent upheaval may or may not be directly related to US intervention. More likely the corruption and incompetence of the Chávez and Maduro regimes provokes genuine lawlessness and anger, but this history – which led to a situation where stranded motorists can be

---

* Narea, Nicole. "Trump's agreements in Central America are dismantling the asylum system as we know it". *Vox*, 20 November 2019. Accessed online at https://www.vox.com/2019/9/26/20870768/trump-agreement-honduras-guatemala-el-salvador-explained

readily gunned down by armed gangs, and government militias can fire on crowds – is a consequence of generations of political and economic damage from imperialism, and it is that which gives Maduro's accusations weight.

More than a century after Türk ordered *Vineta* into Lake Maracaibo to exact revenge on the Venezuelans and attempt to intimidate Castro into conforming to the German debt repayment schedule, Venezuela is still a nation riven by coups, protests and civil violence. Chávez's conspicuous campaign to reject American influence, continued by Maduro, may have an altruistic veneer of improving the lives of Venezuelans, but it is rooted in the same caudillo structures of corruption and authoritarian government which plagued and destabilized the country in the nineteenth century. There is, however, a difference. In 1914, around the time that the settlers on Clipperton Island were abandoned to die, oil was discovered below the lightning-scorched skies of Lake Maracaibo, a deep basin of Jurassic crude oil, one of a number of reserves under Venezuela which are today believed to be the largest and richest in the world.

Venezuela's reserves are not easily accessible. They are buried deep and harder to process than the lighter crude of the Middle East, but they are vast – more than enough to make Venezuela one of the richest nations on earth, and to finance Chávez and Maduro's much-vaunted and never realized social programmes and lift Venezuelans out of poverty. That this wealth has never been fully attained is the legacy of two key factors: the internal corruption of Venezuela's ruling elites, who have consistently chosen personal profit over meaningful national wealth redistri-bution, and the complicated networks of international diplomacy and commerce which provoked the crises of 1895 and 1902 and the years since, undermining efforts to build and sustain legit-imate democratic succession and responsible governance.

Venezuela, and its history of encounter with colonial empires, is but a single example of the ways in which structures of oppres-sion enable exploitation on a colossal scale, which prevent effective opposition through collaboration and corruption, and favour those willing to exploit the system over those who would seek to make it work successfully. The systems devised in this period of history are the foundation of the systems we live in and perpetuate today, and the nations which shaped this world are, for now, the nations who continue to shape it. In the chapters that follow, various aspects of this process will be explored to present a holistic understanding of the extent of the dominance systems of oppression enact.

Chapter Three

ECONOMIC OPPRESSION: HUNTING FOR HEADS

Until very recently, if you wandered into the Pitt Rivers Museum in Oxford, passing though the Museum of Natural History in its grand Victorian sandstone and into the obscured annex at the back through the dark door behind a pillar, you would find a grand hall stuffed with artefacts from peoples all over the world. Hundreds of cases, each one filled with the material culture assembled by a century of curators and based on the core collections of Augustus Pitt Rivers: eclectic collector, British Army general and inveterate racist.

Pitt Rivers was obsessed with the notion that you could, by examining the world's material culture, create a working hierarchy of civilization, with moustachioed British men like himself at the top, and at the bottom those stateless tribal peoples steamrollered by empire whom Pitt Rivers considered less human and more proto-human, whose examination might for example enable an understanding of Neolithic Europeans, based upon racist misreadings of Darwin's theory of evolution. In the Pitt Rivers Museum, founded on his collection and his theories, this theory was put to the test. It was of course nonsense, but in the course of his studies, Pitt Rivers obtained some remarkable objects, including a selection of extravagantly decorated human heads, shrunk to the size of a fist.

These have recently been removed from public view,* but until the autumn of 2020 they were in a case just to the right as you made your way down the entrance steps. Some of these heads look barely human, and that is because they are in fact the heads of sloths or monkeys, but others are unmistakably the miniaturized features of people dangling as curiosities in the fevered White supremacist fantasy of a long-dead colonial general. The modern staff of the museum do not share Pitt Rivers's racist views, and have for generations fought against the racist legacies of their forebear, yet these heads hung there for years, subject to fierce resistance from museum visitors and external commentators whenever efforts were made to remove them.

The heads remain in the collections, and are in the museum as a legacy of a war which waged almost unknown in the jungles of South America among the Shuar, a people denied even the

---

* Adams, Geraldine Kendall. "Pitt Rivers Museum removes shrunken heads from display after ethical review". *Museums Association*, 18 September 2020. Accessed online at https://www.museumsassociation.org/museums-journal/news/2020/09/Pitt-Rivers-museum-removes-shrunken-heads-from-display-after-ethical-review

fig-leaf protection of sovereignty permitted to the Venezuelans. For beset though they have been by corrupt leadership and Imperial exploitation, the people of Venezuela have an advantage many other groups lack: they have independence, if sometimes nominal, and the right – the privilege – of an internationally recognized nation of their own to broadly lead or mislead as they see fit. It is common in the early twenty-first century to talk about the world as a post-colonial place, in which the empires that marked so much of modern history are things of the past, ostensibly dead and buried by the independence movements of the mid-twentieth century and replaced by supposedly more equal communities of nations working together in international organizations like the UN or the Commonwealth of Nations. Yet the imperial legacies in the political structures and borders left behind are not only ongoing factors in disruptive competition between nations, but also a process of the oppression of communities within nations.

For when European empires rolled across the rest of the world, they did not find blank spaces on the map, or wilderness to be claimed. The Spanish who arrived in the Americas in the early sixteenth century found hundreds of civilizations already there, civilizations which stretched from vast empires like those of the Aztecs in Mexico and the Inca in Peru, to individual communities in coasts, mountains, rivers, jungles and deserts. Every single one of these communities had its own complex political, social and technological structures which enabled it to survive, and one by one every single one was systematically destroyed by imperial expansion. Oppression existed in these communities too, of

73

course; the networks by which people oppress one another are a human constant. But to the European invaders these people and their cultures were by and large considered barely human – savages and primitives to be enslaved, exterminated and dominated, the survivors inserted into newly imposed social structures at the very bottom.

It was thus that everywhere that European empires stretched, and there was almost no part of the world their armies and merchants and missionaries did not reach, they damaged and oppressed the societies they found there as a core function of how empire was intended to operate. And even in those few places where they did not rule directly, those corners of the map not coloured according to European political control where their influence and dominance was less than total, the philosophies they brought with them continued to disrupt and harm communities never before exposed to these networks of ideas and the practical structures which sustained them. For these people colonialism did not, at least not immediately, overrun their homes and communities; instead it settled on them more slowly and insidiously until they found themselves enveloped, with borders drawn around them over which they had no say and of which they were often unaware. They became often unrecognized nations within nations, subject to laws and hostile alien practices against which they had limited defence and few tools to cope.

Many of these communities, which today are generally termed Indigenous peoples, denoting the inheritors of the people who claimed these lands before colonialization scarred them, still live in an uneasy half-state, caught between traditional ways of life and European philosophical structures, driven to adapt as best they can to the unfamiliar frames of existence forced upon their communities from outside. For these people the colonial period has never ended and probably never will. They are buffered by outside forces far beyond their control which clash chaotically with the structures they have built for themselves. For them the world is very far from post-colonial – it is colonial, and they are likely to be forever trapped this way. Among the most pernicious and insidious of the forces operating in these systems is something that lies at the very foundations of European cultures, the economic structures of capitalism.

In the late 1890s, armed bands of warriors of the Shuar people, dressed in feathered head-dresses and armbands and carrying rifles and clubs, descended from the rainforested highlands of Ecuador known as the Cordillera de Cutucú. Cut off from most of the rest of the country by high mountains and dense jungles, these highland communities had resisted invasion for generations, successively fighting off the efforts of the Inca, the Spanish and then the independent Ecuadorean government to explore and exploit their homelands, leaving invading forces lost and bloodied by their superior knowledge of combat and terrain in the forested foothills of the Andes.

These raiding parties swept into communities of the neighbouring Achuar people and the more assimilated villages in the lowlands along the Gualaquiza River. Emerging unexpectedly from the forest, they killed all the men first, then most of the women and children, leaving a few young women alive to be taken as prisoners. When survivors of these raids emerged from their hiding places amid the trees and returned to the ruins of their villages, they found that every single person captured and killed by the Shuar warband had been decapitated, their heads severed and carried back into the highlands with the raiders. For the Shuar had learned about the global systems of economics from traders and missionaries, and had come to understand that in this colonial environment, in which they lacked the independence and security to control their own destiny, the only way to gain wealth and keep it, under pressure from rivals and neighbours and the encroaching rubber planters and cattle ranchers backed by the Ecuadorean state, was through a systematic campaign of mass murder.

The Shuar had, for thousands of years, lived in villages based around extended families living together in large communal houses erected in the forest, presided over by chieftains known as kakaram and surrounded by carefully tended gardens. They subsisted on the produce of these gardens, mostly manioc, tended by the women of the village while the men hunted in the forest along loosely defined but widely understood territories. Like any human civilization, they had a process by which food and goods moved between communities along an insular trade network that connected families and communities, a form of what we would call economics but which was in reality a very different social construct maintained through trust and familiarity between

families and communities – contact with outsiders, even neighbouring Indigenous peoples, was limited to the peripheries of
Shuar territory.

Alongside the kakaram, who held formal political authority
among the Shuar, were the shamans. Practitioners of traditional
medicine which combined the therapeutic and the magical,
the shamans were understood as wielding supernatural powers
over life itself, able to cause sickness and death through curses,
and direct Shuar kakaram in their trade, diplomacy and warfare through advice, oracles and spells. The isolation of the
Shuar was a safety measure. Long before the Spanish invaders
crossed the Andes, other outsiders had invaded Shuar lands;
the armies of the Inca Empire had first overrun the lowland
Shuar, driving many families further into the mountains and
turning the survivors into a vassal people under Inca colonial
rule. Inca expeditions deeper into the mountain forests, though,
were defeated again and again. The Shuar disappeared into the
trees at their approach and engaged in guerrilla combat which
whittled down the invaders' numbers and morale.

When Spanish conquistadors murdered the Inca emperor
Atahualpa and upended his empire in 1533, the lowland Shuar
were unable to take advantage of the political chaos to seize their
independence, and were soon overrun in turn by the Spanish,
enslaved and nearly destroyed by disease and mistreatment as
their lowlands were divided up into plantations and Spanish
fiefdoms. Many Shuar communities, though, remained un-
assailable in their highland homelands, and exploring Spanish

armies suffered the same fate as the Inca before them, dying of disease and exhaustion in the high forests until the Shuar war parties emerged to kill or drive off the few survivors. In time, the Spanish learned that the Shuar were too dangerous, their lands too inhospitable and their resources not valuable enough to merit the losses suffered in each failed operation.

The Shuar were not totally unaffected by the Spanish colonization of the continent, suffering from introduced European diseases which in time changed social structures to revolve more closely around the nuclear family unit, fracturing the communal structures which had knitted extended families together into loose aggregations of survivors. These interrelated groups sporadically descended from their mountains to raid Spanish colonial farms and communities in the river valleys, before retreating from counter-attacks, their independent existence a constant threat to the maintenance of Spanish rule. Sometimes in these raids, as in the endemic intertribal warfare of the highlands, particular victims would be beheaded and the heads taken back into the forest. Back in their communities, the Shuar would then shrink the heads in a complex and intricate ceremony essential to Shuar culture and society.

Shrunken heads, known as tsantsas, are a phenomenon peculiar to the Indigenous communities of the high jungles of the western Amazon basin and surrounding areas. Other peoples in other places have taken heads as trophies, from kings of England to the rainforests of New Guinea, but none have turned the removal and preservation of the human head into such a dedicated practice as the Shuar and their neighbours. Using a technique originally practised on the heads of both powerful enemies and beloved leaders, the head was sliced open at the back to remove the skull, the remaining skin envelope then boiled and treated with hot sand around a wooden ball to shrink the skin until it was roughly the size of a human fist, still with lustrous hair, beard and eyelashes attached, becoming the tsantsa. The tsantsa was then coated in ash, this last to prevent the musiak, the angry soul of the deceased, from seeking vengeance on its killer. The heads would then be celebrated at a series of three feasts to which family, allies and rivals would be invited to celebrate the martial achievements of the kakaram, who would distribute food and gifts. Once celebrated at the feast, the tsantsa would lose its power, and could be safely disposed of.*

These feasts are a critical moment in Shuar life, and gift feasts like this are a social phenomenon found in Indigenous communities across the Americas – though usually without the requirement for severed human heads – in which prominent leaders impose obligations on their guests by bestowing gifts which demand repayment with communally understood terms of interest. A Shuar kakaram who created many tsantsas and distributed great wealth could call on the support of his guests in times of war or trade negotiations, relying on their obligations to him until their debts were repaid. This was how the Shuar pursued economics, not by adjustable values of economic

---

* Steel, Daniel, 1999. "Trade Goods and Jívaro Warfare: The Shuar 1850–1957, and the Achuar, 1940–1978". *Ethnohistory* (46:4), pp. 745–776.

goods, represented by raw materials or units of currency, but in personal status within complex networks of debt and obligation between the kakaram. Sitting outside Shuar power structures, and held in a certain feared awe by Shuar society, the shamans were excluded from these complex economic systems which underpinned Shuar politics, and were able to accumulate wealth without participation in the network of debt obligation which governed the kakaram, making them an alternative, supernatural power structure to which the Shuar could turn in times of crisis. It was an economic system which had endured for thousands of years and was to collide with the capitalist systems of Europe, originally imported by the Spanish, with devastating effect.

The Spanish, of course, could not simply leave the Shuar alone in their mountain forests. They were too great a threat to the peace and stability of surrounding territories, both practically, due to their sporadic raiding, and as an example of resistance to Spanish rule which might inspire others. If they could not be brought under Spanish dominion through armed invasion, perhaps the spiritual arm of the Spanish conquest might have more success. Thus it was that the Jesuits were given permission to establish missions on the edge of the Shuar lands, with the hope that God might achieve what the musket could not. They too failed, however. The Shuar showed little interest in the Spanish God or the steel knives the priests offered as enticements, and the Jesuits themselves were purged from the Spanish American colonies after falling foul of King Charles III of Spain, who accused them, probably falsely, of fomenting rebellion against the crown in New Spain.

The expulsion of the Jesuits ended Spanish encroachment into the mountain forests of the Shuar, and for a century they lived on largely undisturbed, emerging occasionally to trade with outlying colonial villages but otherwise determinedly maintaining their autonomy and isolation away from the governments in the lowlands, which had begun to fracture from the Spanish Empire. When the Jesuits returned in the 1880s, more than a hundred years after being driven from Shuar lands, the political climate was very different. The Spanish had been gone for decades, driven out by the same wars that had established Venezuela to the north, and in their place was the government of Ecuador, led at that time by a rapidly rotating succession of caudillos as corrupt and disorganized as those who traded the presidency of Venezuela between them. They were generally marked by their conservatism and adherence to military might and religious conviction: hence the return of the Jesuits to the mountains of southern Ecuador.

As before, the Jesuits found limited success in their efforts, for among the highland Shuar, conversion to Catholicism was much less popular than with the lowland peoples. The Shuar could be lured into visiting the missions, but they were searching less for spiritual enlightenment than for material wealth, the means to influence the debt obligations made at the feasts and break the power of the wealthiest kakaram. Traders accompanied the missionaries, establishing posts alongside the houses of worship from which the Shuar visitors could trade goods obtained from their forests, including pigs and salt, for imported manufactured goods, including metalwork, textiles and other products otherwise unavailable to the Shuar. But what they wanted more than anything else was guns. Access to manufactured goods meant that a kakaram could host more prestigious feasts than their rivals and trap them into debt obligations which they could never hope to meet; access to guns meant that a kakaram could overthrow rivals, seize territory and (most importantly) contest for control of access to the missions. Their war parties would be stronger than their rivals in any encounter and could force those who wished to trade to pay tribute to the kakaram who commanded the mission. European capitalism, unfettered by restraint or authority, became a subjective oppressive force on the Shuar. Within just a few years they had descended into internecine warfare which rapidly upended their political, social and economic structures, turning farming communities embedded within well-established social and political structures into a dystopian war zone of battling kakaram split among unsettled warbands.

It was in this way, in short order, that traders succeeded where soldiers and priests had failed. The Shuar were not politically or militarily dominated, but colonialism had finally, fatally upended their social, economic and political structures without a single soldier penetrating into their forests. Capitalism has ever been a cutting edge of colonialism, a catalyst for driving deeper into the territories and cultures of other people in search of profit, a bow wave of disenfranchisement and dominance. Once colonial capitalism encounters those peoples, it warps their ways of life in response, provoking a scramble for wealth and power that can destroy entire cultures and replace them with something far more amenable to military and bureaucratic overthrow.

So it was for the Shuar. Though their pigs and salt could be traded at colonial valley towns like Macas in exchange for equipment – initially machetes, then increasingly guns – these were low-value items in the Ecuadorean economy, which could be obtained anywhere. No kakaram would become rich this way, nor be able to protect their people and territory from rivals. To survive, the Shuar needed something unique and valuable – they had to supply something no one else could. Thus it was, somewhere in one of these trades, that a trader took a fancy to a tsantsa carried by a kakaram and bought it. Others soon followed, purchased as curiosities and entered into an international network of antiquities trading which in many ways exemplified the ultimate marriage of Enlightenment science and the age of European empire.

Unknown to the Shuar, the preceding century or so had seen new and vast cathedrals of knowledge rising in European and American capitals – the Louvre in Paris, the Kunstkamera in St Petersburg, the Smithsonian Institution in Washington DC, the Royal Museum (now the Altes Museum) in Berlin and, perhaps the most influential of them all, the British Museum in London. Each sat within national networks of hundreds of other museums in towns and cities and universities all dedicated to the collection, preservation and codification of knowledge. From their vast national empires, and the trading networks that branched from them, these institutions extracted material culture from all over the world, through gift, purchase and, in many cases, outright theft.

Though their precise ambitions differed, reflecting the perceived national missions of each country and filtered through the personal ambitions of curators and the availability of funding and access, these institutions often combined materials from across the world. Their mission was to gather archaeological heritage of their own countries and keep it for scholarly study alongside fine art, the so-called ethnological collections from other peoples, vast libraries, and scientific collections of natural history and geology. The British Museum, for example, housed the national collections of natural history until 1878 and the national library of Britain until 1973, when each was branched off into its own institution. These were nothing less than bold efforts to catalogue the world, driven by the European Enlightenment movement which sought to codify, quantify and study everything which made up all that they knew.

Though couched in the language of polite scientific enquiry and public betterment, and often genuinely devoted to these pursuits within the narrow confines of stratified European society, these institutions had another, more sinister purpose: they were not just to catalogue the world and its peoples, but assess and analyse them through an explicitly European lens, and in doing so deliberately create a theoretical hierarchy of peoples which tangentially justified the exploitation of other cultures and lands. In this they were partially successful – they were able to construct their hierarchies, a study known as evolutionary archaeology, and provide governments and colonial authorities with the rationales they needed to extend paternalistic governance to willing, or more usually unwilling, colonial subjects. Pitt Rivers himself was an enthusiastic proponent of this theory.

This bled into the public consciousness through words like 'primitive' and 'savage', a likening of colonially dominated Indigenous peoples such as the Shuar to the Neolithic – the European Stone Age. The assumption ran that by studying the material culture of Native Americans, Africans or Australians, one might gain insight into how European ancestors lived, while simultaneously demonstrating that their repression and destruction were deserved since they could not be compared to modern Europeans, and were thus, in some abstract way, less human and less deserving of respect – innocent children unworthy of the rights or responsibilities of adults. This thinking was not only entirely unscientific and incorrect – there is no valuable insight into European pasts from looking at the recent or contemporary history of peoples on other continents – it is also embedded within a culture of White supremacy, and the legacies of this deeply embedded scientific racism are still with us to this day.

Yet the plan to create hierarchies failed on any objective scientific level. These collections were never even close to comprehensive, nothing more than snapshots of people in place and time which came to represent them to this day as the only authentic depiction of communities from all over the world. The dividing line between an authentic Indigenous person or object and one supposedly corrupted and made inauthentic by the advance of colonialism is one set in the museum, not in the communities affected. In many places, such as Ethiopia in 1868, Benin in West Africa in 1897, and the crumbling Chinese Empire in 1860, among hundreds of others, these collections were formed by invasion and mass killing. European armies stormed the ancient capitals of African or Asian civilizations and burned them to the ground, carrying their treasures back to their museums as evidence of a world of the past, being deliberately destroyed by the present. The Shuar, however, ended up in museums all over the world without ever being invaded; tsantsas flowed from their territories not as loot, but as sales.

In part, the failure of museums to really be scientific institutions was caused by the insistence of curators in focusing their collecting on the spectacular – those parts of material culture which would fascinate, amuse or repel European visitors on whom the museums relied, at the expense of the mundane work of scientific investigation, a process which generated ever greater demands for the extraordinary. There is almost nothing better calculated to achieve this than human remains: curators, and the less scrupulous collectors they sent out searching, scoured the world for the most shocking human remains they could find. Mummies from Egypt were the most popular. The physical remains of pharaohs and queens, priests and noblemen, carefully preserved thousands of years ago for their journeys into the afterlife, were torn from their tombs in thousands and placed on display in glass-fronted cabinets, if they were lucky. Those that were unlucky were sold to private collectors, eager to acquire status symbols of knowledge and scientific curiosity, and unwrapped before gawking crowds at special parties. The sacred contents of their tombs were sold off to the highest bidder, sometimes in very dubious circumstances indeed – hundreds of thousands of sacred mummified cats were brought to Britain and ground up for fertilizer.* More than the material culture of the past, the people too were systematically looted to fill the museums of the empires. The mummies and skeletons and skulls on display in museums across the world were not pre-pared for our amusement, but for journeys into eternity, laid to rest with ceremony and devotion by loved ones who mourned their passing and sought to make meaning by granting them the resources they would need in other worlds. None imagined they would be torn from their rest for scientists to poke and tourists to gawk, and their horror at such a fate is, on reflection, almost palpable.

It was into this world of organized disrespect for the dead, and disdain for those living who did not meet the require-ments of the human hierarchy, that the tsantsas of the Shuar entered this network of fetishized remains of human beings being installed in museums as educational curiosities and among

---

* Daley, Jason. "Tomb Full of Sacred Cats and Beetles Found in Egypt". *Smithsonian Magazine*, 12 November 2018. Accessed online at https://www.smithsonianmag.com/smart-news/tomb-full-cats-and-scarab-found-egypt-180970786

wealthy collectors as mantelpiece decoration to be shown off to friends. As – to European eyes – bizarre, almost horrifying depictions of supposed savagery, torn out of the respectful context they held within Shuar feast politics, they rapidly became wildly popular as grotesque curiosities, and this demand trickled down the trade networks that led from the cities of the wealthy industrial nations all the way back to the traders living in small towns at the edges of the Shuar forests. These traders began to demand more and more tsantsas, refusing the offers of pigs and salt, which could be bought anywhere, and instead insisting on the tsantsas, which could not.

The small supply of tsantsas kept in the communities were soon exhausted, and so the Shuar began to expand their supply. Raiding parties attacked other Shuar villages at first, but soon found that easier prey lay outside their territories. Bands of men, wearing feathered jewellery and carrying clubs, machetes, steel-tipped spears and rifles passed across the tribal boundaries into the neighbouring Achar territory, storming villages and massacring the inhabitants. Other neighbouring tribes, such as the Huambisa and Candoshi to the south, who did not have head-taking traditions, were almost overwhelmed in the 1880s, driven off their lands and fleeing to the safer lowlands as small armies of up to 500 Shuar warriors crossed through their territory month after month.

The heads, tied in knots by their hair, were no longer tsantsas, bearers of the bravery and strength of great warriors celebrated through ceremony. They lost their ceremonial and cultural significance and became 'shrunken heads': no more or less than the heads of people murdered to sustain a trade in human remains. They were for the most part no longer feasted, no longer part of an ancient and complex economic and political system. They were a commodity, to be traded for guns and clothes and tools. So great was the demand that when human heads were not available, the Shuar slaughtered monkeys and sloths, shrinking their little heads just enough that they looked like wizened furry men, and sold them alongside those of their human victims.

Those kakaram who controlled access to the trading posts now expanded their power, using their access to firearms and resources to build forces from the fracturing Shuar communities which enabled them not just to conduct large-scale raids, but also to defend against Shuar rivals seeking to capture the lucrative trade monopolies. These Shuar, more distant from the trading posts, were forced to pay tribute to those with access, and take more heads in their own raids to compensate.

Missionaries, who were increasing their intervention in the Ecuadorean highlands once more and now finding ready converts among the peoples displaced by the Shuar raiding, complained bitterly about the effects of the head-hunting, which was murdering their converts and preventing religious teachings having any effect while there was profit to be made. Head-hunting was illegal of course under Ecuadorean law, but it had never been enforced in the highlands, and though the Dominican and Franciscan missionaries who had replaced the Jesuits prohibited it where they could, their presence once again brought traders less scrupulous and less concerned by the morality of the goods they traded, and the raiding increased in intensity.

The Shuar needed the weapons and the wealth for another reason. Rubber planters had begun to intrude on the Shuar territory, previously considered not valuable enough to risk conflict with the inhabitants. Pushing into the forests with armed mercenary bands, rubber companies cut the old-growth jungle and laid down rows of rubber trees. After a few years, these trees could be tapped and the sap collected and treated, making commercial rubber, increasingly important for production in industrialized nations. The best and most consistent source of rubber was in the rainforests of northern South America, where the rubber tree grew naturally, and plantations had appeared all over northern Brazil and now in Ecuador and Peru.

The rubber planters, and the farmers and ranchers who followed them, used their mercenary bands, supported by the Ecuadorean Army, to drive off the Shuar and other Indigenous peoples from these lands, massacring those who refused to move. A few kakaram were able to make deals to retain their position and people; most commonly they would be granted permission to survive on the condition that they would procure slaves from surrounding communities to be worked, often to death, on the rubber plantations. Due to concerns about the violence of the Shuar, many planters opted instead for the Achar territories, arming Achar warbands with rifles, shotguns and machetes and encouraging them to attack the Shuar in turn. Thus, as the 1890s progressed, an undeclared, disorganized and bloody conflict raged out of sight in the forests of the Ecuadorean highlands as communities attacked and counter-attacked one another in search of slaves and heads.

The conflict was in no small part provoked by a shortage of resources. The forest clearing and pollution from the rubber plantations and ranchers had a disastrous ecological effect on the forests, severely damaging the ecosystem and reducing the productivity of Shuar farmers. The pig herds and gardens were no longer able to support the population as a result. So for many, conflict and head-hunting were now the only reliable way to ensure access to food and basic necessities as well as the weapons necessary to defend communities and conduct one's own raids. A generation had grown up in this dystopia, a martial society of extreme violence in which social and familial bonds were breaking down due to soaring mortality.

Uncontrolled capitalism, unleashed on a population unable to make its own laws or exercise authority, still a colonial vassal of the corrupt and uncaring Ecuadorean government, and un-prepared for its effects and unmanaged or restrained by moral or social code, had created a macro-version of Clipperton Island. In the Shuar territories now, might made right, and to the strongest the spoils. Those Shuar with control of access to trading posts were able to become very wealthy indeed. Shuar from other com-munities could not travel except in large war parties, lest they be waylaid and beheaded, and so Shuar communities became insular and defensive or migrated eastwards away from the threat of further raids, many settling around missions and mission towns where they could live more safely.

It was this migration which in part brought the conflict to a tentative end. In 1915, at around the time that the settlers on Clipperton Island began to die from scurvy, there was a sharp decline in head-hunting raids. Partly this was the result of missionary activity finally taking hold among Shuar communities, especially those driven out of the highlands by the constant warfare, and partly by the consolidation of access by certain kakaram. The primary driver, though, was that both the Shuar and the Achar were suddenly under less pressure from the rubber plantations. The international price of rubber had collapsed so far and so fast that the plantations had been largely abandoned as worthless. The reason why rubber collapsed lies in the network of international trade and imperial competition rooted in the very heart of empire. Britain had decided to use its vast influence and territory to exercise its power and diminish its rubber-trading rivals, because Britain had very little direct access to rubber, a strategic resource of increasing importance found almost exclusively in South America, especially so after the invention of the internal combustion engine which made cars and trucks possible in the 1890s.

The British government knew that many of its territories in East Asia were the perfect climate for growing rubber. These colonies were a loose conglomeration of directly ruled ports and towns and client rajah states stretching from Penang on the border with Thailand through the Malay peninsula to the strategic port city of Singapore and the jungles of Brunei and Sarawak in northern Borneo. They lay sandwiched between the Dutch East Indies to the south and recently invaded and conquered French Indochina to the east, sitting across the main, vital trade routes from China, and worth tens of millions of pounds a year.

Plans had been afoot to seed rubber in these territories for some time, and in 1875 a British agent was dispatched to Brazil. The agent was named Henry Wickham, and he was able to travel freely through the Brazilian Amazon stopping at plantations there and acquiring a vast collection of 70,000 rubber seeds. It was a hazardous journey; as part of his cover Wickham had brought his whole family with him on the trip, all of whom were killed by tropical diseases. With his seeds, Wickham returned to London alone, and there his smuggled rubber plants were carefully planted and nurtured at the Royal Botanic Gardens in Kew. There, after many false starts, rubber trees grew and flourished, and were sent to British colonies all over the world, especially Malaya in Southeast Asia, so that within a few short years British rubber was outstripping South American rubber plantations. The price of rubber fell and the rubber industry collapsed; the plantations encroaching on the Shuar territory were abandoned and the Shuar and Achuar kakarams were plunged into poverty due to decisions taken in a city thousands of miles away by people who had never heard of them, except perhaps as a curiously shrunken human head in a museum labelled with the collective Spanish name of 'Jivaro'.

With their populations in collapse, their economic systems once again undermined and missionary activity increasing in effectiveness among the displaced communities, the Shuar and Achuar began to lean more and more on one another for support. Gradually trading came to replace warfare as their main source of engagement, and though traders could still fetch a price for tsantsas, museums were glutted with them, they were no longer the prestige item they had been, and could not routinely be traded to obtain firearms. The Shuar continued their raids on neighbouring peoples and the lowland communities, but they were smaller and less frequent, calculated to maintain feasting but to avoid reprisals which might jeopardize the trading networks that had replaced the rubber and head-hunting booms. The Shuar had never stopped the tsantsa feasts, though they had receded in importance as head-hunting for profit had become widespread, but now they once again assumed a central role in Shuar ceremonial life.

The period of growing trade saw a greater influx of industrially produced goods into Shuar and Achuar territory. This saw a corresponding increase in the number of men who became shamans – and were thus spared the debt obligations which held together the kakaram. These shamans accumulated followers and weapons and embarked on complicated blood feuds with one another, firing off curses and directing raids. When rubber briefly became popular again during the Second World War, the Shuar and Achuar shamans dominated access to the redeveloped plantations, fighting brutal conflicts within the forests to

94

control access to trade. In the years after the war this attention turned to the significantly increased missionary activity on their eastern borders, driven by American-funded Protestant missions and accompanied by traders, with whom the missionaries had a working relationship to draw in potential converts. The Achuar shamans in particular participated in a series of tit-for-tat killings which in twenty-five years are believed to have caused the deaths of up to 60 per cent of the Achuar male population.

By 1970, a century of arm's-length colonialism, missionary activity and unrestrained imported capitalism had entirely destabilized and depopulated the Ecuadorean highlands. Many of the survivors lived as refugees on the outskirts of missions and lowland towns to avoid the shaman-led warbands of their fellow tribesmen. The violence finally receded in the 1970s as external economic investors lost interest in the region, but the brutality and efficacy of the conflict had not gone unnoticed by the Ecuadorean and Peruvian governments. The border between these two countries, always ill defined and largely uncharted, skirts the southern reaches of the Shuar territory and in 1981, and again more bloodily in 1995, conflict flared up over control of border posts and resources along this disputed line, set as always by a committee in a far-off city (in this case Rio de Janeiro in 1942), which bore little resemblance to conditions on the ground.

Expert forest warriors, Shuar warbands were recruited by Ecuador, armed and sent in to fight, leading raids on outposts manned by Peruvian conscript soldiers on isolated hillsides and along rivers. Peruvian casualties were heavy, and it seemed that the border might collapse. Peru counter-attacked, but after initial massed assaults against Ecuadorean fortified outposts ended in defeats and further casualties were suffered at the hands of the special raiding units of the Shuar, named the Iwia, the Peruvian government deployed its special forces, veterans of decades of scorched-earth combat in the forests of southern Peru against the Marxist guerrillas of the Shining Path. Fighting was fierce, though mercifully brief, leaving several hundred dead before a ceasefire known as the Montevideo Declaration was confirmed and a new border commission established to attempt to finally resolve the conflict. In 1998 a new treaty was signed by the respective governments – without any Shuar representation – formally establishing the border and ending the conflict. Two years later a mining exploration discovered large copper deposits under Shuar lands, which were sold for extraction to multi-national mining companies by the Ecuadorean government, again without consultation with the Shuar. The companies immediately began making fresh encroachments into Shuar territory, felling forests, building roads and once again smashing a hole right through the Shuar way of life, a process which continues unabated to this day.*

The Shuar raiders emerged from their forests in the 1870s

---

* Rudel, Thomas K. "The Extractive Imperative in Populous Indigenous Territories: The Shuar, Copper Mining, and Environmental Injustices in the Ecuadorian Amazon". Human Ecology 46(5), October 2018. Accessed online at http://www.researchgate.net/publication/326654509_The_Extractive_Imperative_in_Populous_Indigenous_Territories_The_Shuar_Copper_Mining_and_Environmental_Injustices_in_the_Ecuadorian_Amazon

because their way of life, transferred down generations for millennia, had been disrupted and displaced by the intrusion of industrialized capitalism and colonialism. Unable to survive through traditional means, the Shuar adopted the ways of the invaders, and in an effort to secure the resources necessary to survive, they turned to war. The lesson of the Shuar is that capitalist economics, unchecked by strong political forces in a colonial environment, can be a highly destructive force. It is one that is influenced and manipulated by people on different continents in small ways which can lead to chaos, social collapse and mass murder. The curators who purchased the tsantsas likely never dreamed that their activities could be provoking wholesale slaughter on the other side of the world, because they failed to understand the interconnected network of economic forces exerting themselves on the people who lay at the other end of the supply chain. Whether they would have cared or not, knowing as they did how much of their collections came via acts of colonial violence, is another question. Understanding the oppression of economics and the predatory ways in which it spreads unchecked is essential to understanding how economic systems within which we all participate can cause misery and destruction even beyond the reach of colonial or post-colonial governments. It is this legacy which lies behind the still reverberating effects of the financial crash of 2008 and the exploitative actions of those making money from the economic upheaval of the COVID-19 pandemic.

A popular idea on the right and centre right of the political spectrum is that 'the market' is capable of finding the best solution to a given problem – that supply and demand work in tandem to meet human needs. Ever since Adam Smith turned economics from a mysterious brand of witchcraft to a science in the late eighteenth century, there have been those who believe that markets and financial systems can operate as methods of ensuring freedom – and there is some evidence that they are not entirely wrong. Market forces, run by more or less responsible governments, have in the last fifty years lifted more people out of poverty and into education and healthcare and employment and the components of a productive and stable life than anything that has come before. There are arguments that on the whole humanity is richer, healthier and more comfortable than it has ever been, and there are those who have made the case that a system of carefully managed capitalism has been the root cause of these improvements.* But that shouldn't be allowed to obscure the fact that capitalism unrestrained by government and justice can create an environment as dangerous and murderous as one without government at all, and a fully free-market capitalist system, as sometimes advocated by those whom it benefits the most, has no barrier to prevent hideous atrocity – disasters of the type that befell the Shuar.

Even when managed, capitalism is unequal and frequently unjust, and too often subject to the unjust control of those who

---

* Heath, Allister. "The World is Richer and Healthier". *The Spectator*, 2 December 2006. Accessed online at https://www.spectator.co.uk/article/the-world-is-richer-and-healthier

would wish to oppress others to make a profit or exert political influence. Like those kakaram governing access to the trading posts, those who control the markets and the means of production are too often in a position to exploit those who work for them, be it in a factory, or in the taking and shrinking of the heads of villagers in the Ecuadorean lowlands. Effective capitalism requires responsible and accountable government, but responsible government can be fragile, and irresponsible government can be merciless.

Colonialism and capitalism, as enacted by the nations whom they benefited the most and represented by the museum collections in which their heads appear, wreaked a disaster on the Shuar, and it was this effect that Aimé Césaire lamented when he wrote that

> All things considered, it would have been better not to have needed [museums]; Europe would have done better to tolerate the non-European civilizations at its side, leaving them alive, dynamic and prosperous, whole and not mutilated ... the museum by itself is nothing, that it means nothing, that it can say nothing.*

---

* Césaire, Aimé, 1972 [2000]. *Discourse on Colonialism*. Monthly Review Press, New York, p. 77

Chapter Four

COLONIAL OPPRESSION: KILLING DEDAN KIMATHI

When protestors tore down the statue raised in honour of the slaver Edward Colston in Bristol in the summer of 2020 and threw it into the harbour, they did not do so just because of his personal past crimes in owning and trading in human life, but also as a symbol of the failures of the post-colonial period to properly acknowledge and respect the damage that the shedding of empire caused. There are those who see the fall of Colston as an indictment of Britain and British history and values, an affront to the pride of the nation and a criminal act of subversive violence. They are in truth not wrong: Colston's statute was torn down in the main because it stood as an icon of pride in a legacy of human misery for which Britain should feel profound shame. We have a national myth that excuses British culpability in the Atlantic slave trade because after 200 years of violence and murder the

British government belatedly took steps to stop it. This myth is harmful because it allows Britain to sidestep acknowledging this cruelty and adequately addressing its ongoing legacy. Protesting this national delusion is precisely what underlay the statue's unceremonial dunking.

The public demolition of Colston's statue is therefore about far more than his personal legacy in the slave trade, or even who Britain chooses to honour with its public monuments. It is also about the repeated and deliberate failures of British society and government to acknowledge that the history of slavery and the empire it sustained and which sustained it continues to cause harm today. For one, it is a falsehood that the retreat from empire in the aftermath of the Second World War was in some way a benevolent act – the gifting of independence to nations who had earned it in that conflict, or as a father allowing their children to leave home and flourish. This idea is a lie, and understanding this lie is essential in understanding our responsibility, national and personal, for the shape of the world and its imbued injustices.

Though Britain, exhausted by war, chose not to commit large armies to engage in major conflicts in retaining its colonies, the retreat from empire was nonetheless one of bloody conflict, overt political manipulation and ongoing exploitation which still shapes and colours the world today in myriad ways. National complicity in the disasters of independence – poorly managed and corrupt – and the millions of deaths in the process has never yet been meaningfully grasped by the former colonial powers, and the issue looms large over the systems of oppression and exploitation within which we all still participate to this day.

In February 1957, a thirty-six-year-old man named Dedan Kimathi, known across the British-ruled Kenya Colony as 'Field Marshal', was taken from his cell in Kamiti Prison in Nairobi, hanged on a gallows in the prison yard, and then buried in an unmarked secret grave. His crime, the one for which he had been sentenced to death, was possession of a pistol. His last wish was for his son to receive a formal education – a luxury then almost unimaginable to the vast majority of the Kenyan population, and something Kimathi understood was his only chance to succeed in the post-independence Kenyan society Kimathi believed and hoped was going to follow his death.

His real crime, for the colonial government, as implicitly judged by the indiscriminate justice of the Kenya Colony court system, was far more significant. Kimathi, the itinerant son of a widowed Kikuyu woman, had spent the last four years directing a sustained campaign of violent resistance to British rule as a senior commander of the Mau Mau, leading Kikuyu partisan units operating from the Aberdare mountain forests. Operating through applied force and passionate rhetoric, Kimathi had ordered ambushes and murders of British Army patrols, colonial police units and local Kikuyu allies of the Nairobi government across a swathe of the Kenyan interior, conducting war so effectively that special squads of askaris, Kenyan soldiers serving the colonial government, were sent to hunt him down. Eventually one succeeded, wounding Kimathi in a skirmish and taking him prisoner. The British press, rather than report this action as one led by Africans against Africans, falsely reported that a team of British settlers wearing blackface had conducted the raid.[*]

The Mau Mau uprising was one of the largest rebellions against the British Empire in the twentieth century; it saw tens of thousands of Kikuyu, an ethnic group native to the Central Kenyan highlands, fighting against British soldiers, askaris and settler police across the Central Kenya region between 1952 and 1958. The war was brutal, with both sides engaging in torture, rape and murder on a mass scale, upending Kikuyu life and creating an internal refugee crisis. Mau Mau squads murdered settler families and Kikuyu accused of collaborating with the government, while government forces conducted massacres of suspected Kikuyu sympathizers and indiscriminately herded tens of thousands more into special protected villages which were little more than concentration camps, where thousands died of typhus and other infectious diseases. During the course of the conflict more than 10,000 Kenyans were killed, including more than 1,000 who were, like Kimathi, judicially executed: sentenced to death and hanged in prison yards and village squares. Collective reprisals were initiated against the Kikuyu, by colonial military and paramilitary groups operating

---

[*] *Liverpool Echo.* "Death Sentence: Mau Mau Leader Who Had Revolver". 27 November 1956. Accessed online via the British Newspaper Archive at https://www. britishnewspaperarchive.co.uk/viewer/bl/0000271/19561127/204/0010

largely without oversight from a colonial government eager to repress the rebellion without taking responsibility for the means. During this campaign, in addition to the judicial executions, many more Kenyans were extrajudicially shot, beaten or tortured to death by a system of colonial oppression running completely out of control.

Kimathi's killing was vengeance, certainly – he had been one of the most effective forest generals of the Mau Mau, often cited inaccurately as the leader of the decentralized movement and certainly its most prominent commander – but it was also about British efforts to shape the future of Kenya. The decision to grant independence to the colony was already privately advanced when Kimathi was executed, and his death was not intended to end the calls for independence so much as to determine to whom it would be granted. Kimathi's death was, for the empire, an apparently small moment in the transition of Britain from a position of colonial dominance to the primary influencer of a network of independent nations, but it marked a brutality and ruthlessness in the nature of that independence and the legacies of colonialism that followed in which so much of the world in which we live was forged.

In the mid-twentieth century, in the aftermath of the Second World War, the empires which had dominated the world for the previous four centuries began to collapse. This was not without relatively recent precedent: most of the Spanish Empire had been lost in the aftermath of the Napoleonic Wars in the early nineteenth century, the last of it was snatched up by Roosevelt in the Spanish-American War of 1898, and the German and Japanese empires had been forcibly dismantled. Others, though – principally the British, French and American – still existed, even if they had finally stopped growing. Even the Russian Empire was still largely intact, though it was now the communist empire of the Soviet Union run by Stalin, rather than the old tsarist empire ruled by an autocratic hereditary king. Part of the compact which had sustained the allies during the Second World War, though, relied on existing promises to grant independence to the more powerful and vocal parts of their empires – the United States, for example, granted independence to the Philippines in 1946, promised since 1916 and guaranteed since 1934, even as much of the country still lay in ruins – but American military bases, armed forces and political and commercial influence remained in control of large portions of the country.

Britain then, more reluctantly, granted independence to its vast colonies in India in 1948, split between the new and British-shaped nations of India and Pakistan, along a border between them drawn under the guidance of a British lawyer, Sir Cyril Ratcliffe, who had never previously been to India, and never before drawn a border. His lack of experience, coupled with the rush to independence and intransigence of some of the new leaders of the two nations, led to a sustained period of civil violence in which up to two million people may have died and more than fourteen million became refugees. Fighting continues along parts of this line to this day – as recently as December 2020 Indian and Pakistani soldiers were killed in clashes along the Line of Control which separates the countries in the heavily disputed mountain province of Kashmir.

In Africa too, the end of empire was wreathed in violence, and the way in which that violence manifested is illustrative of why the world is the way it is, for the independence of Africa was tailored and designed to permanently weaken the continent in ways which still reverberate today, and which explain so much of the ways in which global inequality still operates. It first has to be understood that except for nibbling at the edges, the European invasion of Africa was relatively recent. As late as 1860, inland Africa was a map of African kingdoms and loosely collected polities of independent villages and families, with Europeans limited to small formal colonies on the coasts.

As with Venezuela and the Shuar, though, these coastal colonies were the key to political dominance of the continent because they controlled access to trade with the wider world, and through them the wealth necessary to maintain thrones flowed. African rulers could trade among themselves, but wealth was more concentrated close to ports which could trade overseas, and those ports – in places like Cape Town, Algiers, Zanzibar and Elmina Castle on the Gold Coast – were governed either directly by European empires, or indirectly by client rulers. Trade goods flowed, usually down rivers, from inland African kingdoms to European company ports, once again, on a massive scale, using capitalist economics to enact colonial dominance inland without the need for large-scale warfare or military occupation. Though wars did take place between African kingdoms and European forces, they were much rarer in this earlier period than internecine warfare between African kingdoms on one hand, and between European empires on the other, each battling over riverine trade routes and the raw materials that flowed through them. They were largely content not to fight one another in campaigns in which they would each face considerable disadvantages though geography and technology – the trading arrangement was enough to ensure the rulers on each side all obtained and preserved wealth at the expense of others.

Dominance in the European wars was how Britain and France in particular came between them to control most of the African trading ports by the mid-nineteenth century, leaving only a few, principally Portuguese, in other hands. For hundreds of years the most valuable resource which had flowed from these ports was human: slaves, captured in brutal wars inland during campaigns of ethnic cleansing which threw the continent into turmoil, chained and sold downriver to European slavers who carried them to the Americas where they died in enormous numbers, then to be replaced by new shipments. This atrocity, dragged out over decades and centuries, was one of the most brutal in human history, and is thought to have resulted in more than twelve million deaths.

In the early nineteenth century, under ethical political pressure at home and economic pressure abroad, Britain banned the slave trade on British shipping in 1807, and to prevent other European nations benefiting from it used the Royal Navy to seize and capture foreign slave ships as well. Slavery itself was made illegal in British colonies in 1836, the British government propping up the economies and governments of their colonies by compensating slave owners for the liberation of the people they kept as property. In effect the British government purchased all the slaves in their colonies and set them free into poverty and coercive control by the men who had latterly owned them – often 'free' in name only. Freedom in name is and was an important step ahead of outright slavery, but there was no pretence whatsoever that the no-longer-enslaved people were equal to their former owners or welcomed as anything other than a labour source, unable easily to leave the islands or make their fortune. They were now free, but still oppressed in very crucial ways.

Once the slave trade was prohibited, other goods shipped from Africa replaced slavery, including ivory, rubber and agricultural produce. European efforts to secure both the trade routes themselves and the means of production through imperial intrusion into the African interior became more pronounced. Examples include the 'Great Trek' of 1844 in South Africa, in which Boer settlers migrated north from the Cape Colony into African territory, defeating and driving out the African kingdoms they found there in order to settle; or the British invasion of Abyssinia in 1868, launched in response to the kidnapping of British missionaries and diplomats which saw a British army crossing deep into the country, dethroning the Emperor Tewodros, who committed suicide, and capturing and looting his mountain fortress at Magdala before withdrawing, having massacred the royal guard with concentrated rifle fire and leaving Abyssinia in political chaos.

Competition between European powers continued to grow. In the 1880s German and British companies operated as trading partners with the Sultan of Zanzibar, the regional power on the East African coast, and leased stretches of land for plantations and farms. These relatively small incursions rapidly expanded, fuelled by troop deployments to protect the investments of the companies against rebellions by local rulers who found themselves undercut or overrun. For example, the Hehe Rebellion in German East Africa, now Tanzania, lasted seven years and caused the company to be taken over directly by the German Empire. The war only ended when King Mkwawa was tracked down and forced to commit suicide. His head was taken to Germany as a trophy, where it remained until 1954.

In 1885 the Berlin Conference, an initiative of Chancellor Otto von Bismarck, brought the governments of fourteen imperial powers together to formalize these informal divisions of African influence. Though it was ostensibly an effort to 'civilize' the African peoples, the real goal of the conference was to prevent war breaking out between European powers over control of African territories. It was far from perfect in this ambition – Britain and France nearly came to blows over Sudan in the Fashoda Incident of 1898 – but it roughly delineated which parts of Africa fell under the dominance of which parts of Europe. It therefore limited conflict between the empires while simultaneously clearly indicating that those lands within their demarcated territories were legitimate targets for conquest. Over the following decade European control stretched to their respective determined borders, overwhelming all African resistance militarily or economically. Expeditionary forces put down those African kings and chiefs who resisted the demands of colonial officers and merchant companies, annexing their territories.

This period saw many wars as European armies surged into the African interior – the Belgians up the Congo, the French across the vast sweep of the Sahara, the Portuguese in the lands which would later become Angola and Mozambique, the Germans also in Cameroon and what is now known as Namibia and the British almost everywhere. One of the most famous incidents was the British invasion of the independent Kingdom of Benin, formerly a trading partner and now a rival. The Benin Army was massacred, and their capital city looted and burned down. The spoils remain scattered in museums all over the world. By 1900, only Abyssinia survived as an independent African-ruled kingdom, having weathered invasions by both Britain and Italy. A further Italian invasion in 1935 would result in their loss of independence and as many as 800,000 deaths in massacres, concentration camps and deliberate famine.

The imperial division established in 1885 underwent a major realignment in the aftermath of the First World War, when the captured German colonies, including East Africa, were divided up between Britain and France, who now controlled the majority of the continent. In the 1930s there were further divisions. Britain and France acquiesced in the Italian invasion of Abyssinia, before the three nations turned on one another during the Second World War. Extensive fighting took place across North and Eastern Africa to drive the Italians and Germans off the continent, resulting in severe casualties among the African populations it swept over.

In the aftermath of the war, however, with resistance to empire and calls for independence rising, Britain and France took two very different paths in relation to their colonies, paths which both reflected their different national experiences in that war and indicated very strongly where each nation saw itself in the new world order of glowering superpowers, and which have to an extent marked how they have seen themselves ever since. Britain, as one of the key victorious allies, battered, broke, but undefeated, ultimately settled on a strategy of gradually, reluctantly and violently releasing its African colonies, while France, occupied and colonized for four years, sought determinedly to hang on to its empire at catastrophic cost.

The French intended primarily to retain their colonial possessions through military might. Perhaps most famous in Britain and America are their efforts in Indochina, where up to 400,000 people were killed in a gruelling eight-year conflict which gradually bled into the American intervention in Vietnam, a continuity war lasting another twenty years, in which up to three million people died. Despite efforts to divide their opposition and the deployment of ever greater numbers of troops, the French suffered defeat after defeat to the dedicated armies of the Viet Minh and were ultimately forced to withdraw in 1954, but even as they suffered collapse in Southeast Asia, the French fought another conflict, even more bloody, closer to home in North Africa.

In the aftermath of the Second World War, the French had had initial success in quelling rebellions against their colonial rule, such as in Madagascar, where an uprising in 1947 was met by a sustained terror campaign by the French Army. There collective punishment was meted out, so that if the inhabitants of a village were deemed to have attacked French plantations or soldiers, that entire village would be wiped out in a raid designed to shock neighbouring communities into compliance. Rape, mass murder and torture were employed freely to cow the Madagascan rebels into submission. A year and more than 40,000 lives later, the rebellion was defeated, and the island remained a French colony until 1960. Commentators at the time noted with concern and disgust that the French Army was conspicuously using German terror tactics, so recently meted out on the French population, to enforce control of the island colony. The French Caribbean writer Aimé Césaire noted that 'Each time a head is cut off or an eye put out in Vietnam and in France they accept the fact, each time a little girl is raped and in France they accept the fact, each time a Madagascan is tortured and in France they accept the fact, civilization gains another dead weight.'*

Algeria would prove an altogether harder challenge. It was one of the wealthiest and most important of the French colonies, and perhaps the one most tied to France culturally. It had a large and

---

* Césaire, Aimé, 1972 [2000]. *Discourse on Colonialism*. Monthly Review Press, New York, pp. 35–36

politically active French-descended population and from 1848 was administered as part of France itself rather than a colony. The vote, however, and the citizenship it implied, resided with the French population, the *pieds noirs*, and not the majority Muslim population – apartheid South Africa was only an anomaly in its duration, not in the context of the 1950s.

When the FLN, the Algerian independence movement, began attacking French targets in 1954, the French government deployed the army, prepared to repeat the tactics which had ended the rebellion in Madagascar, and to avenge the failures of Indochina. Torture and massacre became the norm on both sides, leading to a spiralling death toll as Algerian cities descended into chaotic fighting as hundreds of thousands died. The war spread to mainland Europe. Nearly 4,000 people died in France itself as the French-Algerian community there devolved into a period of infighting known as the Cafe Wars, so called for the propensity to shoot up or blow up cafes run by members of the opposing faction.

The war tore Algeria apart, and engendered furious anti-French feeling among the Muslim population, feeding the FLN's ranks. In France itself the French public began to lose enthusiasm for the conflict and by 1958 the government began negotiations with the FLN on moves towards independence. Furious, the French Army launched an abortive coup, seizing Algeria and Corsica but ultimately placated by the imposition of the hawkish war hero Charles de Gaulle as the President of France. De Gaulle was under pressure; the UN had begun condemning French actions in North Africa, and NATO allies complained that too many French resources were being spent on maintaining empire and not enough on facing the Soviet threat in Europe. De Gaulle recognized too that military efforts were failing, as they had failed in Indochina, and he introduced political reforms designed to end the conflict. They failed, and brutal infighting between Muslim Algerians and French Algerians led to renewed tit-for-tat bombings and assassinations which killed many more.

When Algeria finally gained independence from France in 1962, more than 700,000 were dead and nearly a million and a half *pieds noirs* and French-supporting Muslims had fled to Europe as refugees. De Gaulle was pursued by assassins for the rest of his life. The military and humanitarian disaster of French efforts to retain their overseas empire was enormous, a blunt approach to the conflict enforced by mass deployment of troops and open violation of human rights. This contrasted in tone if not intent with the choices Britain made at the same time, which are worthy of study because it was those choices which shaped the world to follow – there is no so-called first world or third world, no developed and undeveloped, without the dichotomy of the colonizer and the colonized, and that distinction was largely drawn by Britain, the nation which dominated a third of the world land surface and a third of its population in 1920, and forty years later had relinquished almost all of it, apparently, if not actually, peacefully.

There were wars fought by the British in the 1950s as French Algeria and French Indochina tore themselves apart, but none remotely on the scale of those humanitarian catastrophes. Low-level guerrilla fighting rumbled on in the jungles of Malaya and the mountain forests of Cyprus, claiming thousands of lives in campaigns of bombing and shootings, punctuated by torture and judicial and extrajudicial killing, but without the tens or hundreds of thousands of deaths the French colonies experienced. In each case, the British forces declined to take on their opponents in the open with large armies, instead operating from isolated bases and ceding control of the hinterland to the rebels. The reason that these campaigns were not prosecuted with the rigour of the French was that Britain was not concerned primarily with preventing its colonies from gaining independence altogether – in both Cyprus and Malaya this had already been promised well in advance. Instead the British were buying time to try to ensure that it was their allies within the colony, not their enemies, who assumed control after independence. This would allow Britain to maintain a measure of economic and political control, operating as a soft power, relieved of the need to dominate militarily or invest in infrastructure as direct government. They could hand off to sympathetic leaders, often educated at British schools and trained in British imperial military or civil service, assured of continued commercial and diplomatic dominance via the mechanism of the Commonwealth.

In Kenya, those settlements which spread out from the coast had deliberately driven deep into the territory of Kenyan kingdoms and communities. The peoples of the land that became Kenya were from a diverse set of disparate social and linguistic groupings, clumped together by the British without any particular regard for existing boundaries or relationships. The Kikuyu, Kimathi's people, lived on the plains and forested mountains of Central Kenya, and parts of their territory were among the most productive land in the colony. British settlers entered Kikuyu lands in large numbers in the early twentieth century and very rapidly upturned Kikuyu economics, undercutting agriculture and seizing land. The blurred line between commercial and government interests enabled the settler government to repeatedly raise taxes on Native Kenyan produce while keeping them low for White settlers, part of a programme designed to gradually drive Kikuyu communities off their lands and into an itinerant system of farm labour, in which each settler-owned farm would be surrounded by encampments of Kikuyu labourers, who could be treated with astonishing brutality without repercussion – beatings and whippings were common. When they were denied the chance to advance beyond a form of near-destitution servitude, and prevented from continuing to live in their traditional communities, frustration and disgruntlement at an overtly racist system policed by a British-run paramilitary colonial police force boiled over into the Mau Mau rebellion.

The Mau Mau grew from an existing collection of oath-sworn societies among Kikuyu labourers, many of whom had served in the Kenyan Battalion of the King's African Rifles fighting in East and North Africa against the Italians and in Burma against the Japanese. These units suffered heavy casualties fighting for the British – nearly a thousand African troops were killed in the sinking of a single troopship alone, the SS *Khedive Ismail*, torpedoed by a Japanese submarine in the Indian Ocean. Those who returned were paid less than promised and forced back into the wage labour system in which they were forcibly shifted from farm to farm, fingerprinted and corralled to ensure compliance and obedience. The British avoided slavery in their colony only on the technicality of offering severe, poverty-level wages, but otherwise controlled the lives of their labourers, preventing their advancement and severely punishing those who refused to comply. When the rebellion began, many of these labourers slipped away from their farms and joined the rebels.

The principal units of the Mau Mau were based in the forested highlands of Kenya, supplied by allies in the capital Nairobi. Their main goals were to put pressure on the colonial system to pursue land redistribution. As in most British colonies, most of the land, and all of the most productive farmland, in Kenya had been seized from traditional rulers and was now controlled by a small elite of White farmers and governors, and the Mau Mau wanted it back.

The Mau Mau mostly initially targeted other African ethnic groups and Kikuyu who refused to join their groups, with occasional assaults on White-run farms and colonial outposts. Striking from the forests, they assassinated local chieftains who worked with the British, burned villages and raided convoys, melting back into the highlands when British troops, principally Africa-recruited askaris serving in police units or East African rifle regiments, reacted to their operations. In time, the Mau

Mau began to expand their operations to larger scale attacks on White settlements and military targets. The British responded with a campaign of brutal repression – Kikuyu leaders were arrested, bombers dropped heavy explosives on villages and armed paramilitary reprisals on Kikuyu communities killed hundreds. Police brutality was so extreme and routine that British soldiers, no strangers to brutality, on occasion refused to hand over prisoners, knowing they would face torture.*

But the British campaign was very successful in one area: they concentrated on the Kikuyu and the highlands. Raids and operations occurred elsewhere, particularly in Nairobi, but the rebellion never spread to other ethnic groups, let alone reaching Britain itself, which was largely unaware and uninterested in the goings on in one distant colony. Though they were able to limit and contain the conflict in a way the French had failed to achieve, the British could not yet win the war, unable to get to grips with the Mau Mau units. The Mau Mau did not cease their attacks, however, so the British expanded operations, ethnically cleansing whole areas of the Kenyan countryside, herding villagers into fortified settlements no different from concentration camps. After being assessed by their guards, the captives were sent to prisons of varying severity. The worst employed torture, starvation, rape and murder to gather information and intimidate the Mau Mau leadership into surrender, and all were rife with disease and abuse. At one stage, the entire Kikuyu population of Nairobi was

---

* Anderson, David, 2005. *Histories of the Hanged: Britain's Dirty War in Kenya and the End of Empire.* W. W. Norton, p. 260.

arrested en masse while British troops searched house to house through the city, smashing in doors and beating suspects in the streets. Prisoners passed to the police were flogged, roasted over fires and had lit cigarettes shoved in their ears.* Many did not survive. At the Hola camp in 1959, during a non-violent work strike, guards beat eleven prisoners to death; the colonial government tried and failed to cover up the atrocity.†

Over time, this campaign of targeted brutality succeeded in lessening the strength of the Mau Mau, aided by psychological operations which divided the Mau Mau leadership and recruited other Kenyan ethnicities, and troops from outside the borders of Kenya, into the fight against the Mau Mau. In late 1956, after six years of conflict, Dedan Kimathi was wounded and captured, taken to prison in Nyeri, tried and executed. After Kimathi's death an amnesty brought many of the Mau Mau down from the hills and the conflict sputtered out, though low-level fighting continued until independence three years later.

The British campaign against the Mau Mau had not really been about denying Kenya its independence. Despite the protests of the White settler community, determined to preserve their privilege and control, and unlike the contemporary French conflicts in Indochina or Algeria, in which hundreds of thousands died in efforts to keep those countries under French dominion, the war in Kenya was less about preventing Kenyan independence, and much more about a longer-term plan to

---

* Anderson, p. 310.

† Anderson, p. 327.

ensure that the leaders of independent Kenya were amenable to the British. Though empire had its defenders and supporters in the British Parliament and population, it was plain that continued British dominance over such a huge swathe of the world was impractical and unjustifiable. International and domestic pressure, along with very serious economic problems, meant that the empire was not profitable or sustainable even in the medium term. It was hoped in some quarters that, by fending off outbreaks of violence like that of the Mau Mau until perhaps the early 1970s, the British could bring in the reform programmes necessary to maintain arm's-reach dominance over its former colonies by ensuring that the successors to the imposed British governors were politicians, democratic or not, who were popular and effective enough to ensure internal stability and amenable enough to enable British commercial interests to continue to exploit the colony's resources.

In this ambition for their colonies, they were only partially successful – for example, within ten years of independence Nigeria descended into the brutal internecine Biafran War which killed more than two million, as disparate populations within the European-designated national borders sought their own self-government. In Rhodesia the White settlers staged a coup and seized control of the independence process. Unwilling to go to war with White British settlers the way they'd gone to war with Black Kikuyu, the British government disapprovingly withdrew, allowing a de facto White supremacist independence which faced a fifteen-year war and which killed more than 20,000 and resulted in the ascent of Robert Mugabe as president of the renamed Zimbabwe, who subsequently led a brutal dictatorship for thirty-seven years.

The British-accepted leader of Kenya after independence was Jomo Kenyatta. Kenyatta, a Kikuyu man, had been educated in London, was married to an Englishwoman and had a good relationship with the governor of Kenya. A long-time vocal and passionate advocate of Kenyan independence, very popular among his faction, he had politically opposed the Mau Mau but was still hated by the colonial government and settler community, and had spent the entire uprising in prison at Lokitaung following a farcically unjust show trial. This meant that he had remained apart from the increasingly bloody tit-for-tat community violence which had riven the Kikuyu while still remaining active and prominent in the independence movement from his cell. Having been despised by the White settlers before his incarceration, he emerged from prison as their moderate preferred choice. With so many other leaders either dead or wanted for murder by the colonial authorities, Kenyatta was in prime position on his release to assume leadership of the peaceful independence movement, rejoining his banned political party, the KAU, and becoming the favoured candidate of the colonial government.

Kenya was granted its independence on 12 December 1963, after last-ditch British efforts to steer governance of the country away from Kenyatta and the KAU failed. Kenyatta won overwhelming electoral support as the Black African population were finally accorded a meaningful vote. Faced with the choice of accepting the result or ordering a massed military deployment to prevent it, for which there was no political or public will, the British brought in Governor Malcolm MacDonald to oversee a smooth transition. MacDonald was chosen because he got on well with Kenyatta, and enacted reforms to the Kenyan political system to strengthen the incoming president's position – better to have a strong Kenyatta ensuring Kenyan continuity than a weak central authority constantly buffered by challenges and coups. The risk of ushering in a dictatorship was strong, but the priority here was not to ensure a Kenyan democracy for the Kenyan people, but instead to create a stable, pliant client state which would continue to support British commercial and political interests. Kenya's independence was thus granted as a dominion within the Commonwealth, with the queen as head of state.

In power, though, Kenyatta turned away from the British in pivotal ways. Dominion status lasted only six months. Kenya became a republic. Kenyatta replaced the queen as head of state with himself, and built a cult of personality though propaganda, charity and significant gifts of wealth and land to prominent supporters. Though he remained within the Commonwealth, maintained links with Britain and retained much of the colonial political and police structure, he supported African nationalism in Kenya and abroad, and gradually worked to nationalize or Africanize key industries, driving out the British corporations and parts of the settler community. These industries were then shared among allies, friends and family, Kenyatta enriching himself and key supporters while adopting only the vaguest pretence of running a democracy or governing on behalf of Kenyan groups beyond his own Kikuyu and their allies.

Rival political parties were broken up or banned, and insulting Kenyatta became a grave criminal offence. Farms belonging to those settlers who left were broken up and shared among the Kikuyu, while those who stayed were courted for their wealth and political clout. Dissent was brutally suppressed, particularly among Somali nationalists along the northern border, who were subject to a brutal campaign every bit as oppressive as that led by the British against the Mau Mau. Elections were entirely rigged in his favour. He died, still president, in 1978, and was succeeded by Daniel arap Moi, his chosen successor, who was, controversially at the time, not a Kikuyu. Moi ruled for twenty-four years, expanding and deepening Kenyatta's web of corruption to the tune of hundreds of millions of pounds while engaging in severe human rights abuses, including torture and murder, of political opponents. His secret police ran an infamous torture centre in the basement of the Nairobi Police Headquarters, Nyayo House.

Moi was forced from office in 2002, and Kenya has been a fragile democracy ever since, though still plagued by terrorist campaigns, deep corruption, regular political violence and election tampering – more than a thousand people are thought to have died in riots which followed the 2007 election. Kenyatta's son Uhuru, a Moi protégé, currently holds the presidency, only the fourth President of Kenya in the last sixty years. The end of empire in Kenya was a violent, corrupt and deeply racist affair. The British government sought not to create a functioning democratic state, but to further their own interests, in the aftermath of a bloody terror campaign, by installing a reliable strongman. It was not an act of philanthropy, but one of corruption which left Kenya, bounded by artificial lines imposed over ancient tribal distinctions, and in the hands of powerful interests running unchecked, a nation built to serve a colonial master left at a severe disadvantage when it came to justice, equality, democracy and the rule of law. More, though, was to come from the war with the Mau Mau and the independence of Kenya, because as bad as its aftermath had been, what subsequently happened in neighbouring Uganda was far worse.

A legacy of the Mau Mau uprising was that among the other African troops brought in by the British to fight the Mau Mau was a Ugandan contingent. Among these soldiers was a cook named Idi Amin. Strong, obedient to authority and unafraid of inflicting violence on people, Amin advanced rapidly during the Mau Mau uprising, and by the time he returned to Uganda he was an *afande* second class, the highest rank an African could attain in the British Army.

Uganda's colonial history was similar to that of Kenya, one of insidious political takeover and commercial exploitation. In what was then the Kingdom of Buganda, a civil war in the 1880s overthrew King Mwanga II. Mwanga launched a campaign to retake his throne, and offered sovereignty of his kingdom to the

Imperial British East Africa Company in exchange for the money and troops to restore him to power. This they duly did, followed by the usual cavalcade of missionaries and merchants. From then on Uganda was administered by the British, primarily through client chieftains from Buganda, who were given authority over their rival kingdoms. Cotton became the principal export, grown on a plantation system which forced minority communities off their traditional land and into the same type of itinerant labourer lifestyle as the Kikuyu in Kenya, while tens of thousands of indentured workers were brought in from India to run the system on behalf of the colonial authorities.

It was under this system that Uganda readied for independence under the rule of the British-groomed heir to the throne of Buganda, President Mutesa II. Literally born in the governor's mansion in Kampala, the colonial capital of Uganda, Mutesa had been privately educated, matriculated at Cambridge and served as an officer in the British Army, apparently nicknamed 'King Freddie' by the British. He initially shared power with the prime minister, Milton Obote, an effective locally raised politician of the Lango people. Within four years of independence, however, amid mounting ethnic and class tensions in Uganda, not least caused by Obote's desire to nationalize British-owned industries, Obote launched a coup against Mutesa and drove him into exile in Britain. Mutesa subsequently died in suspicious circumstances in a flat in Rotherhithe, London, in 1969. In seizing power for himself, Obote relied heavily on support from the army, and in particular Idi Amin, who had risen so rapidly that by 1965 he was in sole command of the Ugandan Army. It was Amin who commanded the attack on Mutesa's residence.

In 1971, while Milton Obote was at a meeting of Commonwealth leaders in Singapore, Amin ordered the army to seize power, racing to act ahead of corruption charges from Obote. He cut off the airports and border crossings and took the presidency, suspending parts of the constitution and instigating a reign of terror. Members of minority groups, especially Lango people, were purged from public administration and Lango soldiers were trapped and massacred. More than 20,000 Ugandans fled the country, principally to Tanzania, and thousands more disappeared into prison camps.

Amin more than doubled the size of the armed forces, recruiting heavily from Sudanese and Congolese populations who owed no loyalty to existing Ugandan power structures. The massacres and oppressions deepened, the death toll spiralling into the hundreds of thousands in indiscriminate purges of supposedly disloyal populations. All Ugandans of Asian descent were expelled from the country, many arriving in Britain as refugees. Though Britain had initially supported Amin, who had promised not to nationalize British-owned industries, he did so in 1972 and they withdrew support, Amin turning to the Soviet Union instead. In 1975 he supported Black September terrorists by offering shelter for a hijacked French airliner carrying mainly Israeli passengers at Entebbe, though the subsequent Israeli attack on the airport and rescue of the hostages shook the Amin regime and led to splits between his loyal soldiers and increasingly rebellious Ugandan groups.

With his regime falling apart, Amin sent troops across the Tanzanian border in pursuit of mutineers. Unwilling to further tolerate Amin's brutality or instability, Tanzania led an alliance of other African nations who invaded Uganda, overran the collapsing Ugandan Army and overthrew Amin, who fled first to Libya and then Saudi Arabia, where he remained until his death in 2003. The fall of Amin's regime led to a period of instability and violence, in which bands of soldiers and bandits known as kondos roamed the country looting and killing. And it was into this situation that Obote returned and rapidly seized power once more, cracking down on rebels, kondos and political rivals. Hundreds of thousands more died in massacres which punctuated the civil war which followed, from which General Yoweri Museveni, who had served both Amin and Obote before turning on them one after the other, emerged victorious. Obote fled the country. Museveni has remained in power ever since, meeting constant low-level rebellions with extreme force. His security services have been repeatedly sanctioned for human rights violations. Most notable among his enemies is Joseph Kony, whose Lord's Resistance Army has been responsible for more than 100,000 deaths and the enslavement of more than 65,000 children. The aftermath of colonialism in Uganda has been one of continual murderous conflict and oppression.

What this chapter illustrates is that colonialism – the pernicious interference which saw German gunboats burn a Venezuelan city, the Shuar turn on one another in economic genocide, and British troops herd Kikuyu villagers into concentration camps – did not end or suddenly heal with independence. It was not a case of old colonial powers like Britain walking away from their colonies, leaving them intact and ready for independence, but of deliberate, systematic and often violent insistence on guaranteeing friendly regimes in these countries so that Britain and the descendants of British settlers could continue to exercise control and avoid the appallingly destructive outcomes of the failed French wars of domination.

That these ambitions subsequently failed so severely in places like Kenya and Uganda is reflective of the weakened state of those colonial powers after the Second World War, and of the continued underestimation of the African leaders they installed, or inadvertently inspired. These are atrocities within living memory, and these nations live today with the political and social oppression these settlements brought. Ending colonialism, ending the domination of countries built and shaped and exploited by European nations, was not an act of altruism but one of further exploitation and control. The processes by which independence was granted were not designed to bring freedom and self-determination to those nations, but to minimize these things from fear that they might turn away from European domination.

The problems that plague colonized nations to this day are not just the responsibility of their own people and their authoritarian leaders, though they do bear a significant portion of this blame, but they are our responsibility too. Our nations did this, and then walked away, leaving Africans to live under war and famine and authoritarian domination by brutal opportunists afforded the ability to manipulate systems designed to preserve and retain power. We cannot undo these actions from the past, but we can and should acknowledge our culpability and responsibility for so much of the political, economic and social oppression and instability these actions brought about, and try to make amends through aid, communication and better and equal travel and economic links between nations. Our nations have caused harm by which we still profit and others still suffer, harm we can mitigate, but on which we choose as a nation to turn our backs. We claim that because we stopped actively oppressing people with troops and land seizures we are somehow absolved of the guilt for having done it in the first place. But colonialism has not ended, and cannot until the poisonous legacy it wrought has been properly addressed and recompensed, a project of generations which we have barely begun.

Chapter Five

ECOLOGICAL OPPRESSION: FOUR PESTS AND THE GREAT CHINESE FAMINE

In the summer of 1958, odd decorations appeared on the trees in villages and towns across China, from the broad central plains to the high mountains, from coastal fishing villages to large factory districts in crowded cities. Pans and kettles were strung up in the branches of trees and from the eaves of buildings, clattering and clashing together in the wind, creating a constant deafening cacophony which echoed across plains and valleys. In the streets of cities and the fields of collective farms millions upon millions of people, marshalled by local authorities and Communist Party officials or acting on their own excited initiative, marched regularly, shouting and pounding drums, as men followed with shotguns, blazing away into the sky.

As the relentless noise continued, the ground in and around these villages and towns was gradually carpeted with hundreds of millions of tiny corpses, stacked in heaps and swept daily into mass graves. Yet each morning more and more little feathery bodies appeared, exhausted, emaciated little birds tumbling down from the sky to die in the fields and streets. The constant noise of drumming and clattering kept them in flight, starting up in terror wherever they tried to land to feed or nest, draining their energy and preventing them from sleeping or pausing, until eventually their fluttering hearts gave out, or shotgun blasts tore their delicate wings apart. China had declared war on the sparrows, and the one-sided conflict led to an ecocide almost unparalleled in human history and which ultimately contributed directly to the death of more than ten million people.

Wherever humans have touched, animals die. The migration of early humans from Africa to all habitable corners of the world can be traced in the extermination of species large and small, from mastodons to snails. As humans move in, they hunt, they clear forests, dam rivers, level hills and change the geography, erasing habitats and turning local ecosystems upside down. It is a constant of humankind. But it usually settles into a balance, or at least a managed imbalance. Useful or insignificant or adaptable species survive the extinctions and are bred into some form of co-resistance with their bipedal neighbours, who seek mostly to systematically exploit rather than destroy the wildlife they encounter in these conditions. There are times, however, when these exterminations have been deliberately targeted on specific species. These go beyond limited or localized efforts to eradicate predators, becoming instead deliberate efforts to drive entire species of creatures, largely harmless, but feared or inconvenient, to extinction. The effects of this sort of campaign, known as ecocide, are widespread, devastating and often unanticipated.

Some of the most famous examples of systematic mass extinctions (or near extinctions) in recent history come from the United States in the late nineteenth century, in which concerted hunting efforts by private enterprise drove various hitherto ubiquitous species to or over the brink of extinction. The buffalo, for example, more properly the American bison, was hunted relentlessly for sport, for profit and as part of a deliberate campaign against the Native Americans who relied on them. The extermination was contracted out to private hunters, who stripped hides from their carcasses and later collected the bones for grinding for industrial purposes.

Their task was simple: when a buffalo was wounded, the instinct of its herdmates was to gather around it in protection, and in this way whole buffalo families could be exterminated in just a few minutes by hunters wielding rifles. Between 1830 and 1890 buffalo numbers dropped from forty million, great black herds blanketing the plains, to just 500 survivors huddled on small reserves and ranches. That the species survived at all was a miracle, as is their recovery; today there are more than 360,000 buffaloes in America and their numbers are rising steadily.

Even more dramatic and tragic was the fate of the passenger pigeon, once the most common bird in North America. More than three billion were thought to swarm across the eastern seaboard in vast flocks whose wings blocked out the sun. Their habitat shrank and shrank as mass settlement moved westwards, and by the late nineteenth century they were a popular target for sport and commercial hunters. They were trapped with nets, their nesting trees were burned or cut down, carrying thousands of young pigeons with them, and they were lured into traps to be slaughtered en masse – the record for a single double-shot blast from a shotgun was sixty-one birds killed in one go. By 1881 there were so many dead pigeons sold as animal feed that they were worth less than the barrels and ice in which they were packed. Attempts to battery farm them failed: the pigeons died of disease and famine when locked in huge cages. By the 1890s they were a rare sight, the few survivors jumping from roost to roost, far too few to maintain a stable population. The last known wild passenger pigeon was shot in 1901. In just fifty years they had gone from the most numerous bird in North America to entirely extinct.

We can simplify and suggest that imperialism killed the buffalo and capitalism the passenger pigeon, while acknowledging that this happened largely not as a systematically directed government campaign, but rather through the economic self-interest of millions of individuals combining to destroy animals for which there was no compelling economic reason for any authority to permit them to survive. Indeed the resurgence of the buffalo in the twentieth century owed more to their value as commercial rarities for tourists, and nostalgia for the way of life their extermination represented, than any noble conservation effort. Likewise, the last sad passenger pigeon died captive in

Cleveland Zoo, stared at as a curiosity by people whose parents and grandparents had treated them as pests and slaughtered them without thought. There was nothing illegal about these exterminations – this was not objective oppression in the sense of being opposed by law; rather, it occurred in a situation in which there were just no frameworks in place at all to protect these animals, and they were slaughtered for merely being in the way.

What happened in China in 1958, though, was something quite different – this was no official carelessness or indifference or excessive individual exploitation. Instead the Chinese government, for no greater reason than to provide their population with an enemy against whom they could unify and prevail, attempted to do to the sparrow in one year what Americans had done to the passenger pigeon in fifty. They tried to wipe them out, and in doing so enlisted the enthusiastic (and often not so enthusiastic) support of millions of their own citizens, persuaded and encouraged to commit a brutal ecocide which brought down a demographic disaster on their own heads.

For control of wealth and levers of public opinion are not the only means by which oppression can be enacted. One of the more powerful alternatives is to enable and encourage populations to turn against nature itself, and in doing so fundamentally reshape the very ecological structures of human life, people forcing adaptation or death on themselves, twisting into new forms more amenable to those in control. These actions are literally recreating the world into new forms with which people are unfamiliar, and they must rely on the state and its institutions to survive, just as destroying the buffalo had forced unwillingly on the Native Americans of the Plains.

In chapter three, I looked at the ways in which exploitation of Shuar territory by rubber industries had a warping effect on both Shuar society and the environment of the Ecuadorean highland forests. The plantations drove communities off their land and into a sort of indentured servitude, spreading poverty, dislocation and war ahead of them like a bow wave. A similar effect occurred in Kenya: the White settlers drove the Kikuyu off their traditional lands and fenced them off into large farm conglomerates. The Kikuyu lived on the edges of these capitalist empires until desperation and fury drove them to rise up in search of freedom from the oppression of the mutually supporting institutions of international colonial capitalist business and government, which cared nothing for their traditions, politics or families.

Capitalism was not the only political system operating in the mid-twentieth century, however, and its great rival, communism, was also an exploitative system of oppression which in China at least was designed to operate in ways that preserved the power of a wealthy elite at the expense of the vast majority of the population. It was developed from a series of political philosophies which emerged in mid-nineteenth-century Europe as a response to exploitative conditions in factories, expanded on the idea of collective bargaining and buoyed by philosophies of historical determinism. These theories dictated that history was a trajectory running from primitivism to a utopia of shared resources and mutual collaboration. It became a movement which in the aftermath of the destruction of the First World War found most success in Russia.

A destructive civil war led to the foundation of the Soviet Union, the first communist nation on earth, in which ostensibly every citizen could participate in national wealth production and share the proceeds equitably. This was never more than an ambition, however, and one largely dishonestly held – power was always reserved for a small coterie of political leaders and their supporters, and resistance and protest were always punished by savage reprisal and violence. Millions died to preserve the integrity of the nation and the rule of the Communist Party, and millions more were forcibly moved around the country in a concerted effort to destroy social and community bonds and replace them with loyalty to the state. It was largely successful.

Though couched in aspirational language and philosophy, Soviet communism shared the colonial system's interest in treating human beings as little more than economic units to be exploited for the benefit of others, supported by the conscious erasure and prevention of personal will and desire. Whatever improvements people saw in their lives under these systems were at the expense of freedom or independent movement or thought, and the constant risk of arbitrary and violent punishment. Indeed, the Soviet Union operated a colonial system of its own, every bit as oppressive and destructive as that of the capitalist powers of Europe; in its first twenty years it crushed independence movements in Central Asia, Ukraine and the

Caucasus and spilled over into neighbouring nations, invading Poland (twice), Finland and the Baltic States, and battling the Japanese for dominance along the Chinese border.

As part of this campaign the Soviets also tacitly encouraged the rise of communist insurgency in northern China during the late 1920s, even while publicly supporting the country's Nationalist government. China as a nation had shattered catastrophically in the aftermath of the collapse of the two-thousand-year-old Chinese Empire a decade earlier, and the Soviet Union sought to exploit this weakened but still wealthy giant on their southern border, keeping it weak and vulnerable and perhaps creating an ally against their ideological enemies in Europe and Asia. Unlike the violent demands for self-determination which drove the fall of the Spanish Empire or the patchier negotiated end of the British Empire fifty years later, the implosion of China was an internal political collapse – the centre fell out from underneath the government rather than the peripheries slipping away.

China had been fading as a power throughout the nineteenth century. The Taiping Rebellion of the 1850s killed between twenty and thirty million people and left most of southeastern China in ruins and the government economically crippled. In the aftermath, small European armies had attacked and crossed China with impunity more than once. A British and French force had captured and sacked Peking in 1860, and in 1900 an eight-nation alliance stormed the capital and sacked it once again during the Boxer Rebellion. British, French and Japanese armies successfully stripped away Chinese influence in neighbouring countries in Southeast Asia and Korea, and rebellions and revolutions scarred the country and destabilized the government, which was unable to raise capital in part due to European dominance of key strategic points on the Chinese coastline and access to sea routes, particularly the British-controlled port of Hong Kong. Increasingly unable to exert authority within its boundaries, the integrity of the state began to crumble, and in 1911 a series of rebellions flared up that the Chinese imperial authority was powerless to put down.

The emperor abdicated and handed power to a Republican government dominated by the authoritarian president Sun Yat-Sen, but right across China generals, administrators and wealthy noblemen seized the opportunity to exert control over their regions, raising armies and declaring quasi-independence. This period is known as the Warlord Era, in which dozens of mini-states appeared across China, battling with one another and the remaining national government for dominance. By 1927 the country had fractured almost completely, independent state-lets stabilizing even as the truncated nation's remaining strength lay with the Nationalist government, now led by Chiang Kai-Shek, whose power base was centred in the coastal cities. The suffering of many ordinary Chinese people, now effectively living under anarchic and unstable rule, was immense, and it shouldn't be surprising that millions of displaced farmers, their villages overrun by bandits and warlord armies, should look elsewhere for support.

China's peasants, always exploited by the government in

Peking and regional governors, now became feudal subjects of the warlords who controlled them, at constant threat of attack by warlord armies disputing territory, or from roving bands of displaced men thrown off their lands, and lacking any kind of large-scale state relief necessary to cope with environmental disaster. A drought in northern China in 1928 led to a famine which killed more than three million people, left to starve by a crumbling bureaucracy unable to do anything to alleviate their suffering. These traumas were fertile breeding ground for communism and its message of collective government to grow and spread among the Chinese population.

In 1927 the Kuomintang (KMT), the leaders of the Republican-ruled parts of China led by Chiang Kai-Shek, moved to purge the communists from their ranks, and the Communist Party of China (CPC) split from the government and seized control of the central city of Wuhan, forming a power base against Chiang's Nationalist KMT forces. Chiang counter-attacked and drove the communists out of Wuhan, consolidating power and capturing most of the east coast, now the largest and most representative government China had. In the Nanchang countryside around Wuhan, though, the communists banded together and formed the Red Army. The Chinese Civil War had begun.

For the next ten years the communists and the KMT battled back and forth for control of parts of China. The attraction of communism to Chinese peasants never previously offered the opportunity to advance was powerful, and the CPC had no difficulty raising forces to oppose the Nationalists right across the country. These conflicts rarely took the form of organized declared warfare, but rather a constant ebb and flow of low-level fighting which occasionally flared into full-scale battles when one side or another felt they had an advantage. Chiang kept pressing the communist forces, launching four distinct campaigns against their strongholds around Wuhan, in what was known as the Ten-Year War or the Central Plains War. Each of these operations failed, and up to half a million people were killed in the fighting.

In 1934 Chiang's armies, now beset by a Japanese invasion of Manchuria to their rear, launched a fifth campaign, pushing deeply into communist territory, encircling and destroying their main force in southern China. A smaller army, led by Mao Zedong, slipped through the KMT cordon and escaped more than 12,500 km into their remaining stronghold in Shaanxi Province, evading KMT pursuit. From there the war continued until 1937, when Chiang was forced to come to an understanding with Mao and the communists to form a united front against the Japanese, who were now once more pushing their armies into Chinese territory.

The ensuing war with Japan lasted eight years, and was later joined by wars in Europe and the Pacific to become the Second World War, in which the Chinese campaign was one of the bloodiest and most brutal theatres of conflict. More than 700,000 Japanese and four million Chinese soldiers were killed in attritional fighting across Chinese territory, which also left up to ten million Chinese civilians dead from massacre and famine.

The KMT, with its organized armies, bore the brunt of the fighting against the Japanese, and the bulk of the casualties. The communists, experienced in and equipped for guerrilla war, were better able to operate behind Japanese lines, raising armies from displaced peasants and plaguing Japanese supply lines and reserves. At the Japanese surrender, the KMT were left exhausted and damaged, the communists reinforced and invigorated.

The wartime truce, never well maintained and frequently broken, lasted mere months after the armistice. A formal agreement was signed between Chiang and Mao, but even as it was being negotiated their forces were skirmishing over large parts of northern China. Within months all-out war began again, the balance shifting from the KMT to the communists and back again, but now each defeat cost Chiang men he could no longer replace, whilst everywhere the communist armies marched they soaked up millions of peasants left displaced and destitute after decades of chaos and conflict. Mao reinforced this movement by giving the peasants in the areas under his control free rein to take revenge on 'landlords', a term which could mean anything from wealthy noble families to slightly wealthier peasants in the same village. During the civil war and in its aftermath it is thought that up to three million people were killed through this campaign alone, many in ritualized public beatings by their neighbours and former friends. Another two million or more died in the renewed fighting.

By November 1948 the KMT were exhausted. Losses from the Japanese war could not be replaced and the war of attrition with the communists favoured Mao. A series of huge communist armies advanced from their strongholds in northern China and, despite dreadful losses, were able to crush the remaining KMT armies. Chiang retreated and retreated again until he and his forces were driven from the Chinese mainland, escaping to the island of Taiwan and fortifying it against further communist attacks. Mao had won the war and China was communist.

The breathing space the victory in the war brought to China was short-lived. Within a year Chinese troops were dying fighting American and UN forces on the Korean peninsula – more than 200,000 Chinese and three million Koreans were killed. In China itself Mao, now paramount leader, set about entirely reorganizing the Chinese state. Abandoning thousands of years of farming technology developed and specialized to local conditions, Mao centralized farms into communes. Forced into this system on pain of severe punishment, the remaining farmers complied, and crop yields began to collapse. This provoked famine and compounded disease; cholera, plague, malaria, smallpox and tuberculosis were rampant across China, whose people were still living amid the wreckage of decades of conflict and disaster. These illnesses killed almost a third of children and persistently affected the production efforts required of the centrally marshalled population.

In an effort to preserve remaining crops, and to eliminate the public health crisis, Mao declared four animals to be traitors to China: rats, flies, mosquitoes and sparrows were to be targeted for extermination – a deliberate ecocide never before so systematically attempted, let alone achieved, and one that flew in the face of both traditional agricultural practice and available technology. Sparrows were included on this list not for their potential as disease carriers, but because they ate the seeds from which next year's grain sprung. Thus came the odd displays in Chinese villages up and down the land, as Chinese people came together into one purpose: the extermination of the sparrow, one of the 'Four Pests', the 'treasonous' animals which were spreading disease and famine across the nation.

All had to participate in what came to be known as the Kill Sparrows Campaign. Driven from their homes and workplaces by party officials, all of China turned on the sparrows, delicate little birds with a wingspan of just 20 cm and weight no more than 25 grams: difficult to target in the air, even in their vast flocks. Mao's instructions were to prevent the sparrows from landing. Sparrows eat on the ground, pecking their food from the soil. If they could be startled into flight over and over, and prevented from staying still long enough to eat, they would soon begin to die from exhaustion and starvation. Thus it was that pans clattered in the trees and drums pounded in the villages day and night, forcing the sparrow flocks ever onwards in a futile search for a safe place to land, rest and eat. When they landed they were set upon with clubs and rakes, their tiny bodies piled and weighed for the bounties the government paid on sparrow carcasses. In just a few weeks as many as a billion sparrows and millions of other birds were dead, the skies of China empty and quiet.

The massacre of the sparrows did not come from nowhere, but was only one stage in a determined effort to modernize China in the aftermath of the war, to replicate the effects of the European industrial revolution – a process which had taken nearly two centuries – in less than a decade. Organized on strict communist principles, it continued the persecutory campaigns of the civil war, deliberately targeting those deemed to be privileged or wealthier than others. It was directed and controlled at all times by Mao, now China's paramount ruler for life, wielding ultimate dictatorial power.

Now called the Anti-Rightist campaign, the oppression of the Chinese population was formalized and organized via a vast bureaucracy, designed and maintained to both effect Mao's modernization and to turn the Chinese people against themselves, to make them compliant, afraid and invested in a system that preserved new social restrictions, no less oppressive than the ones which came before. First targeted, from 1957, were intellectuals. Teachers, politicians and lawyers especially were intimidated, fired from their positions, imprisoned by the thousand and sometimes executed. Two years later a fresh wave of persecutions, larger than the first, reinforced the message – do not think for yourselves.

Among those subject to the ongoing purge were successful farmers who had survived the persecutions during the late civil war and its aftermath. Overturning generations of carefully gathered agricultural knowledge specifically tailored to the diverse soils and climates of China's vast territory, experienced farmers were replaced by Communist Party officials, selected for their loyalty to Mao rather than any agricultural expertise. The myriad farms of Chinese villages were collectivized, pushed together into larger conglomerations in which all were expected to work in order to provide for each other and to produce large surpluses for the wider Chinese state.

The bureaucrats who ran these farms faced enormous pressure from above to demonstrate the effectiveness of communist methods by producing spectacularly large yields. To achieve this they were provided with tools and techniques imported from Soviet Russia, in particular the notion of deep ploughing. This would turn over several yards of soil, rather than the few feet normally moved, supposedly exposing the rich and fertile soils hidden deep below the topsoil. The brainchild of committed Soviet agricultural scientist Trofim Lysenko, this technique, alongside others like close-sowing (putting large quantities of seeds very close together) and focusing particularly on the most fertile land at the expense of larger acreage of less productive fields, had already been shown to be a failure in the Soviet Union, but Lysenko, with the support of the Soviet government, simply falsified his results.

The effects were disastrous, compounded by the imposition of inexperienced and incompetent officials to run major engineering and development projects which failed over and again. The Four Pests campaign and its attack on the defenceless sparrows was a critical step in this worsening situation. The swarms of insects which descended on the Chinese villages destroyed those few crops they had been able to grow under these conditions. Sparrows do not only eat seeds – they also eat insects, and in particular they eat locusts. Sparrows in fact were the principal predator for locusts. A few months after the massacre of the sparrows, the new generation of locusts, unterrorized by the slaughtered sparrows, appeared in numbers so great that they dwarfed the sparrow flocks they replaced. Gnawing at the carefully husbanded crops, they hugely exacerbated the deepening famine, and unlike the sparrows they were indifferent to the clattering pans and drums, and did not care about the marshalled crowds who sought to chase them away, drowning out the human noise with a whirring and clicking which obscured all else.

To try to mitigate some of these problems, millions of peasants were mobilized into relief units and sent to build irrigation systems and dams, to repair damage from flooding and decades of warfare and to try and compensate for the lost agricultural productivity. But this operation often did more harm than good. The units descended on areas already suffering food shortages without supplies and demanded or seized food from the communities already there, draining reserves from surrounding areas as they laboured inefficiently on projects for which they were not trained or prepared. Meanwhile many of the communities from which these men had been conscripted no longer had enough farmers to harvest their crops, and so what excess they grew, withered and died in the fields as their abandoned families starved. Officials, unable to meet targets and fearful of reprisals, began to lie. In one county they reported 11,000 tons of food when they only produced 3,500 due to failed agricultural experiments unsuited to the terrain and crops; government agents then removed 3,000 tons as tax.*

The Chinese peasant farmers were not stupid. They knew that what they were doing was going to lead to disaster – they and their ancestors had farmed these fields for millennia and developed a body of skills and knowledge tailored to their patches of land which was so ingrained as to be almost inviolable. They had grown up in the soil and they knew how to grow crops to feed their families on their own land using the technologies available to them, and in good years to pay taxes and provide surpluses for the imperial state, or whatever warlord happened to be in control at any given time. In times of hardship there were simple economic systems of renting or distributing land and crops to mitigate the worst of the damage, and though shortages were common, the system meant that it was only in extreme circumstances that famine set in, usually the product of war or natural disaster. The farmers, now forced into collectivization, could see their crops yields collapsing, their produce eaten by pests or withering in the sandy rocky soil thrown up by the deep ploughs – they understood that disaster was unfolding.

In other times they might have risked official displeasure and spoken up against these changes, or simply packed up and moved elsewhere. But Mao dominated and controlled China entirely, and there was nowhere to go and nothing that could be

---

* Dikotter, Frank. *Mao's Great Famine: The History of China's Most Devastating Catastrophe, 1958–1962*. Bloomsbury, London, 2011, p. 310.

said. Because the communes were not solely intended to reform farming and distribution techniques, they were also designed to end dissent. Farmers were stripped of personal property and forced to live all together, sharing everything. In each commune the officials who ran it and the soldiers and police who enforced their rule regularly gathered the inhabitants together and invited those with something to say to speak up. Those who praised the government and its initiatives were rewarded, those who offered criticism were punished – sometimes savagely beaten or killed. Soon enough there were no more dissenters. Without the safety mechanisms to protect themselves, when the crops failed the farmers had nowhere to turn and no way to replenish their losses. They began to die.

The causes of the disaster now unfolding across China were not solely man-made. There were some regional droughts and major flooding along the Yellow River which caused lower crop yields than normal, but the significance of these crises was compounded by the economic and social policies of the Chinese government. Unable to move except by official decree and with no support forthcoming as local officials were encouraged to lie about the true state of conditions, villagers turned to their livestock, and then their pets and finally on each other, the desperate feeding on the dead to try and stave off their own, almost inevitable deaths. Across central China entire regions depopulated as skeletal bodies scattered along roadsides in a desperate search for food.

No accurate records were made – none were wanted – but

the most conservative estimate of the death toll is over ten million people, while higher estimates of over thirty or even forty million are sometimes suggested. In just three short years, as many or more Chinese people may have died as were killed in the more than twenty years of warfare and chaos which had preceded Mao's victory. The government was well aware of what was happening, despite efforts by local officials to hide what was happening by dumping corpses in mass graves and rounding up the dying at gunpoint and imprisoning them ahead of government inspections.* The evidence of the vast mortality afflicting the Chinese countryside was everywhere: emaciated bodies piled in heaps or sprawled in the streets where they had fallen; depopulated towns and villages; abandoned fields left to become overgrown with weeds; swarms of orphaned children scavenging rubbish heaps and graveyards.

The sparrow-killing campaign did not cause the ensuing Great Chinese Famine on its own; the repressive and scientifically illiterate policies of China's dictator had already set that train in motion, but in enlisting his people in the world's largest deliberate and co-ordinated state attempt at ecocide, Mao had precipitated and accelerated the slaughter not just of a harmless species of bird, but of between fifteen and forty-five million of his own people through a partially self-inflicted famine. This was not his original intent, but it presaged his planned next stage of China's modernization and the reinforcement of his own power.

---

* Dikotter, p. 314.

He had demonstrated that he could force the hundreds of millions of people of China to take violent vengeance on harmless birds in a manner calculated to cause chaos and resulting in agricultural disaster.

For Mao, the famine was initially an embarrassment. In 1962 he was forced to publicly acknowledge his mistakes in front of a national conference in a move intended by his rivals at the top of China's ruling elite, especially Liu Shaoqi, to force the old war hero into retirement. Mao's humiliation, though, was short-lived, and if he felt any concern at the millions who died, he never expressed it. Instead he traded on his personal popularity to initiate a programme of re-education, a further wave of purges of officials loyal to his rivals, even as Liu sought to reverse Mao's economic and agricultural programmes to end the famine and re-establish economic prosperity in China. Mao's campaign succeeded in removing, among many others, the leader of the Red Army, Luo Ruiqing, solidifying his dominance over the most powerful military force in Asia, as well as the leaders of China's state press service and the civil service.

With the levers of the state firmly under his control once more, Mao was now in a position to put into practice the chief lesson he had learned in the Four Pests campaign and the other initiatives of the previous decade: that power could be efficiently consolidated by forcing populations to work against their own interests and their own knowledge. This time it was not harmless sparrows he targeted, but the very heritage of what it meant to be Chinese. He was able, in the spring of 1966, to raise armies of student protestors and concentrate them at points of political pressure, using the weight of the furious crowds, unimpeded by police, army or hostile press to intimidate his opponents. These crowds formed paramilitary organizations known as the Red Guards which battled the supporters of Mao's opponents in the streets, leading to sustained violence which killed between 250,000 and half a million people.

A key strategy of this campaign, and a main target of the Red Guards, was the 'Four Olds' – not physical vermin this time, but Ideas, Culture, Habits and Customs, the very components of what it meant to be Chinese, to come from the thousands of years of philosophy, religion, heritage and ancestry of that nation. Now everything which had existed before Mao's seizure of power was not just obsolete, but actively poisonous to China's future, and had to be destroyed for the greater good. Temples and museums were burned to the ground, libraries destroyed and ancient archaeological sites dug up and smashed in an effort to publicly demonstrate the erasure of Chinese history. Those who promoted history – professors, teachers and historians – as well as anyone suspected of sympathy with China's past or Mao's opponents were denounced, disgraced and, in many cases, were killed.

Tens of thousands, particularly urban students unaffiliated with the Red Guards, were driven from their homes and into the countryside to work in the fields. Effectively they were used as slave labour, and many died under the conditions into which they forced. In Tibet, invaded and occupied by the Red Army in the aftermath of the civil war, monks were forced at gunpoint to tear down their own monasteries. Through all of this, certain sites of particular value were protected, but thousands of others were wrecked in a campaign, part spontaneous and part directed, against the very meaning of China as a nation. These were not a few statues removed by activists, but the organized machinery of a state within a state systematically seeking to publicly humiliate and eradicate the history of an entire country and reform it anew.

The whole period is known as the Cultural Revolution, and it caused almost incalculable damage – the economy stumbled again in the midst of continual social strife and conflict, and permanent harm was inflicted on China's material heritage. Millions more died violently, adding to the toll of China's bloodiest century as Mao and Liu fought out their power struggle in the streets between their armies of supporters. In truth, though, Mao's careful preparations and popular public persona always held the advantage, and Liu was arrested, imprisoned and killed, along with his supporters and anyone who might challenge the dominance of Mao.

Mao died in 1976, having weathered another coup attempt in 1972, but his legacy did not long survive – his wife and chosen successors lacked his political nous or sway with the masses, and were denounced, removed and imprisoned. Nor was China finished with upheavals. In the late 1980s a fresh round of student protests, this time demanding more freedom rather than repression of political opponents, was brutally put down by the Red Army in the infamous massacre at Tiananmen Square. In the years since Mao's death the Chinese government has reformed its economic approaches, favouring state-supported private industries run by favoured oligarchs and riven with endemic corruption which keeps large portions of the population barred from participation in the ensuing explosion of wealth.

Chinese state control of the population has only slightly relented, with fewer massacres and no famines, but with a constant coercive intrusion into everyday life, and the merciless persecution of religious or racial groups deemed disruptive or corrosive to the sense of Chinese national identity and loyalty demanded by the autocratic and now only nominally communist central state. The Chinese people no longer publicly protest en masse, except in independent-minded Hong Kong, where they have been aggressively suppressed under national security laws. Generations of oppression have not only crushed domestic opposition, but also turned the population in on itself and provided – in most cases – a minimum of stability and opportunity sufficient to quell domestic demands for improved conditions, held in check by memories of past violence and oppression.

This has most recently manifested in the campaign by the Communist Party and Chinese government against the Uyghur people, who live in the mountainous region of Xinjiang in the far west of China. Always fractiously independent, the Uyghur are one of China's designated ethnic minorities and majority Muslim. Xinjiang declared independence in the Warlord Era and remained functionally so until overrun by Mao's Red Army in 1949. In 2009, riots broke out there over increasing Han Chinese control of politics and jobs that spread into a terrorist campaign by Xinjiang nationalists. The Chinese response has been to deploy all the lessons of the Maoist repression of the previous century. More than a million Uyghur are in Chinese detention camps; mosques, cemeteries and religious buildings have been closed, demolished or defaced; and Uyghur religious and political leaders have been arrested, harassed and in some cases, such as Uyghur professors at Xinjiang University, simply disappeared without trace. Just as Mao reshaped China in his own image, so China is re-enacting this repression on the Uyghurs of Xinjiang.*

China may no longer organize the systematic ecocide of harmless songbirds, but the lessons of that campaign were learned and internalized, and in the meantime nature in China has not escaped unscathed. Rapid industrialization in a nation uninterested in environmental standards and in which workers left sick or injured from poor conditions have no one to whom to turn has allowed water and air quality to deteriorate to hazardous standards across the country, especially in urban areas and on major rivers. Among the fatalities are the Yangtze river dolphin, a species unique to the river, driven to extinction by 2005. China, while maintaining communist rhetoric and the

---

* Haitiwaji, Gulbahar and Rozenn Morgat, 2021. "'Our souls are dead': How I survived a Chinese re-education camp for Uighurs." *Guardian*, 12 January 2021. Accessed online at https://www.theguardian.com/world/2021/jan/12/uighur-xinjiang-re-education-camp-china-gulbahar-haitiwaji

oppressive politics of the Maoist era, has, it seems, replaced the systematic ecological damage of Mao's Four Pests campaign with the same careless capitalist exploitation of nature at work in the United States of the nineteenth century.

Mao's ecocide of the Chinese sparrows is emblematic of a desire to enforce control not only over human subjects, but natural ones as well. The exploitation of natural resources, flora, fauna and mineral, has always been a staple part of human social and technological development. Where Mao's campaign diverged was in the explicit targeting of certain fauna not as a form of practical exploitation, but in an ideological campaign driven by ill-informed hysteria and pseudoscience. Mao did not want to kill the sparrows because they ate crops, but because the Chinese people, brutalized by war and sullenly resistant to official oppression and badly designed economic reforms, needed somewhere to turn their frustration.

The people of China died in vast numbers during the Great Famine because they had allowed themselves to be persuaded, by force, propaganda or desperation, to undertake actions which they knew, from generations of experience and education, were destructive. The murder of the sparrows is only one example in this trajectory to self-imposed disaster but it is illustrative of a culture which had stopped questioning the intelligence and sense of the orders they were receiving and instead obeyed, in the hope of evading punishment and turning their frustration and anger against helpless birds. Soon enough it would be turned against friends and family, when in the desperate throes of famine they had nowhere to turn except to a government who despised them as nothing more than numbers in a ledger.

Ecocide undoes our world. Whether it's a case of careless disregard for the natural environment in an effort to turn a profit, or the conspicuous and deliberate extermination of species for political gain, it upends both the ecology of a region and ultimately the social fabric of the people who live there. In mid-twentieth-century China ecocide was a sign of the power of a government built to overawe the people it claimed to serve. The killing of the sparrows and the broader agricultural reforms of the time were part of a social and ecological upheaval designed to crush traditional Chinese life and reform the nation. The people trapped within it and unable to escape knew they were facing disaster, but could do nothing to stop it, a terrifying kind of helplessness which it is hard perhaps for people in democracies to imagine, but which enacts an all-encompassing oppression without checks or balances that can, as in China, lead to death on a catastrophic scale.

Chapter Six

CULTURAL OPPRESSION: NATIVE AMERICANS AND THE HOLLYWOOD GENOCIDE

In November 2017, in a typically graceless moment of racist cruelty, President Donald Trump used an event in the White House celebrating the sacrifices and service of a group of Native American veterans of the Second World War to attack a political rival about her claimed ethnic origin.

The veterans were the code talkers, sometimes nicknamed the wind talkers: men from the Navajo reservation in Arizona recruited into the US Army to send messages between units in the Pacific theatre of the war, using codes based on the Navajo language and functionally untranslatable for the Japanese as long as the code talkers remained out of Japanese hands. By repute each translator was accompanied by a soldier tasked with killing him rather than allowing him to be captured. Their service remained top secret at the time and was not publicly recognized until 1968. The ceremony held in 2017 was intended to recognize and honour some of the surviving code talkers at the White House.

Commenting offhand during the ceremony of the Navajo that 'you were here long before any of us were here', the president then continued, 'Although we have a representative in Congress who they say was here a long time ago. They call her "Pocahontas".' Donald Trump's intent in this moment, standing prominently, and I'm sure deliberately, before a painting of President Andrew Jackson, was not to directly demean the code talkers, although he clearly did not care about any effect it might have on them, but to insult his rival by mocking her claims to Indigenous ancestry through a term conspicuously understood in context to be a racial slur. The political opponent in question was Senator Elizabeth Warren, who had long claimed to be of Native descent, having by family legend Cherokee ancestry – a claim long under dispute from both Republican opponents, who mocked the Indigenous claims of a White-presenting politician as identity politics, and from Indigenous communities for whom a possible remote and distant ancestry alone is meaningless as a marker of Indigenous identity.*

What this sordid moment revealed was not just a man utterly uninterested in the sensitivities of his visitors and wider nation,

---

* Fonseca, Felicia and Kellman, Laurie. "Families of Navajo Code Talkers decry Trump's use of 'Pocahontas'." *PBS*, 28 November 2017. Accessed online at https://www.pbs.org/newshour/politics/families-of-navajo-code-talkers-decry-trumps-use-of-pocahontas

but an entire system in which claim and counter-claim of Native American descent had become a joke, one to be thrown around as a casual insult by a president who made racial insults his particular brand. Elizabeth Warren, who had been asserting Native ancestry for several decades, eventually responded to the president's goading a year later, releasing DNA test results suggesting that she probably did have a Native ancestor six or more generations back. This response seemingly settled the debate for Warren. Trump barely acknowledged her riposte and continued his insults unabashed, but for many Native Americans Warren's response was as insulting as Trump's original comments, displaying as it did a fundamental misunderstanding of what it means to be Native American.*

Warren's assertions of Native ancestry may or may not have had political advantage for her personally, but they afforded her, in principle at least, some association with the original inhabitants of the continent, some legitimacy in left-wing circles otherwise unobtainable by a White middle-class Anglo-American, and some association with the oppressed. This, however, whatever far distant ancestor she may or may not have had, was an association to which she probably had no right – she faced no oppression for her Native 'background', which was no more than a family anecdote, and she had no association with any particular community. Native American identity is far more

---

* Dugyala, Rishika. "Native American critics still wary of Warren despite apology tour". *Politico*, 27 May 2019. Accessed online at https://www.politico.com/story/2019/08/27/native-american-critics-elizabeth-warren-1475903

than blood; it is redolent with a culture and history which requires engagement with historic and contemporary oppression as a fundamental part of its make-up. It thus requires not just genetic heritage but community engagement, and is not a mantle for politicians to assume or discard as convenient based on family myth.

Through ignorance, clumsiness and the demise of respect in American politics, Trump and Warren had stumbled into one of the great lies which underpin American identity and history – the fate and future of the Native American, and the ongoing battle over the rights to tell Native stories. Because in unpacking this particular racist insult, we can understand how a genocide on which the United States was founded – the wholesale military destruction of Native American peoples – was followed by a cultural genocide – a sustained attack on the very identity of Indigenous Americans – which did exponential further damage and continues to cause grief and loss to communities which have already lost so much.

The name Pocahontas should not in theory be insulting. She is widely known in the United States through schooling which cursorily teaches her as an American icon bridging Native and settler society, and internationally from a Disney animated movie made in 1995 which romanticized her 1615 relationship with settler captain John Smith, on film a blond hunk played by Mel Gibson, in reality a heavily bearded and much older man with whom any potential romantic attachments are not recounted in the historical record.

Pocahontas, whose actual name was Matoaka, is reputed at

around the age of twelve to have saved Smith's life from her ambitious relatives as part of the early uneasy interactions between European settlers and her people along the river on which they settled, then known as the James to the settlers after the English king, and now as the Powhatan after the Indigenous people driven from its banks. Four years later she was abducted from her family in a settler raid and held hostage, likely raped, and coerced into baptism. During her captivity she is said to have turned against her people, and was subsequently married to another settler, John Rolfe, who brought her back to Britain, where she was briefly feted by society before she died of a fever aged just twenty or so. She was buried at Gravesend in Kent, leaving her son to be raised by English relatives.

Matoaka, a young woman whose voice is only known in any form through the prism of the European men who met her, imprisoned her, probably assaulted her, coerced her and married her, has been co-opted in the centuries since as a unifying figure, a woman – no more than a girl, really – who is presented as having understood the compromises necessary to enable her people and Europeans to coexist and to work together rather than falling apart into conflict. The fact that these paper-thin compromises took place at gunpoint, under constant threat of sexual and physical violence has been conspicuously lost in translation, so that it is this story of an American union which is above all the message of the Disney biopic of her early life, not the reality of her kidnapping and the brutal war against her people in which it took place.

She has also, as President Trump demonstrated, become in the process a racist shorthand for the epitome of Native American women – a beautiful savage princess who is brave and determined and yet who recognizes that the future can only lie with favouring the strange men from overseas over the requirements of her family. Pocahontas is an American hero: she saves the White men and marries them, wows at courts and dies tragically, still young and beautiful but now tamed, in a strange, more civilized land. This is an invented and selective narrative history, much of it legend or misunderstanding surrounding the actions of a teenager taken captive, threatened and pushed into a baptism and marriage with a much older man. Matoaka is a tragic figure, seized from her homeland and convinced, perhaps in the end willingly but likely with great reluctance, that her only future lay to accede to her captors' demands to convert to Christianity, to marry and to turn against her people as part of a complex settler plot to try to secure her family's land through misunderstood Indigenous inheritance laws. They are the same woman, and only one story is true.

It is this mixture of legend and myth, compounded by centuries of military campaigns, massacres, epidemics and ultimately one of the world's most substantial and successful propaganda campaigns, which Donald Trump, ignorant of almost all this history and its complexities, used to insult Elizabeth Warren, comparing her all at once to a savage, a princess, a Disney character and ultimately, and most importantly, a stereotype. For President Trump, it is just another childish insult to be flung at an opponent, but for Native Americans it is another reminder of

164

the murderous genocide their ancestors suffered at the hands of the US government and its colonial predecessors, as well as the determined effort at cultural oppression they and their parents and grandparents experienced and in many ways still experience.

To understand how Trump and Warren got into this situation, we have to look again at something with which we are all familiar, something we've all seen and most of us have enjoyed, but which has had a direct effect on both Trump's crudity and the ongoing cultural degradation of the Native American people – Hollywood Westerns. In the course of the twentieth century, Hollywood produced more than 4,400 Westerns – films set in and around the Western United States – which created, or more properly furthered, a legend about the West and its role in the first century or so of the US's history which only tangentially connects with reality. These thousands of films told a series of stories about the process by which these lands, their prairies, deserts, mountains and forests, were steadily 'tamed', their wildlife, geography and Indigenous populations eliminated or reduced to less threatening forms, more pleasing to White settler opinion. And they re-enact over and over again, for White entertainment, the systematic murder of the Indigenous inhabitants. In doing so they deliberately dehumanize Native Americans, making them savages, near-beasts, both dangerous and laughable, relegating them to a bygone age of American imperialism, a dead threat from the past, no more worthy of attention than any other extinct animal. This narrative was at the centre of a cultural genocide which, as Donald Trump showed in the Oval Office, has never really ended, let alone been meaningfully confronted or compensated.

A cultural genocide is one in which an oppressor seeks not to kill a population, or at least not directly, but to destroy the things that make that population unique – to eradicate any distinguishing features, stamp out anything that marks them as different from the dominant society and which might pose a threat or risk to the cohesion and control of those in power. It is often termed assimilation, the process of drawing in the oppressed population until they have been forced by necessity or persecution to abandon the things that made them a separate society – language, dress, music, religion and custom – and to conform with the demands of the government run by and for, and in the American case elected on behalf of, the majority population. In this it is schoolyard peer pressure writ large, enacted by brutal punishment for transgressors, and capable of creating a cascading network of psychological harm stretching across generations.

It was for this reason that Native children were crowded into government-run schools where they died in shocking numbers, their bodies dumped in unmarked graves in the grounds, the survivors dislocated and traumatized. This was done, so it was said, purportedly by Richard Henry Pratt, architect of the system, to 'kill the Indian, save the man',* to preserve their humanity

---

* Carlisle Indian School Digital Resource Center. "Kill the Indian in him, and save the man": R. H. Pratt on the Education of Native Americans. Accessed online at https://carlisleindian.dickinson.edu/teach/kill-indian-him-and-save-man-r-h-pratt-education-native-americans

by burning out that which was different and deemed inferior or subversive to the American narrative of savages and civilization. It is also a lie, for the government never really wanted the Indigenous children to assimilate. They were never offered the benefit of access to White society and economy, but were instead abducted, abused, disconnected from their families and communities, and then cast adrift as second-class citizens in a nation which had little more than a fascinated contempt for them.

The assimilation efforts alone do not begin to adequately describe the cultural genocide Native Americans experienced during the nineteenth and twentieth centuries, because they were not simply encouraged or threatened to assimilate into White American society, they were also simultaneously prohibited by racist laws or societies from doing so. Trapped in a limbo between what was demanded of them and what was possible, they were unable to resist when their entire cultural outputs were seized by White entrepreneurs, repackaged as entertainment and reshaped, in the process taking their history captive and reframing it for the convenience and comfort of the White moviegoers who made up the majority of the cinematic audience. What was repackaged the most was the Old West – overwhelmingly any Native American storylines were of the West and often explicitly of their expulsion from most of it. In simple terms, the cultural genocide re-enacted, over and over again, an actual physical genocide packaged as entertainment, until that became the story told about who Native Americans were, and where, for most viewers, they had gone. And it did so by almost entirely erasing Native Americans from the process, either behind or in front of the camera.

So successful was the propaganda campaign of the Western, so that narrative goes, that for much of this period the greatest threat indeed was not these original inhabitants, so alien to the White writers of these works, but other settlers, who battled each other for the land left behind, resulting in a century or so of violence and lawlessness known colloquially as the Old West. This period has, in major part as a result of this vast body of heroic settler narratives, come to be a significant part of the foundational myth of the United States and a major impetus behind such totemic legal stances as the ongoing maintenance and support for the Second Amendment – the right to bear arms – which holds in part that such a lawless country can only have been tamed by men with guns, and thus can only be maintained by men with guns. Though ironically enough, the actual Old West had tougher gun laws than the contemporary United States.*

This body of films, and the vast paraphernalia of books, magazines, toys and costumes which reached its heights with the Hollywood Western in the mid-twentieth century, marks one of the most spectacular multi-generational engagements with what we now term 'fake news', the twisting of information to produce narratives of convenience that only tangentially accord with the reality of a situation. They did not invent the narrative – it was

---

* Jancer, Matt. "Gun Control Is as Old as the Old West". *Smithsonian Magazine*, 5 January 2018. Accessed online at https://www.smithsonianmag.com/history/gun-control-old-west-180968013

one already under construction even as the Old West played out and settlers ploughed and mined and dynamited the landscape and Native Americans deemed to be in the way were exterminated or herded onto barren reservations which were little more than concentration camps.

By the twentieth century, though, the battle for control of the West was over, and by the mid-century all who remembered it first hand were dead. There was then an opportunity to reframe that narrative, to justify what was done to new audiences less enthusiastic than their forebears about the mass murder which the conquest of the West had required; and there was a widespread desire to reframe ancestors real or imagined as classic American heroes – to create a heroic ancestry for modern America in the burgeoning Cold War. This required the integration of the history of the West into the American narrative of a justified, legitimate and above all White conquest which reflected the American future that White Americans, both those of long heritage and recent immigrants, desired to see. For this, certain groups had to be not just defeated, but seen to be defeated, to be erased, dehumanized and kept separate and unequal both in practice and ultimately in the American mind.

We have become wearily familiar with politicians and media figures lying to our faces in recent years, practising confidence tricks large and small to muster support for their political goals and in the process trying to persuade us that what we see in front of our eyes and what we work out for ourselves is wrong simply on their say-so. But this is not a new phenomenon – disinformation has been the staple of oppressive regimes for millennia. What happened in the American West, however, was the marriage of new technologies and naked imperialism in a way which involved telling original lies about the heritage of the United States, lies which unless confronted will continue to permit the continuation of the idea that the conquest of the West was anything other than a genocide, and one which has been replicated on film, for entertainment, in a way that has made the victims the villains.

Exercising physical control over people is an arduous task, one which drains resources and attention. As Mao demonstrated, to contain a population you need fences and guards, an entire oppressive military or paramilitary infrastructure to prohibit and prevent the free movement of people. In the nineteenth-century West, this infrastructure was perhaps best exemplified by the Bureau of Indian Affairs and the US Cavalry. The West was huge, without roads, often unmapped and consisting of rough terrain. It was also home, across its full extent, to Native American peoples. The term 'tribes' has been generally used to describe Native American communities both then and now, but it is very much an imposed description which bore little resemblance to the complex and interwoven nature of Native American community interrelations. What we call a tribe really refers only to people who share a language – thus the names Sioux or Apache did not historically refer to an organized political entity, but rather to many bands of extended families who spoke the same language and through it traded, intermarried and operated in concert, but rarely within a defined central political organization. These groups in turn interacted, sometimes violently, with other neighbouring 'tribes' – groups who spoke different languages and followed different cultural practices. Today there are organized tribes which operate as political entities, the successor states to these historic peoples based largely on the imposed reservation system, but these are not and never were unifying authorities for entire populations before mass colonization of their lands by White settlement.

Indigenous communities drew on thousands of years of accumulated knowledge, living within complex economic, political and social systems which understood and incorporated things like the buffalo or passenger pigeon migratory patterns, and defined their worlds often along the flow of rivers and trading trails. When White Americans first crossed the continent – such as Lewis and Clark's famous expedition to the Pacific from 1804 – these networks, furnished by Native guides, facilitated the explorers' journeys. Already by this time, aggressive settler colonialism was impinging on life for the people of the American West. In the Southwest, Spanish missions had long studded the landscape, and epidemics of diseases like influenza, smallpox and measles came rolling out of the East on a regular basis, brought by immigrants to the long-conquered eastern seaboard and gradually transmitted along the trading routes until they reached unprotected populations, where they killed huge numbers.

By the 1820s, the US government was already directly impinging on land previously designated as owned and governed by Indigenous peoples – the Indian Office, formalized in 1824, was explicitly designed for this purpose. Six years later it was President Andrew Jackson, he of the picture so proudly hanging on President's Trump's Oval Office wall behind the Navajo code talkers as he greeted them, who initiated one of the most notorious genocidal campaigns: the Trail of Tears. In 1830, Jackson legitimized the ongoing military subjugation of the Native communities in what is now Georgia and Alabama. Jackson said

> The condition and ulterior destiny of the Indian tribes within the limits of some of our States have become objects of much interest and importance. It has long been the policy of Government to introduce among them the arts of civilization, in the hope of gradually reclaiming them from a wandering life. This policy has, however, been coupled with another wholly incompatible with its success. Professing a desire to civilize and settle them, we have at the same time lost no opportunity to purchase their lands and thrust them farther into the wilderness. By this means they have not only been kept in a wandering state, but been led to look upon us as unjust and indifferent to their fate . . . It is too late to inquire whether it was just in the United States to include them and their territory within the bounds of new States, whose limits they could control. That step can not be retraced.

Jackson's solution was the removal of the Native peoples to territory reserved for them west of the Mississippi River, hence the term 'reservation', and though he publicly ordered that this removal would be voluntary, his intentions were otherwise. Indeed, shortly thereafter Jackson essentially ordered the ethnic cleansing of the South, and force-marched the populations of five Native American tribes, known at the time as the Five Civilized Tribes for their organized political structures and long alliances and trade arrangements with settlers in the region, to territory hundreds of miles away in what would later become Oklahoma. Tens of thousands died in the round-up and freezing winter marches across mountain ranges. Oklahoma, then called the Indian Territory, was of course already home to numerous Native peoples whose ancestors had lived there for thousands of years. Jackson had a solution to this problem – the Southern tribes were simply relocated on top of the existing residents and the survivors invited to fight it out for resources as settlers crept ever closer. Sixty years on, and despite promises and treaties sworn and signed by the US government, these lands were simply opened for White settlers, who moved in in their thousands and destroyed the Native lands in their way. This piece of ethnic cleansing has since been whimsically portrayed on stage and screen in the Rodgers and Hammerstein musical *Oklahoma!*, which glosses over the appalling violence of the subject nearly entirely, indulging instead in a murderous love triangle between settler families, accompanied by jaunty songs and dances.

At around the same time that Oklahoma was being settled by White farmers and the relocated Native populations displaced once more, the final stage in the centuries-long 'Indian Wars' came to a bloody and remorseless conclusion a thousand miles to the north. On 29 December 1890, several hundred Lakota people were gathered in the snowdrifts beside a frozen creek in territory which had once been entirely theirs but which was now part of the Pine Ridge Reservation, a tract of land carved from the grassy plains and hills which would later become South Dakota. The Lakota speak a dialect of the Sioux language, and in 1876 had organized under the leadership of Chief Sitting Bull with other Sioux communities to fight the US Cavalry in the Black Hills War. The Black Hills was land assigned to the Sioux in a treaty with the US government, but the discovery of gold and an influx of White settlers led to conflict and a concerted effort by the Cavalry to drive the Sioux off their lands and onto the barren lands around Pine Ridge and other designated Reservations.

The Sioux achieved remarkable success in their war, cutting off and destroying a detachment of the 7th Cavalry at a place named Greasy Grass (better known as Little Bighorn), but ultimately the vast resources of the US Army proved far too powerful and the Sioux were overwhelmed, rounded up and imprisoned on the reservation. Many of their children were seized by government agents and sent to boarding schools far away, with the express intent of teaching them to be less Native and more like White Americans, partially assimilated though never equal.

The people imprisoned at Pine Ridge had been systematically shifted from place to place for more than a decade, denied rations and forbidden to hunt, forced to become entirely dependent on government handouts and subject to the capricious will of overtly racist bureaucrats from the Department of Indian Affairs. Any practice of traditional Sioux culture was forbidden, deemed to be both heathen and, more seriously, a possible presage of renewed rebellion; cultural genocide was thus well underway even as the last violent stages of the military genocide played out. The Lakota who gathered by the creek were cold and hungry, suffering the cumulative effects of a century of colonial incursion which had spread disease, carved up their lands, stolen their children and resulted in long, bloody but ultimately futile wars with the ever-growing strength of the United States of America and its blue-coated soldiers who dominated the changed landscape.

The leader of the band, a man named Spotted Elk, knew that he was being hunted. Fourteen days earlier Native police and government agents had arrived at the house of Sitting Bull and shot him dead without trial or provocation. Cavalry units in the area continued to threaten further violence against the captive population, and 200 of Sitting Bull's people had fled the murder and joined with Spotted Elk's people at Cheyenne River. Fearing for his safety, Spotted Elk had assembled his people and the refugees and begun a punishing march through the snow, hoping to join with Red Cloud's band at Pine Ridge and find safety in numbers. Approaching Pine Ridge, however, they were intercepted by a US Cavalry unit sent to halt their advance and diverted to the creekside campsite. The name of the creek was Wounded Knee.

Within hours, machine guns had been set up surrounding the camp. When soldiers entered it and began seizing weapons from the Lakota people within, firing broke out. In the ensuing massacre the soldiers murdered as many as 300 of the Lakota, primarily women and children, and dumped their bodies in mass graves. Twenty-five soldiers were also killed, the majority by friendly fire from other soldiers on the other side of the circle shooting wildly into the panicked crowds. Twenty soldiers were given the Medal of Honor, the highest recognition of bravery and courage a US military service member can receive, awarded for their part in the wholesale slaughter of cold, hungry families by the banks of a frozen creek.

The Wounded Knee massacre, described at the time as a battle for political reasons, was the last major armed confrontation between the US Army and Native Americans. Successive systemic oppression, defeats in battle followed by massacre, imprisonment, assimilation and, in the case of the Lakota, further massacre, had destroyed the last vestiges of Native military resistance and taught the Native communities that there was only death in continuing to actively resist the armed strength of the US Army.

From then on, their access to food was strictly controlled and the land they needed to be independent was fenced off and distributed to settlers. The buffalo herds on which the Plains communities depended for survival had been all but exterminated by industrial hunting, and other resources were stolen, such as the fishing grounds on which many coastal peoples relied, which were now turned over to non-Native fishing fleets and patrolled by the coastguard, who would burn Native boats which entered these waters. With their reservations far from economic opportunity and deliberately lacking in meaningful mineral wealth, the Indigenous peoples had little opportunity to harness the American economic boom of the late nineteenth and early twentieth centuries, and with their cultural traditions strictly policed and their children abducted into residential schools, a concerted effort was well underway to destroy not just the reality of Native American life, but the memory of it too.

Control of Native Americans had thus yielded America to settlers. Right across the continent, the US government used the law and law enforcement to ensure that Native people either stayed where they were put, reliant on the government for survival, or moved away and were compelled to assimilate into mainstream American society. Those who stayed, either by force or choice, were now officially wards of the state and mostly reliant for food on government rations, which were subject to corruption and spoilage. Those who could leave their communities often reluctantly, and only partially, integrated into settler society (consider for a moment the cruel irony within the oft-repeated but rarely considered axiom 'gone off the reservation', to mean someone operating erratically, perhaps dangerously, outside the norms of society). Among those who stayed, some made a small living dressing up in imitation ceremonial robes and performing pastiches of traditional ceremonial events for tourists, tailoring their performances to what the tourists expected to see – increasingly a war-bonneted, war-painted movie caricature – in a phenomenon known as ethnodrama, the staging of fictional ceremony as reality. With Native people consigned out of sight and out of mind to mainstream American society, the rewriting of Native history had begun.

The exoticization of Native society was nothing new. Almost from the earliest encounters, those in which Pocahontas featured so heavily, European settlers had recast Native peoples as simultaneously a savage and dangerous threat, and a naive and childlike race of non-humans connected to the earth and nature and not long to survive. Both constructions enabled settlers to dehumanize and exploit the Indigenous population, whose access to military technology and particularly their resistance to imported diseases put them at a disadvantage. They also suffered from their fractured political systems, which allowed communities to be isolated and destroyed piecemeal, and their different economic and legal systems – complex and sophisticated, but frequently incompatible with European legal systems, which asserted absolute ownership of property rather than negotiated access to resources.

Bestselling books like *The Last of the Mohicans* (1826) continued and developed the narrative that was already circulating of Native Americans as a noble, innocent but ultimately doomed people, who belonged to a world of the past, to be assimilated and erased by the Europeans coming to America and asserting their right to seize the land and the wealth they found there. This attitude drove much of the settlement in the early part of the nineteenth century, including the purges of Andrew Jackson which led to the Trail of Tears. In the 1840s a new phrase was

coined to describe the sense that it was the right and responsibility of White America to seize the entire continent: manifest
destiny.

It was, as described earlier, this movement that led American
expeditionary forces out into the Pacific in the second half of the
nineteenth century, and drove laws and declarations like that
asserting US sovereignty over barren reefs and atolls that might
hold guano reserves. It was also that which led to the slaughter
of the buffalo and the massacre at Wounded Knee. Manifest
Destiny was thus used as a justification for the assertiveness of an
American government in which Natives were wards of the state
and Black citizens, now freed, were unable to vote in large parts
of the country without the constant threat of violence. Manifest
Destiny, like the British and French colonial expansion across
Africa happening almost simultaneously, was a determination of
might making right which justified the exploitation and eradica-
tion of other peoples, especially those of other races, across the
globe. It founded the American Empire just as assuredly as the
British, and it demanded a noble story to be told of how it came
to be. And a noble story requires villains.

The conquest of the West therefore was not nearly enough in
itself. To confirm this victory required America to control not
only the Indigenous peoples of the region, but also their very
history. Thus they could control their future, and rewrite it as one
of noble exploration and adventure, taming an empty wilderness
and turning it into a civilized paradise. Indeed, the suffusion of
the West with an almost religious aspect in the founding story of

modern America made this a story less of a disorganized, murderous and chaotic invasion and more of a courageous, Christian, American operation to bring the continent into the modern era, shedding those parts which no longer had anything more than symbolic value. It took on an overt or implicit religious aspect, depending on the context, demanding obedience and encouraging a patriotic unity in memory of an adventurous and exciting past sanitized of all but the mildest horrors.

As noted, film did not start this process – it was already underway well before Hollywood was invented. Not least among these efforts were the Wild West shows, including the most famous one, belonging to Buffalo Bill, which toured for decades across North America and Europe before millions of people, hosting displays of horsemanship and mock battles in which actors representing the 7th Cavalry or cowboys saw off Indian attacks on innocent women and children, leaving the stage covered with bloody bodies who would rise up once more and repeat the performance twice a day.

The mock slaughter ingrained a series of interrelated ideas – the West as an inherently violent and savage place in which the Native people were the aggressors; that the American Army and settlers were heroes defending their homes, not invaders in someone else's home; and that the Native people were gone and no longer practising their traditions except under these controlled conditions. Indeed, several of the Native performers in Buffalo Bill's shows were only permitted to perform under parole, and were rearrested by Indian Agents and sent back to their reservations the moment they were no longer needed on the show. Finally, it fixed in popular imagination the ideal of a Native person as a bronzed warrior, wearing a feathered war bonnet and riding a horse into hopeless battle before an array of totem poles, a noble figure quite unlike most of the reality of warfare on the Plains and utterly unlike the experiences, clothing and image of the vast majority of Native peoples across an entire continent.

It was in this way that Buffalo Bill and his imitators began the process of reshaping the Native American in popular imagination into something valuable to the founding myth – the lie – at the heart of America: they became a useful tool to their oppressors whose exaggerated legend justifies their destruction: too innocent, too naive, too savage, too dangerous and too obsolete to survive.

Where Bill, who died in 1917, left off, the movies picked up. The first known Western was probably directly inspired by one of Bill's shows. A silent film shot in 1899 in Blackburn, Lancashire and lasting just a minute, *Kidnapped by Indians* set the tone for the following century. For the next six decades, Westerns dominated as one of the most successful and popular genres of film Hollywood put out. For a time, it seemed that every story under the sun could be retold as a Western, and retold over and over again. The vast majority of these Westerns were produced in Hollywood studios and filmed either on set or in the easily reached mountains and deserts of Southern California or, if you had a bit of money, further afield in the Southwest, particularly in the spectacular Monument Valley on the Navajo Reservation on the Utah–Arizona border.

In this way the sandy deserts and rocky mountains of this far Western region soon came to stand for the entirety of the plains and forests and mountains of the real Old West. Within them were told the stories of the Westerns, which either featured Native American characters or did not – and in neither case did the films present either an authentic story or a sensitive one. For when Native Americans did not appear, the films effectively erased them from the West, from the territories on which they used to live, from the reservations, and from the towns and communities where they, and their many mixed-race children, were forced to live on the periphery of White society, not quite afforded the rights of a full human citizen, not quite inhuman enough to the authorities not to be exploited.

But when they did appear it was often worse, because until the mid-century in almost none of these depictions were they presented in a favourable light. Capricious, murderous and savage, brutal and unknowable but easily mown down by John Wayne with a rifle, they were a constant danger, an inevitable source of fear and ultimately a direct threat, particularly to the innocent virtue of White women. They were in essence there to be deservedly eliminated. For all their screen nobility and strange beauty, they were a relic of a past best disposed of and remembered in the lies of others, not their own telling. Indeed, during the Second World War the Office of War Information actually laid down guidelines on how minorities, including Native peoples, should be depicted, noting that 'Our sincerity is judged by the attitude and treatment we accord those dark-skinned peoples within our own borders,' a warning which extended only to depictions on film, and not to actual treatment.*

The history of Native Americans in Hollywood is one of half-truths and outright lies – lies such as in John Wayne's *Hondo* of 1953, in which the Apache warriors are lauded as the dying remnants of a once-noble race, now reduced to barbarism in the present and a direct threat to White women. Ultimately they are protected by a White man who is able to shoot them all down, his superior tactical skills and technology overwhelming wave after wave of faceless, unnamed feather-wearing savages. Or think of Audie Murphy's *The Guns of Fort Petticoat* of 1957, in which a warband of the Pawnee are defeated by a ragtag band of women who string up the Pawnee 'medicine man' and dangle his body before his horrified compatriots, who flee in terror. Or *White Comanche* (1968), a Spanish-made Western, where William Shatner – on a break from filming *Star Trek* – plays Comanche twin brothers separated at birth with all the subtlety and sensitivity you might expect of such a film.

In many Westerns, like John Ford's 1939 *Stagecoach*, or Gregory Peck's 1951 *Only the Valiant*, the Native Americans are nothing more than an insidious threat, without names or characters, something on the edge of the world, a faceless

---

* Aleiss, Angela, 2005. *Making the White Man's Indian*. Praeger, Westport, p. 75.

mass of danger and fear to be shot down by heroes wearing Cavalry blue. Even in *The Searchers* of 1958, one of the more nuanced Westerns of the 1950s, the ever-implicit threat of violence and violation to White women drives the hatred in John Wayne's character, hatreds which are critiqued in the film, but in ways subtle enough to be mistaken for acceptance. In almost all these films, with very few exceptions, the Native characters were played by White actors in redface make-up, dancing mocking pastiches of Native ceremonies, wearing clumsy approximations of Native dress and falling dramatically from their horses at every opportunity. Hollywood didn't just steal a Native genocide and turn it into entertainment; it simultaneously erased all Native presence and agency from the telling of the tale.

This is not a historical problem alone. Revisionist Westerns from the 1970s onwards challenged the hero myths of the Old West and even started to introduce Native actors to play Native characters. Yet in almost all these stories it was the White outsiders who took on the hero role – from Richard Harris's *A Man Called Horse* of 1970 to Kevin Costner in *Dances with Wolves* in 1990, it was the White men who assumed leadership positions, who taught the unruly savages how to fight, and more often than not retired to the mountains, leaving the remnants of their adopted people behind to die in captivity. Even in the film *Geronimo* of 1993, featuring veteran Cherokee actor Wes Studi as the eponymous Apache war chief and hailed as a turning point in the depiction of Native Americans on film, Studi is at best the third most significant role, with young cavalry officers played by Jason Patric and Matt Damon having far more screen time and lines, as well as providing the narrative voice. By the time Disney's *Pocahontas* rolled around in 1995, generation after generation of Americans were used to seeing Native Americans as both wild and untamed children of nature, as well as dangerous, murderous outsiders who could not be trusted or reasoned with.

The truth of course is that Native Americans fought, and fought hard. They were expert trackers and hunters and fighters whose defeat lay more in attrition, internal factionalism and ecological disaster than any great military success from the Cavalry. They did not waste their lives in frontal attacks on forts or military formations unless there was little choice. Their wars were guerrilla campaigns conducted over decades, and only when the alternative was a fate akin to death, the slow degradation and humiliation of imprisonment, as Geronimo ended his days, or the ever-present possibility of murder by your captors, which Sitting Bull discovered.

This narrative is one that has never been adequately addressed. There is a structural and institutional racism in Hollywood and among its audiences that both reflects and amplifies the structural and institutional racism embedded in the United States. In 2015's *Bone Tomahawk* the cannibal Natives are deliberately dehumanized as troglodytes – sub-humans incapable of civilization or reason. In 2017's Emmy award-winning miniseries *Godless*, magical Native characters appear to guide the White characters before slipping away without explanation. As recently as 2013 Johnny Depp was cast as Tonto, a grotesque Native servant caricature in his own right, in the Disney blockbuster of *The Lone Ranger*. Hollywood is still doing this, and even efforts to get it right are a battle. When Eugene Brave Rock, of the Kainai people, was cast as the character 'Chief' in 2017's *Wonder Woman*, he had to explain to the director that to his people the very term, as applied indiscriminately to Native men by White characters, is a racial slur. He added the Blackfoot language to the film, and had direct input in character development and costume. The character's name was changed to Napi, short for Napioa, a Kainai spirit who created the Earth, yet this distinction does not seem to have made it into the film's credits, where Brave Rock is still credited as 'Chief'.*

Modern news and social media are riven with lies, and recent times have seen countless discussions about fake news and its pernicious effects. This is often interpreted as a modern phenomenon, but in reality its roots are ancient, and found one of their strongest occurrences in the demonization of an entire continent of peoples who stood in the way of the American Empire.

But for all the desire of the US government to eradicate them, Native Americans held some small value to them; they were an ideal symbol of America's past and a warning to the future about

---

* Davy, Jack. "A Conversation with Eugene Brave Rock". Beyond the Spectacle, University of Kent, 20 August 2018. Accessed online at https://blogs.kent.ac.uk/bts/2018/08/20/a-conversation-with-eugene-brave-rock

what civilization could do. It was thus, seventy-five years after the massacre by the creek at Wounded Knee, that a Hollywood movie was released which purportedly covered the events at Wounded Knee, entitled *The Great Sioux Massacre* (1965). The film was poorly made, expressing sympathy for the Sioux at one turn and hatred for them at another, before ultimately ending with the message that to trust the Sioux was to invite murder and mayhem, and that the massacre, while regrettable, was the fault of a few bad apples in the US Cavalry, a phrase which in American contexts is wildly overused and misused in the context of racial violence. The film's main intent was to indirectly suggest that the massacre at Wounded Knee, and the hundreds of massacres which preceded it, were justified as part of the inevitable progress of American civilization at the expense of the Native communities who had lived there before.

The Great Sioux Massacre was not widely watched; it was poorly received, won no major awards, and its individual significance is slight. But it was also one of the more than 4,000 Westerns made between 1900 and 1980 which together carry the same message of a West made over the remains of a people whose fate was, if not deserved, inevitable. Not all of these films featured Native Americans, and not all were entirely unsympathetic to them, but the Western genre of film sat at the heart of vast cultural apparatus of books, TV programmes and toys which fetishized and stereotyped Native Americans and the Native American way of life, focusing almost exclusively on one small sliver of time and one small group of people to consciously make them into the idolized representation of American life. It is this dichotomy which enables Native people to be portrayed in multi-million selling books and films by non-Native writers and actors, with the profits of their stolen stories never reaching the communities from which they were taken.

Which brings us to the *Twilight* movies, a story of a teen love triangle involving vampires and werewolves set in the forests of the Olympic peninsula of Washington state. The werewolves are Native people of the Quileute Tribe. The author Stephenie Meyer appropriated reserved Indigenous stories of skinwalkers and shapeshifters for a story laden with cultural stereotypes for which the tribe depicted received no financial benefit. Worse still, though several secondary characters were played by Indigenous actors, the lead werewolf, named Jacob, was played by Taylor Lautner, an actor of no known Native ancestry, the continuation of a harmful Hollywood trope and an example of representation without authenticity.*

Twilight aside, most of the Westerns discussed here are set in a period in which Indigenous peoples lived in the midst of genocide, making the typical and traditional out of the desperate and disastrous – what most of us think of as typical Native culture from the movies is in fact ancient peoples at the brink of collapse under violent and continual oppression by a government overtly hostile to their very existence. Very few

---

* Vassar, Shea. "The Twilight Saga's Issue with Indigenous Culture". FilmDaze, 20 May 2020. Accessed online at https://filmdaze.net/twilight-sagas-issue-with-indigenous-culture

Native Americans had any say in how they were portrayed on screen; few actors and no directors or producers were Native, or could speak with any authority on Native identity or culture. The cultural descendants of those who had persecuted and murdered Native men, women and children did so over and over again on film before the eyes of millions of Americans over multiple generations.

Native Americans, who spoke more than 500 distinct languages and lived in thousands of distinct communities, became bonneted caricatures of the fading past to be replaced by the American future, ludicrous figures of menace and buffoonish simplicity, economically valuable only to the degree to which they could be dehumanized. They were rendered as savage children deserving only of sympathy in their fruitless resistance to modernity or as worthy of no more than adoption and re-education, taught to abandon their heritage in favour of a blanket oppressive non-Indigenous identity.

Militarily defeated, economically excluded, Native Americans were easy targets for an entertainment machine seeking villains to be killed, and thus for more than a century after the massacre of Wounded Knee this was the role they held in American popular understanding: culturally oppressed, represented by those who did not respect or have interest in them and reduced to irrelevance. This process cut them off from their cultures and deliberately disrupted their ability to identify with their ancestors and to integrate with non-Native American society.

Native Americans survived. They did so by enduring remark-able horrors in a demographic and cultural genocide which still reverberates through their communities. They resisted by surviving, and by retaining what they could in the face of determined efforts to destroy them and eliminate, physically, emotionally and legally, any claims to the millions of square miles of territory seized from them and reallocated to White settlers. For Native people the colonial era from which Kenya or Algeria tentatively emerged has never ended and probably never will. Suicide rates, drug dependency, life expectancy and employment statistics on Native reservations are consist-ently among the worse in the United States. People there are denied access to basic provisions even as thousands of Native women and girls simply vanish in an ongoing toll of murderous exploitation.

Native Americans became symbols for the nation which sought to destroy them, a people hailed as the noble and heroic past based on an invented story while being simultaneously despised, mistreated and ignored by the nation. They became icons in Hollywood. Racial slurs against them are used to this day by major American sporting franchises and their stories of suffering and military service were co-opted by the president for use in childish games of political theatre. Many still occupy destructive positions of poverty and suffering, but through cultural, economic and political activism, they actively resist. To resist is to survive and to survive is to resist, and in such a state the very act of living day to day becomes a protest against the literal and metaphorical massacres of their history. When people lie publicly, and lie loud enough, the results can be devastating, and when we are complicit in those lies and participate in them unchecked as liars or audiences, we personally exacerbate that damage.

Chapter Seven

POLICE OPPRESSION: FREE DERRY AND BLACK LIVES MATTER

On the evening of 19 April 1969, a squad of men kicked in the door of a family home on William Street in Derry, Northern Ireland, a terraced row of inner-city houses ostensibly like any other in the UK. Finding the inhabitants in their hallway and living room, the assailants set about them with batons, knocking the family to the floor and smashing their possessions. They proceeded to mob the father, Samuel Devenny, landing blow after blow until he was so battered his own son could no longer recognize him. Devenny, a forty-two-year-old father of nine children, died in hospital three months later. The coroner reported his death as the result of a pre-existing heart condition and a paper-thin police investigation, still never publicly released, found no trace of the suspects. No one from the police ever directly spoke with the family during or after the investigation.*

The reasons for this cover-up were simple: everyone – the family, the coroner, the neighbours and the police themselves – knew that the men who attacked Devenny were police officers, and apart from his local Member of the Parliament of Northern Ireland, future Nobel Prize recipient John Hume, who was later shot in the chest with a police gas canister while protesting the murder,† no one in any official position at the time was interested in exposing this fact. The family, from the Catholic community of the Bogside in Derry, had no power or connections to get attention, and though a subsequent independent investigation, led by the Metropolitan Police and also never publicly released, identified that the attack was conducted by police officers of the Royal Ulster Constabulary (RUC), operating as a riot squad that night, no official action was ever taken to try and establish who the men who murdered Samuel Devenny were, or to bring them to justice. The crime remains, and likely always will remain, unsolved.‡

---

* O'Neill, Leona. "First Troubles victim was beaten unconscious alongside daughter by RUC – We just want the Truth, says family". *Belfast Telegraph*, 15 July 2019. Accessed online at https://www.belfasttelegraph.co.uk/news/northern-ireland/first-troubles-victim-was-beaten-unconscious-alongside-daughter-by-ruc-we-just-want-the-truth-says-family-38311730.html

† Coogan, Tim Pat, 1996. *The Troubles: Ireland's Ordeal 1966–1996 and the Search for Peace.* Arrow Books, London, pp. 88 and 141.

‡ BBC News, 2014. "Samuel Devenny death: documents to stay secret", 11 February 2014. Accessed online at https://www.bbc.co.uk/news/uk-northern-ireland-foyle-west-26132996

The officers who killed Devenny were supposed to be maintaining law and order under the authority of the Parliament of Northern Ireland, a representative body empowered by the Parliament of the United Kingdom in London, but they understood implicitly in public and explicitly in private that their role was far more political and conspicuously one-sided. They were to clamp down on protests – violent or non-violent – from Derry's Catholic community as part of a worsening campaign of inter-community violence in which one side, the Catholics, were conspicuously oppressed and another, the Protestants, were tolerated and encouraged by the police. The RUC officers who attacked the family were likely all Protestants; Devenny was a Catholic with no ties to violent groups or recorded involvement even in the peaceful protest movement. In Northern Ireland in 1969 there was no justice for a Catholic taxi driver in the wrong place (his home) at the wrong time (early evening), and everyone knew it. His death was part of a sequence of events which saw the breakdown in policing by consent across Northern Ireland, a collapse triggered in large part by police violence, which would lead quite rapidly to a war which cost thousands of other lives.

I will look specifically at the role of the RUC and its failures, which contributed to the slide to war in Northern Ireland, but then more generally at the breakdown in trust and obedience to police authority from stigmatized and oppressed parts of the community which precipitated it. We are always expected to respect and obey the police, but when the police are providing not even justice, or a partial justice which is hardly justice at all, it is essential that we explore that relationship.

The catastrophic, cascading failures of the British government response to intercommunity violence in Northern Ireland are a salutary lesson in understanding that policing is not always about separating good from bad or legal from illegal. All too often the police, either deliberately or systemically, choose sides – whether directly instructed to do so by unrepresentative government or via a series of individual choices in police forces riven by institutional biases, thus enforcing the unjust and highly subjective oppression of the state.

The brutal murder of Samuel Devenny was one of the first in a growing number of tit-for-tat killings between the Protestant and Catholic communities of Northern Ireland in the spring of 1969 which marked the start of a thirty-year conflict, the Troubles.

The causes of this conflict reach far back into the bitter and violent British colonization of Ireland, but more immediate were the consequence of a total breakdown in the practice of principled and democratic government in the province, and in particular the legitimacy of policing in Northern Ireland. The people of Northern Ireland were split, then as more or less now, by a religious divide. First there were the Unionists, who controlled political power and wished to preserve the political link with the United Kingdom. They were largely Protestants, and their paramilitary wing, a coalition of violent groups, was known collectively as Loyalists. Opposing them were the Nationalists, largely politically powerless through mainstream structures, who sought a union with the Republic of Ireland to the south. They were largely Catholic, and their paramilitary wing was dominated by the Irish Republican Army (IRA) and its various splinter groups and subdivisions. Between them were millions of British citizens of Northern Ireland like Samuel Devenny, Catholics and Protestants alike, whose sympathies lay perhaps with one side or another, but whose main desire was to be allowed to live their lives without the threat of unexpected death in bombings, shootings and beatings by one faction or another.

Keeping the supposed peace over this volatile and dangerous political rivalry, which had already sparked campaigns of bombing and assassination three times in the preceding fifty years, was the RUC. And yet the RUC in the late 1960s was not a police force dedicated to the preservation of law and order, but one dedicated to the maintenance of Protestant supremacy through deliberate and systematic unequal policing. In pursuing this goal, they actively and aggressively oppressed the Catholic community by targeting them with overtly unjust and brutal police tactics aimed not just at community leaders, but at the broader Catholic population. This included random beatings and murders, either by constables in or out of uniform, or through collusion with armed Loyalist groups (and often the line between police and Loyalists was blurred entirely).

The second part of this process was active non-policing, the failure to make any serious attempt to preserve law and order in Catholic communities, leaving them undefended against criminal operations from within and without. Though it was rarely stated openly or conspicuously, the approach of the RUC in 1969 was to make it clear to the Catholic communities of Northern Ireland that they were not only unprotected, but that the organization tasked with protecting them could also enact brutal, fatal violence at random – that no one could ever be fully safe. This was the context within which Samuel Devenny was beaten to death.

The result was an escalating series of violent attacks as Republican paramilitaries assumed the protection role for their community the RUC had abandoned, as well as an offensive capability striking back against both the Loyalist paramilitaries and the state security apparatus which conspicuously aided and sheltered them. In a clumsy and counter-productive effort to keep the peace between the communities, the British Army was subsequently deployed to the streets of Northern Ireland. It was a tragic mistake. The government was responding to a failure of policing with an army trained, as in Kenya, to keep the peace not though reconciliation, but through explicit violence.

We all live under at least the theoretical protection of a police force to which we turn when we are victims or witnesses of a crime – there are very few places on earth like Clipperton Island, where there are simply no law enforcement agencies at all. However, as witnessed again and again in the preceding chapters, all police and security forces are answerable to the governments from which they derive their authority and therefore are, at the very best, no less corrupt than the government which runs them. Thus it was that the police in Kenya during the Mau Mau uprising were empowered to arrest and torture Kikuyu men without trial or oversight, and that revolutionary police in communist China could arrest and kill people unchallenged for imagined political crimes such as shirking or travelling without permission.

But these were authoritarian regimes, in which the persons being repressed had no vote and thus no stake in government or worth for the men attacking them. Modern democracies like Britain and the United States are not supposed to permit this kind of abuse of power within their own borders, because politicians who do so will be punished by the voters at the ballot box.

And yet they do. They did when the RUC killed Samuel Devenny in 1969, and they did when a Minneapolis police officer choked George Floyd to death in the summer of 2020. And this is because Devenny and Floyd came from communities for whom the police were no longer protectors, but oppressors, acting without accountability or oversight, and with a mission – explicit or implicit – to demonstrate to other members of that community that they were less valuable than other citizens, and protected by majority White electorates who saw the police as on their side against minority communities they found threatening.

Floyd, a forty-six-year-old African American man recently laid off from his work as a nightclub bouncer due to the coronavirus pandemic, died on 25 May 2020. He had been shopping at a market in Powderhorn Park, a suburb of Minneapolis, and was accused by the clerk of paying with a fake $20 bill. An argument ensued and the police were called. Hauling Floyd from his vehicle at gunpoint, the officers restrained him and tried to place him in a police car, which Floyd resisted, leading to a struggle which ended with Floyd, by now in a state of panic, lying face down in the street with his hands cuffed behind his back. A crowd gathered to watch, some filming the arrest on their cellphones.

It was at this point that a White police officer named Derek Chauvin chose to kneel directly on Floyd's neck, apparently in an effort to subdue him. This was an entirely illegal method of restraint, and one repeatedly demonstrated to be dangerous – in another famous case of police brutality six years earlier, a street merchant in New York named Eric Garner had died when a NYPD officer choked him with a baton; the killing was filmed and broadcast in seconds on social media. Chauvin continued this illegal use of excessive force for more than nine minutes, despite calls from bystanders that Floyd was in distress and Floyd's own increasingly desperate pleas that he could not breathe. Three other officers on the scene did nothing to intervene or prevent Chauvin's fatal assault. Floyd died under Chauvin's knee, the entire murder captured on cameraphone recordings and instantly sent and shared around the world, watched by hundreds of millions of appalled viewers.

Chauvin's murder of Floyd was, horrifyingly, not in itself unusual. Police forces in the United States kill US citizens at rates which would be considered a national crisis almost anywhere else in the developed world. In 2020 alone 999 people were shot and killed by American police forces, five fewer than 2019 and three more than in 2018. More still are killed in the manner of George Floyd, choked or beaten to death in restraints. In a modern nation of laws, even one as large as the United States, these numbers are enormous, exceeded only by active warzones such as Syria and Afghanistan, or authoritarian nations with a history of political repression such as Brazil or the Philippines. The worst, by a considerable distance, is Venezuela, where the police kill more than 5,000 people a year in a nation with a population a tenth that of the US. By contrast, neighbouring Mexico, still fighting a major drug war on its northern border, had 371 deaths at police hands in the same year, a figure roughly in proportion by population with the United States, while Canada had thirty-six. European and Asian developed countries have much lower numbers: French police killed twenty-six people, Germans eleven, Australians four, British three and Japanese two. The number in the US is not even close to proportional, and is indicative of serious structural problems, not least of which is that for many African Americans, the police are not protectors, but oppressors.*

The statistics on police killings bear this out: African Americans make up approximately 13 per cent of the US population, but African Americans, predominantly men, are killed by US police at more than twice the rate of their White fellow citizens, making up more than 26 per cent of all cases. Nearly 70 per cent of US police officers are White, with African American representation

---

* These figures are based on the data compiled from numerous sources at https://en.wikipedia.org/wiki/List_of_killings_by_law_enforcement_officers_by_country

at or around their levels in the general population. Put simply, if somewhat reductively, predominantly White officers kill Black citizens at a startlingly disproportionate rate. The historic reasons for these tragic statistics are complex and discussed in a later chapter, but it is worth clarifying here that this was the context in which Derek Chauvin killed George Floyd. The footage of Floyd's death was far from the first video of such a killing to emerge from Minneapolis. Cafeteria worker Philando Castile was shot dead in front of his partner and daughter for possession of a legal handgun during a traffic stop near Minneapolis in 2016, for example. By 2020, Americans were very familiar with unaccountable police violence on their phone screens.

But something about the callous and pointless killing of George Floyd reverberated around American society. Perhaps it was the chaos and panic of the COVID-19 pandemic, in which so many found themselves unemployed and under threat. It is likely also to be linked to the presidency of Donald Trump, who had publicly advocated for increased police brutality, suggesting to police cadets in New York that under his rule they could bang suspects' heads on police cars with impunity, a statement met with applause.* In the aftermath of Floyd's murder, Trump could only lament that US police kill more White people than Black people, casually dismissing the disproportionate likelihood of

---

* Berman, Mark. "Trump tells police not to worry about injuring suspects during arrests". *Washington Post*, 28 July 2017. Accessed online at https://www.washingtonpost.com/news/post-nation/wp/2017/07/28/trump-tells-police-not-to-worry-about-injuring-suspects-during-arrests

death at the hands of police that is a feature of African American life.*

Protests began across the country, people marching against this unaccountable and seemingly intractable legacy of police violence against men, and women, of colour. Some participating in the protests recalled Breonna Taylor, a young woman in Louisville, Kentucky, shot dead three months earlier by police who smashed their way into her house in the middle of the night in search of an ex-boyfriend. Beginning in Minneapolis, people spilled out onto the streets in cities across the United States in protests which were mostly peaceful by day but marred by outbreaks of rioting and looting at night.

The police response to these protests was ferocious. Making no distinction between legal peaceful protests and rioters, police forces across the United States launched an apparently spontaneous, though officially encouraged, campaign of fearsome violence. Heavily armed and armoured, accompanied by military surplus vehicles, police units waded among the protestors, using pepper spray and tear gas to disperse groups and leaving hundreds injured. In Los Angeles a man in a wheelchair was thrown to the floor and beaten; in Buffalo, New York, a man in his seventies was shoved to the floor and left unconscious and bleeding; and in Atlanta a young Black couple were dragged from their car and tasered for doing nothing more than driving past a protest.

---

* Walters, Joanna. "Trump twists stats on police brutality: 'more white people' are killed", *Guardian*, 15 July 2020. Accessed online at https://www.theguardian.com/us-news/2020/jul/14/donald-trump-george-floyd-police-killings

Just as the murder of George Floyd was transmitted around the world, so were pictures of police brutality shared by tens of millions: pictures and videos of police in New York City using their bikes to strike at commuters on street corners, or police vehicles in Detroit deliberately running into crowds, and in particular the deliberate targeting of journalists covering the protest – at least 328 incidents of attacks on the press were reported.*

Even as much of America recoiled at this naked display of official strength and brutality, spokesmen for police unions went on television demanding further powers to brutalize without restraint, echoing that violent rhetoric of the president.† It was an immediate and obvious display, as if one more were needed, that the police infrastructure in the United States was geared not solely or perhaps even mainly towards public protection, but to the oppression and restrain of specific parts of the population. The police were in effect demanding the right to choke, beat or shoot to death whomever they chose, without accountability or reprisal, and demonstrating that they would deliberately target anyone who attempted to call out their hypocrisy.

With the US government paralysed by indecision and incompetence at the highest level, and unwilling in any case to offer

---

* Klebnikov, Sergei. "Journalists targeted while covering protests". *Forbes*, 4 June 2020. Accessed online at https://www.forbes.com/sites/sergeiklebnikov/2020/06/04/journalists-targeted-while-covering-protests-279-press-freedom-violations-and-counting

† Roberts, William. "After 2020's BLM protests, real police reform proves a struggle". Al Jazeera, 13 April 2021. Accessed online at https://www.aljazeera.com/news/2021/4/13/after-2020s-blm-protests-police-reform-still-a-struggle-in-us

support or condolence to a suffering minority the president had publicly castigated, this crisis was, like the COVID-19 crisis within which it took place, allowed to billow and accelerate. Protests and violence spread and more people lost their lives, leading to fresh rounds of protest. In a grotesque effort to project strength, President Trump's solution was to order an attack on protestors in Washington DC. Unidentified, heavily armed paramilitary units apparently drawn from staff in the federal prison system and accompanied by uniformed army officers, including the Chairman of the Joint Chiefs, the nation's most senior uniformed military commander, brutally assaulted the protestors with tear gas and baton charges. Peaceful protestors were driven from the vicinity of St John's Church just across the road from the White House, so that Donald Trump could stand before it, clasping a Bible and mouthing campaign slogans as photographers took pictures, the tear gas swirling. The message, to people of colour and other marginalized groups, could not be clearer: we do not serve you, we do not respect you, and if we want to beat, gas and kill you with impunity, we will do so. If you protest, it will get worse.

In the Northern Ireland of 1969, there were no cameraphones to record what was done to Samuel Devenny, nor Francis McCloskey, a pensioner beaten to death in the street by an RUC riot squad in Dungiven in July; or nine-year-old Patrick Rooney, killed by bullets fired from a machine gun mounted on an RUC armoured car which punched through his bedroom wall in the Divis Tower housing estate on 14 August; or Hugh McCabe, an off-duty British soldier visiting family on the Divis Flats estate shot by an RUC sniper; or John Gallagher, Samuel McLarnon, Michael Lynch or fifteen-year-old aspiring IRA volunteer Gerald McAuley, all killed in two days of running Belfast street battles between Loyalist gangs and the RUC on one side and Republican gangs, already rapidly coalescing into the reformed IRA, on the other. In Derry, Northern Ireland's second city, similar though less murderous rioting broke out which saw parts of the city barricaded and cut off, the inhabitants declaring the areas as de facto independent Free Derry. The Troubles had begun.

The IRA were nothing new for Northern Ireland. The organization stemmed from the bloody days of the War for Independence fifty years earlier, when gun battles flared across all of Ireland, the IRA facing the British Army, the Royal Irish Constabulary and the Ulster Special Constabulary in a vicious shadow war. When Ulster was partitioned from the rest of Ireland, the British Army withdrew from front-line security duties and the police forces re-formed as the Royal Ulster Constabulary, which had skirmished with the IRA ever since, including flare-ups of the conflict in the late 1930s and the mid-1950s. When Loyalists and the RUC began to attack Catholic areas like the Divis Flats, the IRA's numbers swelled once more, and the fighting spread across the country, the police unable and largely unwilling to curb the growing civil unrest.

Police brutality was a response to a concerted political and social effort to end decades of anti-Catholic discrimination by the Parliament of Northern Ireland and the other institutions of state. Northern Ireland's government was carefully constructed to prevent Catholics attaining a meaningful representation in the Parliament, with constituency boundaries carefully drawn and a series of restrictions in place to limit the numbers of Catholics who could vote. Unrepresented at the highest levels, and disdained by those in power, the Catholic half of the country was shut out of government positions and denied access to many government services – housing, tied to vote rigging, was disproportionately made available to Protestant families, and Catholics were three times more likely to be unemployed than their Protestant neighbours.

In response to these pressures, a group called the Northern Ireland Civil Rights Association was established in the mid-1960s. A peaceful protest organization, developed along the lines of the American civil rights associations which had achieved so much success in eliminating legal barriers to voting, the group began to organize voting drives and protests, including peaceful marches through cities and towns. In October 1968, however, a march in Derry was blocked by a police barricade and then attacked by a police charge. A Republican MP who was leading the march was among those severely beaten, and images of the violence made international news. Among the marchers were IRA volunteers, who were swift to take note of the violence and launch a recruiting drive.

The attack on the march in Derry signalled a new phase of the battle for representation in Northern Ireland. It was now clear that the Stormont Assembly and the RUC who answered to it had no intention of allowing a peaceful protest movement to make inroads into their hegemony. Further marches were organized and passed unmolested, but in January another march was attacked just outside the city by a Loyalist mob. Police sent to control the violence initially refused to act, and then spread through the city smashing their way into Catholic homes and beating residents.

In response, the Catholic communities of Derry began forming militias and manning barricades to defend their homes from attacks by police and Loyalists, as well as launching attacks themselves on patrols – initially just with stones and debris. Skirmishes continued as Northern Ireland's second city descended into sectarian chaos. It was on one such night of clashes and mobs in April that Devenny died. Standing on his doorstep watching as Bogside kids clashed with RUC and irregular Ulster Special Constabulary riot squads, he began to close his door as the conflict surged closer. He was too slow, and boys scattering from a police charge in the street took a short cut through his home and out of the back door. And then suddenly the house was full of noise, the door smashed in and police, armoured and carrying batons, were among his family, battering his wife and daughters to the floor. As Devenny pleaded for the officers to leave his family alone, his sixteen-year-old daughter Catherine, recovering from surgery, was hauled from her bed on the sofa and kicked into unconsciousness. Her eighteen-year-old sister Anne tried to get between the officers and her father, who had recently been released from hospital following treatment for a heart condition, but was kicked and beaten in turn and thrown against the fireplace. She was then held by her hair and forced to watch as the officers laid into her father with their batons, administering such a savage beating to Samuel Devenny that by the time they finished even his children could no longer recognize him. His eldest son later recalled picking fragments of broken teeth out of his father's shattered face. The son and two other men in the house were also brutally beaten. A month after Devenny's death, Belfast exploded into violence and Free Derry was declared, an independent Catholic enclave which blocked the RUC or Loyalist mobs from entering Catholic homes and repeating the violence of the previous six months.

The violence of the RUC in the late 1960s bears some parallels with the violence meted out by US police forces against members of the African American community, though on a less consistent or organized scale. As the statistics show, police officers act frequently against unarmed and unthreatening Black citizens with impunity, killing, arresting and injuring them on a scale which proportionally far outstrips their representation in the population. At the same time, they frequently barely bother to investigate violence and crime inflicted on Black communities by White or Black-on-Black crimes, particularly in poorer communities. This has been the case for decades, and led directly to the bloody gang wars which sent murder rates soaring in the late 1980s and 1990s, a period which saw murders in the United States reach a total of more than 24,000 a year, driven by a national crime wave focused particularly on the decaying inner cities where African Americans, through conspicuously racist housing policies, formed the majority of the population. For the best part of three decades, nearly nothing was done on a national level to bring this crime wave under control except to introduce harsher and harsher prison sentences for crimes, many of which were never successfully prosecuted and continued on the streets unabated.

Resentment built up in the African American population at their treatment by brutal police officers and a court system which seemed to go out of its way to persecute their communities in particular, but it was a resentment which only rarely spilled over into organized public violence against the state. When it did, though, the results were spectacular and terrible. Probably the most significant race rioting of the post-civil rights era before 2020 occurred in Los Angeles in 1992, part of the response to four police officers savagely beating an African American motorist named Rodney King on 3 March 1991. King, who was drunk and on parole for several violent offences, had fled from a traffic stop before eventually surrendering to police, but there was little remarkable about the chase. Once stopped however he was tasered, beaten, stomped and hogtied by the officers without provocation or resistance.

Though senior police officers expressed their shock, this type of violence was common in arrests by the LAPD, and particularly well known to the Black community, who lived in many cases in a neat constant state of semi-siege with police patrols and raids punctuating neighbourhood life as crime continued to soar. When the officers were charged with the beating and placed on trial, it seemed that perhaps some redress might be found. In court the officers lied about the circumstances of the arrest, and the jury, one or possibly none of whom were African American, acquitted the officers after seven days of deliberations, despite camera footage of their attack on King. A White jury trusted the word of White police officers over actual video evidence before their eyes.

Rioting broke out almost immediately, spreading through several Black neighbourhoods but centred on Los Angeles' Koreatown district. Shops were looted and city blocks burned. Large-scale police deployments were backed up by 10,000 National Guardsmen and 3,500 regular soldiers and marines, who effectively occupied the city to enforce the curfew and bring the riots to an end after four days. Sixty-three people were killed. Crucially, once peace had been restored, the LAPD, uniformed and institutionally racist though they were, resumed control. Most troops had been stood down by 9 May, and all had left by the end of the year. There was no ongoing armed resistance or paramilitary blockades of the affected communities.

In Northern Ireland, the events of August 1969, less bloody or widespread than the violence in Los Angeles, provoked a different reaction. There the underlying factionalism of the RUC and the Parliament, coupled with the ongoing violence of the Loyalist reaction, meant that the Catholic community was reluctant to return to the arrangements of the past. Two things then happened which were to change Northern Ireland for ever. The first was that the IRA, still centred on the vestigial remains of the armed force operating since 1921, had been totally unprepared for the extent of the Loyalist attacks on Catholic communities in Belfast. A schism formed between the old Official IRA and a new Provisional IRA, furious at the failures of leadership, which demanded a far more aggressive approach to armed action in Northern Ireland. This division would eventually see the Provisionals assume leadership over the paramilitary Republican movement and initiate a violent campaign against the Parliament.

The second was that the British government, led at that time by Harold Wilson's Labour Party, was finally forced to take the violence in Northern Ireland seriously – for decades they had been content to ignore flare-ups and civil inequality as long as disruption was kept to a minimum. Indeed the Conservative Party had long forged a parliamentary alliance with the Unionists which encouraged them to turn a blind eye to the rampant corruption at Stormont. Wilson deployed the British Army to Belfast and Derry, drawing a dividing line between the communities, though conspicuously avoiding Catholic-controlled districts. For several months an uneasy peace descended, punctuated by periodic riots and sporadic attacks which left another five people dead, including the first RUC officer to die, Constable Victor Arbuckle, shot dead by Loyalists on the Shankill Road. The British Army did not leave, could not leave, in the absence of a trusted police force to keep tensions low, and instead began constructing walls and roadblocks to keep the communities apart.

Thus began, almost accidentally, the occupation of Northern Ireland, sovereign British territory, by the British Army who, it is worth remembering, were barely ten years on from their brutal repression of the Mau Mau. Thus it was that, during 1970, Northern Ireland was faced with a deteriorating situation. The IRA, resurgent in the Catholic communities terrorized by Loyalist gangs, were arming. The Loyalists, openly encouraged to target Catholics by fanatical Protestant preachers, were doing likewise. The police and Northern Irish security forces were openly supporting the Loyalists and refusing to protect the Catholic communities, and the British Army, heavily armed and in a civilian control context but only really trained for the type of colonial counter-insurgency they'd fought in Kenya (and Cyprus and Malaya and elsewhere), were stationed in the middle, ostensibly to keep the peace.

In July, nearly a year after the riots which had brought them to the province, the Army stepped over the bounds that kept the fragile peace during the Falls Curfew. On 3 July a riot in the Catholic areas around the Falls Road in Belfast clashed with Army units, now operating in these areas instead of the police. This escalated into an exchange of gunfire with IRA units in the neighbourhood. No one was killed in the skirmish, but the Army responded using the lessons they had learned while policing the now-fallen empire, with much the same counter-productive result. They cut off the area from the outside with roadblocks and then smashed their way into houses, one by one. The searches were violent and illegal, journalists were arrested to prevent records being taken of the operation, and residents reported severe damage to homes and property amid violent and abusive interrogation. For three days, no one was allowed in or out of the curfew area; residents were trapped without access to food, work or basic amenities. It was only when 3,000 women and children from surrounding Catholic areas marched peacefully on the roadblock and pushed through them that the Army withdrew. The Parliament of Northern Ireland praised the soldiers for their restraint in the operation, but no one was convinced – the Army had picked a side.

The Provisional IRA saw in this situation an opportunity, and they took it. Their main rivals had been hit hard by the searches and weapons seizures, and the Provisionals had the upper hand. Recruiting extensively on the back of the Army's overreach with the Falls curfew, from early in 1971 they began specifically to target the RUC and the British Army, hoping to cause such heavy casualties among what they saw primarily as an unwelcome occupying force (an attitude not initially shared by much of the Catholic community) that the British government would give up its always lacklustre investment in Northern Ireland and allow it, one way or another, to rejoin the independent south. Hasty efforts by the Wilson government and local politicians to alleviate the main concerns of the civil rights movement came far too late to forestall the snowballing conflict.

People began to die in increasing numbers: ambushes, sniper attacks, bombings and raids punctuated 1971 as an increasingly

assertive Provisional IRA began its organized campaign of terrorism against the government of Northern Ireland and the
British state. In the absence of a trustworthy police force,
the British Army took up more and more policing duties, for
which they were over-armed and insufficiently trained. This was
not Kenya, where atrocities could be hidden in remote forests or
downplayed in the press as some kind of benevolent civilizing
expedition – this was an integral part of the United Kingdom
and the British Army was acting more and more like an occupying force, and an increasingly brutal and unwelcome one.
The introduction of internment, the arrest and imprisonment
of people on suspicion, not guilt, of association with banned
political groups – a measure applied inconsistently, illiberally
and targeted heavily against Catholic communities – exacerbated
the situation, leading resentful Catholics to mingle with IRA
volunteers in squalid conditions.

Though the war had already begun, it still might at this point
have been deferred or at least turned away, but then in January
1972 came Bloody Sunday, a day of infamy and murder which
ended any hope of a negotiated resolution to the conflict in the
near future. On 30 January a peaceful march emerging from
what was still Free Derry in the Bogside area passed down William Street, the same road on which Samuel Devenny had been
murdered nearly three years before, marching past his very front
door. There they encountered Army blockades manned by troops
from the Parachute Regiment, an elite Army strike force which
had no business being involved in civil enforcement in Northern

Ireland – their training was not to de-escalate, but to respond to threats with overwhelming force.

Corralled away from the city centre, some marchers on the periphery began throwing stones at the soldiers, who responded by taking up firing positions around the march. All it took was one man to open fire, and someone, somewhere did. Scattering in panic, the crowd of thousands fled in all directions, soldiers pursuing and firing indiscriminately. Twenty-six people were shot, not one of whom was later determined to have been armed. Ultimately fourteen died, including six seventeen-year-olds. Most were shot in the back, several while attempting to administer first aid to other wounded marchers. Though never ordered from above or explicitly intended in advance, Bloody Sunday was a deliberate massacre of British citizens by the British Army on the streets of a British city. It was photographed and widely reported, and though efforts were made to officially whitewash what happened, it changed the face of the conflict in Northern Ireland and remains a permanent stain on the history of the British government and the British Army. It was entirely and completely avoidable – the soldiers should never have been in a position to police a peaceful march, and would never have been there had the Northern Irish government been willing to maintain a police force capable of mediation and restraint towards Catholic communities. The lack of moderate, professional and even-handed policing directly precipitated a conflict in which more than 3,000 people would be killed.

*

Though deaths in the United States at the hands of the police are horrendous, both in overall numbers and what they reveal about police biases in that country, they have not precipitated a full-scale domestic insurgency. There have been isolated incidents of anti-police terrorism, and some rioting such as that which hit Los Angeles in 1992, as well as sporadic efforts to build Black militant organizations seeking violent action against prejudice and segregation in the United States. These have been met with consistently violent responses by American law enforcement. In 1968, the Oakland chapter of the Black Panther Party ambushed a police patrol and a seventeen-year-old activist was shot while surrendering; the following year the leader of the Chicago chapter, Fred Hampton, was shot and killed in a police raid while lying unconscious in bed. In another notorious case, in 1985 in Philadelphia a police siege of the headquarters of the cult-like militant group MOVE was ended when police dropped a fire bomb on the building from a helicopter, killing eleven people including five children, and burning down sixty-five surrounding homes. There have been other groups over the years – the Black Liberation Army of the 1970s, most of whom either fled to Cuba or remained in prison, and isolated militants of recent years like Ismaaiyl Abdullah Brinsley, who ambushed and killed two NYPD officers in 2014, and Micah Xavier Johnson, who killed five police officers in Dallas in 2016.

These, however, are isolated events and groups, notable as exceptions. Protests against the police, like those that occurred during most of the summer of 2020, have followed the lead of the 1960s civil rights movement and remained largely peaceful demonstrations of civil disobedience. Aside from the Black Panthers, dissipated as an effective force by the 1970s, there has never been a widespread effort to create an organized violent paramilitary force to defend Black neighbourhoods from police brutality as there was in Northern Ireland, and it is this which has, in part, forestalled any descent into large-scale civil conflict. This is to some degree because since the 1960s the US government has spoken the language of, if not often acted as, a moderating factor, responding with the suppression of violence but also an effort to listen and make changes, even if these are rarely sufficient or consistently enforced. It is also due to the commendable restraint in the face of extreme provocation on the behalf of the organizers, leaders and protestors themselves in the civil rights movement, but the United States only barely avoided a massacre of the nature of Bloody Sunday during the summer of 2020, thanks more to luck than good planning or leadership. Across the country heavily armed police forces faced off against protestors, and any one could have become a murderous flashpoint triggering a wider cycle of escalating violence.

There was some killing; both protestors and rioters on the fringe were shot by police, and in Kenosha, Wisconsin a vigilante identifying with the police killed two protestors with an assault rifle and was allowed at first to leave the scene, and then released on bail, reflecting a lack of concern on the part of the authorities. But deaths were kept low, and the protests eventually ebbed away as the summer continued and the 2020 election campaign season began in earnest. The violent rhetoric of the US government during the protests, coupled with widespread and indiscriminate police violence by unmarked federal riot squads, meant that many people stopped believing that the government would or could impose order and act as a negotiator, but was, in this instance, an instigator and participant in the violence.

A major factor in maintaining protest over the decades while limiting its extent to non-violent means is the importance and prevalence of Black churches. Enormously influential and popular among many Black communities, the churches consistently advocate in religious terms the importance of non-violent resistance to prejudice and oppression,* and their long-term influence has become the standard approach to civil rights issues, including the protests during the summer of 2020. In Northern Ireland there was, despite many isolated voices, no such restraint. Churches on both sides played their part in factionalism and precipitated more violence; as early as 1964 the firebrand Protestant preacher Rev. Ian Paisley was directing RUC squads to smash in doors and tear down the Irish tricolour when it flew in Sinn Fein offices.†

The Black Lives Matter protests in the summer of 2020 died down as summer turned to autumn, as the COVID-19 pandemic gripped the country harder, and the news media turned towards the dramatic 2020 presidential election and its bizarre

---

* Calhoun-Brown, Alison. "Upon This Rock: The Black Church, Nonviolence, and the Civil Rights Movement." *PS: Political Science and Politics* 33(2) (June, 2000). pp. 168–174. Accessed via jstor at https://www.jstor.org/stable/420886

† Coogan, Tim Pat, 1996. *The Troubles: Ireland's Ordeal 1966–1996 and the Search for Peace.* Arrow Books, London, p. 56.

and ultimately tragic aftermath. But the underlying issues remain strong and serious. Unless and until the police in the United States address their relationship with the Black community, on a national level, more Black men and women will die unjustly, the protest movement will surge once more, and violence will follow. It is a national crisis which demands leadership, the kind of leadership so sorely lacking in Northern Ireland in 1969 when Samuel Devenny was murdered, and the kind of leadership very thin on the ground in twenty-first-century America.

Policing is one of the most sensitive and intimate roles of the state. The police are supposed to protect civilians, catch and punish criminals and ensure the smooth operation of daily life. What happened in Northern Ireland occurred in no small part because the police were not protectors of the peace, but oppressors of the population, permitted by the government to act as a tool of violent repression and terror to avoid giving up power.

Chapter Eight

RELIGIOUS OPPRESSION: AMERICAN ABORTION AND THE OLYMPIC BOMBING

In the early morning of 31 May 2003, a twenty-one-year-old police officer named Jeffrey Scott Postell was driving through the town of Murphy, North Carolina – a community of about 1,500 people nestled in a forested valley deep in the southern Appalachians. Murphy is situated in Cherokee Country, a name reflecting the fact that the land was part of that vast tract seized by Andrew Jackson from its Indigenous inhabitants some 165 years earlier.

On his patrol, Postell noticed a man squatting in the road behind a supermarket. As his headlights shone on him, the man, dressed in black clothing, scrambled to his feet and disappeared amid the crates and dumpsters at the rear of the store. Postell gave chase and cornered the fugitive, who surrendered without a fight. The man was fit, with a neat moustache and heavy stubble, and Postell arrested him on suspicion of attempted burglary of the store. The man gave his name as Jerry Wilson. Later, when 'Wilson' was being processed at the local jail, he was asked his name again. This time he replied that it was Eric Robert Rudolph, a name the police instantly recognized, and one of the most prolonged and fervent manhunts in modern US history came to an end.

Rudolph, last reported five years earlier stealing supplies and a vehicle from another supermarket, had evaded the full weight of the FBI and local and state law enforcement agencies apparently by hiding in the backwoods of the Nantahala National Forest, a preserved wilderness of more than 500,000 acres of forested mountains riddled with cave systems and abandoned mine workings. He had foraged and scavenged, living like an animal on the very edges of human society even as law enforcement had scoured the region for him. For Rudolph was not just a fugitive, but a man who had tried to lead a holy war in America, to encourage his fellow citizens to rise up and replace American democracy with Christian theocracy, and provoke a civil war to preserve and maintain his version of a uniquely American religion.

To achieve this, Rudolph had planned and executed a terrorist campaign across the southern United States, detonating home-made improvised bombs at an abortion clinic in Birmingham, Alabama in January 1998, killing an off-duty police officer; at a lesbian bar in Atlanta, Georgia in February 1997, injuring five people; at another clinic in Sandy Springs, Georgia in January 1997; and most notoriously at Centennial Park, Atlanta during the 1996 Olympic Games.

On 27 July 1996, at the concert venue at the centre of the Olympic Village a Jack Mack and the Heart Attack concert was in full swing when a security guard named Richard Jewell discovered a backpack discarded under a bench. He notified state law enforcement and began to move people away from the suspicious bag, as word came through that a bomb alert had been phoned in to the FBI a few minutes before. The alert suggested that there were fifteen minutes before the bomb detonated, yet only two minutes passed before three pipe bombs, stuffed with nails, detonated. Debris sprayed into the crowds, killing a woman and injuring more than a hundred others.

The investigation was rushed and lazy, focusing far longer than it should have on Jewell, whose name was leaked to the press as a suspect and who endured a sustained and aggressive campaign of harassment by the media and FBI. After their myriad investigative incompetence was exposed, the FBI was forced to admit it had no suspects, and the investigation ran cold and trailed off. Rudolph had escaped, and was free to continue his campaign to bring religious enlightenment to America through violence.

Many years later, Rudolph attempted to explain his reasoning behind the campaign as a form of resistance to what he saw as burgeoning socialism in the United States, a socialism which, he claimed, was exemplified by the availability of 'abortion on demand' for American women. His attack on the Olympic Games was an effort to embarrass the United States government on an international stage and in doing so promote his efforts to bring about a change in government policy towards abortion and, as his later efforts demonstrated, the free and open practice of homosexuality in America.

Rudolph's understandings of socialism, abortion, government or homosexuality were clearly little more than the ravings of a stupid, angry and maladjusted man. He evaded the death penalty through co-operation with US authorities after his capture, but will spend the rest of his life behind bars: he currently resides in the ADX Florence Supermax prison in Colorado, notorious as the most restrictive prison in all the vast incarceration infrastructure of the United States, home to mass murderers, mafia dons and terrorists like Rudolph.

But Rudolph's ignorant understanding of political philosophy did not emerge from within his own twisted perception of reality. It was born and fostered and fed to him from elsewhere, translated and mistranslated into his own unique brand of the American religion, a concoction of Christianity and fervent American patriotism rooted deeply in the genocidal origins of the nation, and the belief that it is, by virtue of this combination, the greatest nation on earth and must be preserved as such. The notion of America as a religion is not a new one. It is indeed an idea as old as the United States of America, and perhaps older, a political philosophy doused in quasi-Christian symbolism that establishes the US as the pre-eminent moral authority, a chosen nation and people who, by virtue of their holiness, can excuse their cruelties and lather their successes as gifts – even collaborations – with God.*

God and the United States have always had a peculiar relationship, one founded on a combination of convenience, exploitation and devoutly held but highly selective religious faith. It is a canard widely understood that there is a separation in the United States between church and state, a principle rooted in European Enlightenment philosophy and repeated by Thomas Jefferson, but actually never enshrined in the Constitution directly. Rather it was the First Amendment of the Bill of Rights, the one which guarantees the right to free speech, which also mandated that the US government shall 'make no law respecting an establishment of religion, or prohibiting the free exercise thereof'.

This is a long way from being an actual separation of church and state, for while it prevents politicians from mandating state religions or imposing unreasonable restrictions on religious practice, it does nothing to prevent the imposition of religious doctrine into law as long as it doesn't impede the practice of other faiths. Even this limited constitutional protection was not held to apply below the federal level until after the Second World War, when a series of court judgements around the integration of religious schools in the South interpreted it as applying to the states as well as the federal government.

---

* For a dissection of this theory, see Bellah, Robert, 1967. "Civil Religion in America". *Daedalus* 96(1) Religion in America (Winter 1967), pp. 1–21. Accessed via jstor at https://www.jstor.org/stable/20027022

Perhaps the most glaring example of the conflict zone between religious doctrine and state government in the United States was one of Rudolph's confused obsessions: abortion. Abortion, the voluntary termination of a pregnancy, has had a complex intersection with American law, being largely illegal for most of American history, at least in part because of the enormous risks to the mother through historic techniques, but also tied to religious objections from Christian churches. In the 1960s a high-profile case linked to thalidomide poisoning focused attention on the issue when a woman named Sherri Finkbine discovered that her fifth child was suffering probably fatal foetal deformities, but was denied an abortion on medical grounds under Arizona state law. She took her case to the papers, and later obtained an abortion in Sweden. Two years later a woman named Gerri Santoro from Connecticut became a cause célèbre after she bled to death from a botched self-abortion. Clearly the abortion laws were failing to adequately fulfil their intended role of protecting American women, and were now actively harming them.

The result was a series of court cases and legalization initiatives led by women's rights activists and organizations designed to make access to abortion safe and legal. Facing them was a growing coalition of socially conservative and religious groups determined to maintain the criminalization and restriction of abortion, principally led by the Catholic Church. In 1973 these campaigns reached a head with the contentious yet thus far definitive Supreme Court case known as Roe v. Wade. This case determined that laws prohibiting abortion were unconstitutional, and set firm limitations on abortion laws based on medical necessity and gestational period. What it did not do was lay down specific rules on accessibility of abortion – only that states could not prohibit it outright.

Though the ongoing conservative campaign to tip the balance of American politics permanently in favour of one side over another has many roots, a case can be made that it was the decision in Roe v. Wade, almost more than any other, which has driven and motivated efforts by the Republican Party to defeat their opponents by any means necessary and deliberately destabilize the balance of power on which the United States was founded. Likely no other decision in Supreme Court history has elicited so much debate and recrimination – certainly not in the post-Second World War period.

Overturning abortion has been the motivating factor for conservatives and the religious right ever since, and there are millions of voters in the US who vote on this issue and this issue alone. This 'pro-life' faction is driven by a religious conviction that life begins at conception and that by opposing abortion they are saving the lives of babies. The inherent contradiction that the same party which wears the clothes of pro-life actively harms the life choices of the children they save by blocking affordable medical care, good schools and a social safety net is irrelevant – it is paramount to this section of the voting population that abortion is prevented. In 1988 abortion was an issue which influenced

Democrats more than Republicans, but by 2020 these positions had been reversed.*

The principal reason it has become such an important issue in the United States when it has done so in very few other countries – and almost none which lack a state religion – is that to devout Christians, both Protestant and Catholic, abortion is seen as a specific and serious sin, contradictory to religious teaching and thus, in a spiritual sense, as harmful to the person seeking the abortion as to the foetus. To a religious person this is a corrosive act which harms not only a child and its mother, but the entire fabric of a nation which would permit it. And this is the key to understanding many branches of the Christian faith in the United States: that for this large sub-set of the voting population, Christianity and patriotism are not only intertwined, but in fact co-equal parts of a whole which determines a person's identity almost entirely.

For such people, always prominent in American politics and culture but latterly also directly partisan, a faith in America is akin to a faith in God, and the two are indivisible and righteous. Thus any widespread legal practice which so flagrantly flies in the face of religious teaching, such as abortion, is a corruption not

---

* Bolce, Lewis, 1988. "Abortion and Presidential Elections: The Impact of Public Perceptions of Party and Candidate Positions". *Presidential Studies Quarterly* 18(4) Images and Issues (Fall 1988), pp. 815–289. Accessed via jstor at https://www.jstor.org/stable/40574732

Brenan, Megan. "One in Four Americans Consider Abortion a Key Voting Issue". *Gallup*, 7 July 2020. Accessed online at https://news.gallup.com/poll/313316/one-four-americans-consider-abortion-key-voting-issue.aspx

only of religious faith, but of faith in the very nation. Few take this stance as far as the Westboro Baptist Church in Kansas, who for many years picketed public events and military funerals to protest the legal access to abortion and legal practice of homosexuality which they saw as directly responsible for the moral and religious degradation of their society, but that sentiment lurks within much American religious practice, particularly among those faiths intimately engaged with national American politics. It was this understanding of abortion and its place within the nation that drove Rudolph to conduct a murderous terror campaign, and it is this understanding which is critical to appreciating the depth of feeling which elevated President Trump and supported successful Republican efforts to stack the US federal court system, up to and including the Supreme Court, with anti-abortion activist judges.

This chapter isn't really specifically about religion and religious teachings themselves. It's rather about that liminal moment in which conviction and faith turn from concepts designed to nurture and support a productive and constructive life into something corrosive and destructive. This applies equally to religious faith as to political belief as to patriotic identity. For it is one thing to seek to belong and to follow a set of cohesive moral values as part of a mutually supportive collective, and quite another to demand the right to impose those values on others and judge them evil if they fail to follow them. Rudolph did not think that he was villain or a terrorist. He recognized that that was how others saw him, hence the hiding in the Carolina backwoods, but he believed that his cause was just and his murderous campaign justified because the people he was targeting were betraying the very notion of the United States as he saw it, and that his violence towards them was a means of punishing them and attracting attention to his campaign. He viewed the United States as a religious icon to be protected from sin by justified murder, and expected he would be exonerated when the promised paradise was achieved.

It is easy to write Rudolph off as insane, just as one would Timothy McVeigh, who killed 168 people by detonating a truck bomb at a federal building in Oklahoma City in the same year as Rudolph began his terrorist campaign, and for broadly similar reasons. McVeigh, though, was targeting not Americans he saw as sinful, but the federal government itself, a monolithic organization which he believed was corrupting his version of the American ideal and thus it, and the people occupying one of its buildings, were legitimate targets. These men's shared ambition was to commit murders using terrorist tactics to change the political and culture make-up of their nation. But while they were capable of understanding how they would be seen by the government and many of their fellow citizens, they did not consider themselves terrorists. They considered themselves patriots.

And this is the broader point of this chapter: that violent extremist patriotism and violent extremist religious terrorism are effectively the same problem, driven by a desire to reshape nations and populations through overt acts and threats of violence designed and intended to cause oppression across a broad sweep of the population, to force people to change their beliefs, habits and behaviours. And these roots of religious and nationalist patriotic terrorism were not the end result of decades of conflicted messaging and engagement on the relationship between the state and the convictions of the Christian church in the US, but a step on the way to a more dangerous and potentially far more destructive place, where movements demonize and condemn their political opponents not as fellow citizens with different points of view but as traitors and sinners who must be defeated at all costs.

This divide, this problem, has only worsened in the quarter-century since the Olympic bombing, and it is critical that informed readers learn to understand why this has come about, and how we as citizens of nations worldwide have a duty to be alert to this risk. All nations have their trigger issues which are akin to religious belief and which can, in the right circumstances or the wrong hands, become the kind of totemic political issue which can radicalize murderers like Eric Robert Rudolph. And this is relevant to all of us, because we all, no matter how liberal or agnostic, take on national and religious allegiances as part of our shared cultural identity. There is nothing inherently wrong with this – it is a normal part of human interaction – but it also means that we bear a responsibility to listen and think carefully about the allegiances we adopt, to ensure that they are not being manipulated or directed in ways which we find abhorrent, and to speak out, protest or change the direction where we can, when our identities promote values we disagree with or encourage violence. We must have a grown-up relationship with the institutions we align with, recognizing their flaws as well as their benefits and achievements, and refusing to make excuses for those we like, or which we feel might reflect poorly on us. If you are tempted to wave away abuses or prejudice because they come from those you happen to agree with, then you are halfway to participating in those abuses and all the way to facilitating them, rendering the positive aspects of these institutions near worthless with hypocrisy.

Religious faith provides a guide to life based on a series of moral codes developed in most cases centuries or even millennia ago. It should be no surprise that when these codes are applied to modern cultural contexts, conflicts will arise and orthodoxies will be challenged. Religions schism and split; brothers and sisters in faith often become bitter rivals in the process. These schisms occur in secular faiths, too – those rooted in blind belief in righteousness and moral supremacy, such as nation-alism. When religious and secular faiths combine, as they did with Rudolph, a binary notion of good and evil can become entrenched, and intractable. The result is that politics, the earnest dispute on the best course of action for a nature which even at its most poisonous is supposed to recognize that one's opponents have the nation's best interests at heart, become a conflict with a good and bad side, a war between heaven and hell.

Falling on one side of this divide or the other marks one as not a politician doing a job, but an enemy to be destroyed, and that is the road to political violence and ultimately even to civil war.

This is a situation exacerbated in the US by the overt trappings of religious entanglement which adorn the tools of the state – from the words 'In God we trust' on currency to the overtly religious act of the pledge of allegiance in which schoolchildren are encouraged, if not forced via peer pressure, to reaffirm their faith in their nation, which since 1954 has specifically cited a God – officially non-denominational but widely understood to be the Christian God – as its inspiration and protection. As its promoter and defender George Docherty noted, 'To omit the words "Under God" from the Pledge of Allegiance is to omit the definitive character of the American Way of Life.'* The pledge thus reads: 'I pledge allegiance to the Flag of the United States of America, and to the Republic for which it stands, one Nation under God, indivisible, with liberty and justice for all.'

Forty-five US states demand by law that the pledge is recited in schools on a regular basis, and of the others California requires a 'patriotic exercise' every day, which is usually fulfilled by the pledge, though students cannot be forced to recite it or officially punished if they choose not to.

Its widespread adoption and amendment under President Eisenhower was in part a deliberate Christian response to perception of the growing atheist communist threat from the Soviet Union and China, but went further than rejecting atheism, going so far as to equate American capitalism, Christianity and patriotism into a simple, repetitive mantra which reaffirmed the faith

---

* Kruse, Kevin, 2015. *One Nation Under God*. Basic Books, New York, p. 106.

of those saying it. Eisenhower himself said, straightforwardly if illogically, 'Every free government is embedded soundly in a deeply felt religious faith or it makes no sense.'* This sense of religion at the heart of US government has become so entrenched that President Trump could – as already discussed – attempt to manage his struggles with civil unrest in the summer of 2020 by teargassing protestors and then standing awkwardly outside a church clutching a Bible, a typically crude reaffirmation of the explicit propaganda of the pledge all schoolchildren know intimately. Trump was thus able, in the bluntest way possible, to connect himself with the holy foundation of the nation and aligning his opponents, protesting the murder of George Floyd, not as civil rights activists or mere political rivals, but as dangerously un-American traitors to the country and to God.

Trump was merely following in his own crude way the symbolism employed by his predecessors, such as Reagan's 'Evil Empire' of the Soviet Union, described in a speech to the National Association of Evangelicals:

> Let us pray for the salvation of all of those who live in that totalitarian darkness – pray they will discover the joy of knowing God. But until they do, let us be aware that while they preach the supremacy of the State, declare its omnipotence over individual man, and predict its eventual domination of all peoples on the earth, they are the focus of evil in the modern world.

---

* Kruse, p. xii.

Reagan then used the speech to urge his audience not 'to ignore the facts of history and the aggressive impulses of an evil empire . . . and thereby remove yourself from the struggle between right and wrong and good and evil'.

Twenty years on, George W. Bush's comment that 'States like [Iran, Iraq and North Korea] and their terrorist allies constitute an Axis of Evil' in the State of the Union address in 2002, in the aftermath of the 9/11 terrorist attacks, was a similar effort to enlist the Christian God in an American struggle against a non-Christian enemy. 'Evil is real, and it must be opposed,' he said, followed by the assertion that 'Deep in the American character there is honour, and it is stronger than cynicism. And many have discovered again that even in tragedy – especially in tragedy – God is near.'*

Both of these speeches connect America's enemies with the enemies of God and send a clear message that to be opposed to America – and the specific ambitions of certain American politicians – is to be sacrilegious, to be violating heavenly taboos as well as earthly ones. It shouldn't be surprising therefore that those who take on the mantle of America's protectors unbidden turn that religious ire against their fellow citizens who have, in their opinion, failed to reach the high standards of a Holy War.

*

---

* *Washington Post*, 2002. *Text of President Bush's 2002 State of the Union Address.* 29 January 2002. Accessed online via https://www.washingtonpost.com/wp-srv/onpolitics/transcripts/sou012902.htm

We all live in societies which are susceptible to this kind of manipulation, even where religious faith is less a pillar of national identity than it is in the United States. We all play a role in it whenever we engage in reflexive nationalism or assume that our enemies are bad people rather than those who simply hold an alternative point of view. This is not a call for everybody to be nice, for both sides to come together and for a consensus – there are too many in politics and particularly in the media whose influence on this type of divide is too severe, people who often do not believe the things they say and encourage, but do so for profit or fame. They build up conspiracy-laden networks of 'alternative facts' designed to demonize political opponents and turn the worst of their supporters, who include murderous extremists like Rudolph, loose on their opponents.

Likewise, there are many commentators and voters for whom the mere peaceful existence of other people from categories they dislike is enough to provoke a religious or pseudo-religious condemnation. The notion of being 'anti-American' was a common canard against Jews and African Americans of previous centuries; it is still widely deployed against the LGBT community and Muslims. In other nations other categories are stigmatized in similar terms. These are not points of view with which reasonable people can or should reason. They are vicious, vindictive pseudo-religious positions which need to be combatted through peaceful debate and social ostracization. Being rational and non-violent does not ever mean being passive or accepting of attitudes and actions which harm our fellow citizens living their peaceful lives.

There are many on both sides of the abortion argument, for example, who believe that their opponents are unreasonable or wrong. There are many who believe that their opponents are authoritarian, misogynistic or alternatively sinful and destructive. And then there are those who encourage the notion that their enemies are so wrong, so steeped in destructive qualities, that they must be destroyed, and there are those who listen. A personal opinion on abortion is one thing – a view privately held to which we are all entitled. Acting to strip that right from others, demonizing them in the process, is a destructive and damaging stance which harms us all.

As responsible citizens it is not enough to maintain and hold your own view, nor to respect those of your opponents so long as they do not infringe on your rights. It is incumbent on citizens to be aware of those who would commit violence, and to be aware of those who would encourage and further it for their own selfish ends and their own interpretations of scripture, both religious and secular. We must be capable of critical assessment and political empathy, but also determined to call out and confront those who would do us harm by conspicuously polarizing the debate further.

Organized religion, always self-described as a force of positive hope and love, and one of the world's biggest drivers or organized charity, support and comfort, is of course just as capable of enacting oppression as governments or corporations. In fact, the divisive aspects inherent to most, if not all major religions, which state that some people are worthy and others are not, can lead to oppressions which punish and reward based not on human happiness, but on the institutional prejudices and desires of the church itself, and of its leaders. This chapter has examined this phenomenon through the oppressive effects of evangelical faith in the United States and its impact particularly on women's healthcare.

Our faiths, religious, personal and political, are things that define us, and yet they are capable of being vehicles of division and persecution. When we join a church or a movement and incorporate its beliefs and orthodoxies into our daily lives we align ourselves with its values, just as we so often do with those of the nations into which we are born, or into which we move. And yet there are organizations whose values are used to turn people against others, to sow division and hatred and to provoke the more fanatical followers to acts of violence and terrorism. If we choose to align ourselves to such views, it is cowardly to cite a church or supreme being as inspiration for such hatreds – we are adults with personal responsibility, and these hatreds are ours to own, and for which we may face social, legal and personal consequences.

The fate of Rudolph, a man temperamentally unable to understand the hates which drove him, is less relevant than his targets of choice. Rudolph chose the Olympics to generate publicity, but he chose the abortion clinics because to him they symbolized the enemies of the America he wished to recreate. To Rudolph, abortion was the totemic issue which defined the difference between the America he desired and the America which was.

To him it was the great crisis, the great evil to be driven out. Though in method he was an outlier, in sentiment he shared and shares his beliefs with tens of millions of Americans, including former Vice-President Mike Pence, who has spoken of his pride in his opposition to abortion and his efforts to prohibit it in the United States.*

Abortion as an issue sits at the divergence of America between right and left, and most specifically between the right-wing conservative Christian tradition and the more liberal religious traditions on the centre and left of American politics. Over time it has come to define political standpoints – abortion is the key issue on which conservative evangelical Americans vote, and the defining statement which dictates stances on a wide range of other issues. Despite clear legal precedent permitting abortion in the United States, it has become the unifying issue of the American conservative movement, a motivator for their voting base and the subject of strenuous efforts to eliminate it through restrictive state laws and burdensome regulations – as governor, Pence himself signed into Indiana state law mandatory funerals for aborted foetuses, and invasive checks on women undergoing procedures, laws later ruled unconstitutional.†

---

* Gera, Vanessa & Kaufmann, Balazs. *Pence hopeful the Supreme Court will restrict abortion in US*. AP News, 23 September 2021. Accessed online via https://apnews.com/article/lifestyle-donald-trump-health-courts-summits-f135330d4d7cd945ce90e279725f4d21

† Foran, Clare. *Indiana abortion law signed by Mike Pence ruled unconstitutional*. CNN, 20 April 2018. Accessed online via https://edition.cnn.com/2018/04/20/politics/mike-pence-indiana-abortion-law-court-unconstitutional/index.html

In a nation which prides itself on the separation of the state from any established church, abortion access is a subject into which the state intrudes continually, and on nakedly religious terms. In American discourse and media, abortion and the religious objections to it have come to matter far beyond the issue itself, concerning the bodily autonomy of women and the right to make their own choices about their lives. Abortion is now an issue which for some people is an excuse to dehumanize, even kill, fellow Americans.

From the story of the Olympic bombing and its legacy for the politics and religion in the United States comes a lesson on always being vigilant to think about the ideologies to which we attach ourselves, the effects they have on other people, and how we might use our own influences within these organizations for positive rather than divisive ends.

Chapter Nine

RACIAL OPPRESSION:
WHITE ROADS THROUGH BLACK BEDROOMS

Oppression can be imposed on the very land upon which people live, an all-permeating and semi-permanent oppression which consciously traps people into subordinate underclass status. This is nowhere more true than in the case of racially based oppression in which the simple differences in skin-surface melanin levels and cultural activities are an unchallengeable badge of status which relegates certain peoples into certain places. This was the story of twentieth-century America, and the ghettoization of the American city.

The causes of this phenomenon are many, but two events that took place thousands of miles and nearly twenty years apart illustrate its origins. The first is in Tulsa, Oklahoma, where on 1 July 1921, mobs of White men, many recently demobilized servicemen returning from the First World War, marched through the streets. As I explained in chapter six, Oklahoma is a state built on land seized from the Native Americans who had been promised it as their homeland by Andrew Jackson before having it sold from under them when convenient by a later president. During the First World War, Black families from across the Southern United States had migrated to Tulsa and hundreds of other cities in search of employment away from the Deep South and its long history of entrenched poverty, violence, exploitation and disenfranchisement, seeking the jobs vacated by the White soldiers recruited to fight in France. In Tulsa as elsewhere, Black residents were legally discriminated against and forced to live in separate communities, but they found economic prosperity and success. In Tulsa, the Black neighbourhood was called Green-wood.

All this changed in a single day, as White mobs systematically burned and dynamited the Greenwood suburb, at one point flinging high explosives onto the town from a biplane. At least fifty people, and perhaps hundreds more, were murdered. The message was clear: Black Americans should not expect to live alongside White Americans as anything approaching equals and survive. Other Black neighbourhoods were attacked in other cities, and as more and more black families migrated north and west to escape the crushing oppression of the South, restrictions on where and how African Americans could live grew tighter and tighter.

The other event occurred in 1939, when there was only one attraction the people of New York wanted to see: the World's Fair. Constructed on 900 acres of polluted wetland at Flushing,

Queens, it was a showcase of all that America, gradually struggling out of the Great Depression, wanted to be. There were rides and attractions and restaurants, all serviced by a newly rebuilt subway track and, most importantly, large car parks so that visitors from across the country could drive to see the world of the future.

And it was with this focus that the Fair, largely funded by big American corporations and explicitly promoting their interests and products, was designed. At its centre was a huge ride, starting in a silver orb, on which visitors were taken by rail car over a miniature city featuring aspects of most major American cities, except this one was gleaming white, with beautiful clean streets serviced from distant suburbs by wide flowing freeways containing more than 50,000 model cars. Tiny commuters could zip from work to home in minutes, and if roads weren't your thing, flying cars complemented the transport needs of modern Americans.

In between, dotted across the one-acre model America, were futuristic farms and power stations bringing the wonders of modern and future technology to improve the lives of ordinary Americans who could look forward to a bright, clean future in specially designed cities of smooth lines and shapely curves. It was a dreamlike place, moulded by a corporate democracy which, the model suggested, was entirely at the service of the ordinary American. Like all miniatures, it was a lie, and it was a sinister one. The tiny world, dubbed Futurama by its designer Norman Bel Geddes, was intended to be a gigantic advert not for a sleeker future for the American public, but for its sponsor – the automotive behemoth General Motors.

The world of Futurama was one in which the new way of American life was entirely dependent on the motor car – a civilization in thrall to an invention which certainly made life much easier and enabled cities for the first time to properly spread out into the countryside, but also made it dirtier and ever more unequal. For missing from Futurama was all dirt and dust and smoke and pollution and, most tellingly at all, a key component of American life was absent – there were no poor people; no slums or Hoovervilles, no abandoned farms or shuttered factories. Everyone here was rich and happy, and that necessitated one more absence: there were no Black people.

It was never stated; it never had to be. The scale was too large for the most part for the colour of the inhabitants to be identified, but the visitors all knew it to be true. There was no trace of the Black communities already rapidly growing in cities across the nation as the Great Migration began. This movement of millions of Black people from the agricultural poverty of the South to the promise of industrial wealth in the North and the West was already producing large Black districts in every American city. These were people contained within the streets permitted to them, which had an individual and noticeable character already recognizable to the casual motorist. And yet here, in the heart of what it was hoped America would become, there were no Black people, and it is likely that no one among the three million people who toured Futurama in the two years it was open really believed that their absence was due to some assimilated ambition of racial harmony. Black Americans had been designed out of the picture, and it was done without anyone ever explicitly ordering it to be so. It was just how it had to be. And while Black people are easy to remove from a model future city you are building from scratch, almost unnoticed as they are omitted from the designs drawn up in all-White corporate boardrooms, they are much, much harder to eradicate from a city hundreds of thousands already call home. But that didn't stop American architects and city planners from spending the next few decades trying very hard.

The Great Migration of the Depression era accelerated dramatically during the Second World War, as millions more young Black men and women left the farms and plantations of the South on which they had been born and travelled north to find work in factories and shipyards to feed the war effort, while once again the White men for whom those jobs had been so long reserved were conscripted into the armed forces. For people who had grown up in the enforced poverty of the South, the wages and relative freedom of a society where they were not under quite such constant observation and restriction were a revelation. Northern cities were hardly places of racial harmony and equality, but they were far removed from the brutally enforced legal segregation of the South, and there were opportunities for education, entrepreneurship and economic success for those African Americans able to take them.

Inevitably, this mass influx of Black Southerners into cities such as Chicago, New York and Los Angeles caused consternation among the White residents. The idea of having to work and live alongside Black Americans on a legally equal basis filled a significant proportion of them with a collective horror, and steps began almost instantly to ensure that Black people remained in their designated areas and dared not step outside them. The process began in earnest after the creation of the Federal Housing Administration in 1934, designed to co-ordinate the thousands of state and local administrations which had failed so spectacularly during the first years of the Great Depression in stemming the tide of foreclosures and mortgage collapses.

In an effort to regularize how home loans were issued by banks and reduce the risks involved, the Home Owners' Loan Corporation (HOLC), funded by the government, was established to provide financing for homeowners in danger of losing their homes due to default. The loans were purchased by the HOLC and reissued on more favourable terms. The HOLC and the Federal Home Loan Bank Board required detailed data on where housing stock was worth investment, and commissioned a vast survey of so-called residential security maps which designated property in 239 US cities as being of a certain quality, rated from A to D. A was the highest-quality property, likely to increase in value and thus most worthy of loan and investments. D was little better than slum housing, ineligible for loans.

D districts, concentrated amid the oldest and most dilapidated housing stock in the old inner cities, were marked on the maps in red. These districts were predominantly Black communities, in which Black residents and new arrivals had been concentrated by either law, custom or a combination of both. Confined to the worst-quality housing, and denied any meaningful public or private investment, these areas had deteriorated badly, riven by the shadow economies forced on Black citizens excluded from mainstream reliable employment and commerce, and consequently suffering all the social problems which come with poverty, criminal activity and the neglectful under-policing and oppressive over-policing which accompany such a state. The D designation, soon termed redlining, meant that homeowners in these areas could no longer sell their properties, as it became impossible to obtain a mortgage for their value.

Inevitably this led to a collapsing property market in redlined areas, even as the extensive federal support enabled surrounding Whiter areas to begin to recover and for their value to accelerate. The suburbs, generally A-designated in blue, accelerated further and faster, attracting wealthier residents and consequently building a tax and infrastructure base to fund public services such as schools, police and roads, which gave them accruing advantages over the inner cities. This was the informal ghettoization of the American city, already long established in custom, and now it had a legal basis. For places without laws restricting where Black people could live, there was now a legal mechanism to keep them restricted to poorer, more dilapidated parts of the city, a situation that grew worse as more and more Black migrants arrived into already overcrowded inner city areas.

Those who could, left. Black residents with good, stable jobs were able to migrate to other areas – still segregated formally or informally, but with stronger tax bases and less overt or intrusive criminal activity. Millions of Black Americans, however, were trapped in the redlined areas, unable to move out due to the cost of doing so, but watching their assets depreciate and their neighbourhoods struggle. In the aftermath of the Second World War, many of those Black workers who had migrated to sustain the war effort were laid off in favour of returning White soldiers, while returning Black soldiers were often compelled through lack of options to add to the overcrowding in redlined districts.

What followed was a period of economic exploitation in housing caused by a law which was ostensibly intended to reduce segregation, but phrased in such a way that it was easy to use it to entrench segregation across the United States. Since 1917, the US Supreme Court had maintained that local laws which restricted Black residency to specific areas were constitutional, a patchwork of racist legislation formalized and enshrined by redlining in the insurance and mortgage markets. In 1948, though, this ruling was reversed, and states and municipalities were forced to remove the restrictions and theoretically allow Black people to buy homes in A–C neighbourhoods formerly reserved for White residents. It didn't work out that way.

Instead, what followed was an orgy of economic exploitation known as blockbusting. This process enabled wealthy White American developers and corporations to begin to buy homes in those C-grade neighbourhoods which bordered the D-grade redlined Black neighbourhoods, and sell them on to

Black homeowners at considerable mark-up. To ensure max-
imum profits, the prospectors would stir up racial panic in the
neighbourhoods they targeted, generating a fear of increased
crime from the new Black residents and, most damning of all,
warning of a precipitate collapse in the value of property as the
area became more racially mixed. Then as now, property was one
of the safest methods of storing and increasing wealth, but more
than that, there was increasingly a real fear that if the value of
your property fell too fast, you would be unable to sell and buy
elsewhere and become trapped in a neighbourhood becoming
ever more ethnically diverse and consequently ever less desirable
for White residents. Motived to sell and encouraged by increasing
innovations in the mass transit and automobiles Futurama predicted, White populations decamped en masse for the suburbs
and left behind an expanding Black population trapped in neighbourhoods often still riven with the inequality and deprivation
brought about by political neglect and economic hardship.

Not all Black residents were trapped or struggling. Many
retained their jobs, gained promotion, opened their businesses
and maintained their homes. Many Black neighbourhoods
did not suffer in the way the old redlined districts did and
a Black middle class, always present but often precarious,
expanded and developed cultural and economic structures of
its own within the cities. However, in many other areas the
Black population was unable to maintain this level of stability
and the modern Black ghettos were born in areas neglected
by public services, targeted by over-zealous law enforcement

and scorned by White politicians and citizens as dangerous, criminal and undesirable.

Thus they became trapped by both poverty and race by an economic and social machine designed to punish those lacking socially desirable traits. The result was an intersectionality in which converging oppressive systems condemned those unable to move. But this decay was not inevitable or accidental – these areas were working-class districts serving factories and commercial districts before they were unceremoniously and quite deliberately cut off from the rest of the city. They weren't so much ignored as strangled.

It was at this point that they were targeted by infrastructure projects: cheap homes and land due to the price collapses, especially by comparison with wealthier districts around them, and less likely to have political representation to protect them; roads built for the White commuters in their new suburbs smashing right through Black communities, because the new White suburbs needed to be connected with the inner-city financial districts and small local roads simply couldn't handle the weight of traffic. The dreams of Bel Geddes realized in Futurama were coming true, perhaps not as cleanly or as smoothly as he had imagined, but in a way entirely in keeping with the exploitative nature of the American economy: those with money have the strength to make more; those without are abandoned to their fate and ordered to pull themselves up with broken bootstraps.

Roads, great gleaming channels of tarmac and cement, were thus laid right though redlined communities. Homes were seized

through the government power of eminent domain and bull-
dozed, along with the communities to which they belonged.
These highways stretching into the city like a web rarely connected with the Black communities through which they were
driven. By design, commuters never had to stop or even pass
through Black streets; the money flowed back and forth over
the heads of the inhabitants but never reached them. The citizens of these districts, predominantly poor and Black, were
trapped.* Those who could get out did, moving to suburbs or
other districts. Those who could not – unable or unwilling to
move elsewhere – watched as their neighbourhoods stagnated.
Jobs went elsewhere; pollution caused smog and filth to stain
houses and streets, causing respiratory illness and contributing
to increased demand on increasingly over-stretched health and
public services. In many cases these roads were actually built
with racist intent – the roads that connected New York City to
the beaches of Long Island were deliberately built with bridges
too low to allow buses to pass under them, cutting off poorer
residents who did not own cars, as always predominantly Black,
from the Long Island suburbs.†

As the wealthier residents retreated from the inner-city neighbourhoods, they took their taxes with them, leaving behind fewer
and fewer people able to pay them. Public services in America are

---

* Miller, Johnny. "Roads to nowhere: how infrastructure built on American inequality". *Guardian*, 21 February 2018. Accessed online via https://www.theguardian.
com/cities/2018/feb/21/roads-nowhere-infrastructure-american-inequality
† Caro, Robert A., 1974. *The Power Broker: Robert Moses and the Fall of New York*.
The Bodley Head, London, p. 546.

largely based on locally raised revenues by city or county, sup-
plemented by resources and grants from state and federal level.
These are locally controlled and raised, so if the tax revenues fall,
public services such as schools and public healthcare are starved
of funds. The result is a poverty trap in which children struggle
to access the resources necessary to procure an education which
can lead them to college and employment sufficient to increase
the local tax base or, more likely, buy their way into a better
neighbourhood. This creates an environment in which roads,
public transit and the basic necessities of modern life become
dilapidated, unobtainable and inadequate.

The populations of these areas, facing systematic discrimination, high unemployment, generational poverty and a total lack
of interest from the political class, are forced to find livelihoods
in whatever jobs will accept them based on their education, skills
and address. These jobs are rarely high-paying or secure, and so
the cycle of poverty is maintained.

For many, particularly young men, there was another option.
Organized crime among the Black ghettos of American cities
was a perennial presence, but from the late 1960s, as the inner
cities began to die, young men began to turn in large numbers
to a black market in something Americans began to demand in
ever greater quantities; drugs.

Drugs are nothing new in America – cocaine and opioids
were routinely used in readily available medicinal products in
the nineteenth and twentieth centuries, and efforts to ban them

broadly coincided with the Prohibition era of the 1920s, when alcohol was banned in the United States with catastrophic consequences for law and order. Making such a popular product illegal on moral grounds simply forced what had been a taxable and profitable industry into the hands of criminal gangs with no interest in quality control or social cohesion. The murder rate soared and organized crime groups and federal agents battled for control across US cities for a decade until the constitutional amendment was repealed. Demonstrating ably that they had apparently learned nothing from this experience, the federal government made the same mistake again with the Comprehensive Drug Abuse Prevention and Control Act of 1970.

This legislation particularly targeted heroin, a narcotic wreaking havoc among US forces fighting in the Vietnam War and increasingly arriving on the streets of American cities, but also a wide range of drugs deemed to be anti-social in nature, including of course the non-addictive mood-altering cannabis which continued and continues to be criminalized largely to target Black and counter-culture communities with disruption by law enforcement. The Nixon administration intended to target the drugs fuelling the counter-cultural revolution which he and his supporters so opposed, in co-ordination with federal and local police enforcement.

Prohibition once again caused crisis on American streets. With cities dying from the inside out, tax bases crumbling and large portions of the population, particularly African Americans, living in severe poverty, there was a growing opportunity for people willing to flout the new law to make a very large amount of money. Though traditional organized crime groups were swift to act on these prohibited markets, it was in the disintegrating inner cities where drug supply found a ready market, of both addicts creating demand and dealers fuelling supply. The drugs crisis was felt across the United States and has complex origins and effects, but nowhere were these more pronounced than in the ghettoized Black communities living under the highways.

Already subject to oppressive and racist policing, these communities increasingly came under siege by local, state and federal police forces enforcing prohibition of drugs, more interested in arresting the flow of heroin and cocaine than in protecting the communities in which it was sold. The creation of a large, outlawed drugs market free from any official sanction or intervention beyond paltry efforts at prevention and never-successful policing generated the perfect conditions for a massive breakdown in law and order. With so much at stake and with such limited viable alternatives for those living in the areas in which it took place, it gave licence for those engaged in it to operate entirely unregulated. There was no quality control, no management of the addiction epidemic as it spiralled out of control, and no means of easily arresting the tide of violence which ensued.

This brings us to 'ghettoside', a term discussed by Jill Leovy in her book of the same name. It is a geographic space – the Black ghettos of US cities like Los Angeles – but also a state of mind, a lawlessness and abandonment that bring home the third meaning, that of an endemic slaughter, predominantly of young Black men, in the illegal drug market and the gang culture it fostered.* Racist groups hardly needed lynching and terror tactics, when poorly managed social and economic systems killed tens of thousands every year, and when a vastly disproportionate number of them were Black. In the nineteenth and early twentieth centuries a plague of lynching was endemic to the Southern United States – the deliberate, cruel and public torture and murder of Black men and women for usually nothing more than the suspicion they might have committed crimes against White people or property. Sometimes not even that: some 6,000 people were murdered in hideous circumstances in these acts of racial terrorism. Ghettocide, though manifesting as a different phenomenon, mostly Black-on-Black rather than White-on-Black, killed far, far more. Black men and women died in every American city: emaciated addicts overdosing on street corners or in abandoned buildings; sick people dying of preventable diseases as they lacked the money and resources to obtain routine medical treatment; an elevated suicide rate against the backdrop of hopelessness of the economic and social situation from which there seemed no escape; and most prominently of all, a murder rate which soared in the 1980s from the thousands to the tens of thousands as violent gang warfare gripped America's inner cities and spread out beyond them.

With the absence of any investment or interest by civil authorities and with the police forces increasingly acting as clean-up

---

* Leovy, Jill, 2014. *Ghettoside: A True Story of Murder in America*. Vintage, London, pp. 40–1.

crews rather than offering meaningful prevention or prosecution of the rampaging crime rates, gangs assumed leadership roles in communities based on a combination of financial incentive, fear and a lack of opportunity. Able and resourceful young men, those who survived the murderous drug wars which raged across inner cities in the 1980s, could make millions. Far more died. With crime rates increasingly out of control, flight from the ghettos and to the suburbs continued. People no longer spoke of fixing or reforming the communities but of getting out, and when they left they took the money with them for city taxes to begin the long process of repairing the damage.

It was perhaps inevitable, in the Cold War context of the 1970s and the winding down of the Vietnam War, that America would need another unholy enemy to fight. Drugs, given their disastrous effect on the inner cities and their association with the Black community, were a convenient target. Nixon was the first to declare the War on Drugs in 1971, but it was Reagan in the 1980s who expanded it with an emphasis on military tactics for the police and increasingly harsh penalties for drug possession and sale. There was now limited opportunity for people born and brought up in the once redlined Black communities of American cities to get the education and skills necessary for other work, even when it was available, and yet the black economy which thrived in these areas was targeted with aggressive policing and those who participated in it were locked up with a remorseless regularity.

As the border with Mexico was militarized to prevent

trafficking, and US armed forces engaged in military adventurism against communism and narcotics across South America, so incarceration among Black Americans soared to encompass vast numbers of people herded into inadequate and often grossly overcrowded prisons. However, the huge folly of the War on Drugs was that this oppressive regime of restriction and punishment for engaging in prohibited commercial activity in the capitalist melting pot of the United States was that none of this worked. As more and more men were locked up and gang membership spread through the prison system as a means of survival, the murder rate only increased. The fracturing nature of street gangs under police pressure only resulted in further conflict and social disorder.

So many died that there was hardly any time for serious investigations. Conviction rates for serious violent crime fell even as rates for drug offences rose and the preventative role of law enforcement evaporated. They were now merely responsive, scooping bodies off the streets and solving no more than a fraction of the cases they faced. Most of these murders remain unsolved to this day, as no one cared enough that Black men died day in and day out for it to be a national priority or emergency. They were just victims of the war on drugs, and considered by many White Americans not to be innocent victims either, but contributors to their own fates. The structural racism of the circumstances in which they found themselves was rarely acknowledged or addressed by anyone in a position to change it.

This violence continued well into the 1990s, as shifting

political landscapes saw a Democratic president come to power and introduce ever more restrictive and draconian punishments, sending many thousands of young men to prison for life for drug offences alone. Those Americans, particularly Black Americans, incarcerated in numbers larger than any peacetime nation ever before did not only lose their freedom for a defined period, often for the non-violent sale of banned and unregulated substances. They also lost a huge and essential part of their citizenship – to an American their personhood – for in many states conviction for drug-related offences confers a permanent or effectively permanent cessation of rights. Felons were no longer allowed to vote on release, banned from federal jobs such as postal worker or soldier, and excluded from the vast majority of American professions and public life.

All of this collectively caused immense damage not only to millions of individual Black Americans on an individual level, but to Black Americans collectively. Splashed in print and beamed across America's living rooms day after day was imagery of Black people, particularly Black men, as murderers, thieves and participants in a trade that was both illegal and directly contributing to the deterioration of American cities. Twenty-four-hour news contributed further, seeking content for its predominantly White audience that would thrill, titillate and terrify them.

All the weight of these oppressive systems, which tell Black Americans they are part of the freest and greatest nation on earth while repeatedly emphasizing that for a significant proportion of them such things are not for them, did not prevent a Black man becoming president in 2008. It was a phenomenon which would, just a few years earlier, have been thought outlandish, and yet by February 2009 a Black family was living in the White House. Barack Obama, a constitutional law professor turned senator, and the son of a Kenyan father and a White American mother, was ostensibly far removed from the reviled inhabitants of the American ghettos, well-educated and conspicuously eloquent, a figurehead of that Black middle class. Yet he, like his wife Michelle, lived in a majority-Black district of Chicago and had a long history of community engagement with deprived and struggling parts of his own city and country.

And yet even this, the election of a Black man to the highest office in the United States, did not make noticeable differences to the structural problems plaguing so many Black Americans. Distracted by ongoing wars in the Middle East and bitterly resisted by his political opponents, President Obama was stymied and hampered in all his efforts, and it has been noted by some commentators that the election of his successor Donald Trump, a man who enthusiastically endorsed and promulgated racist conspiracy theories about Obama's birthplace and eligibility for the presidency, was in no small part made possible by an upswell in racist animus to a Black president. Certainly, Trump devoted considerable effort to the destruction of Obama's legacy in the most insulting terms, while continuing to support and strengthen the racist systems which cause such targeted misery to America's Black population.

The oppression of the built environment – architectural

oppression might be a better term – is exemplified by the effect that civil planning, housing development and major road-building projects had already victimized suffering African American communities, operating within a series of social systems designed quite effectively to ensure that Black citizens knew their place in the American hierarchy and were punished for stepping beyond it. Though many White citizens operating in these systems knew and participated in the bigotry they enforced willingly, there were just as many who tolerated and took part in them not out of any animosity towards Black people as individuals or even en masse, but from an understanding that this was how society should be organized – that a structure which oppressed some for the benefit of the majority was one that benefited them and minimized the risk of violent disorder and disaster which might place them and their privileges in danger.

This is not by any means an American system alone. In every nation and amid every society there are those oppressed by the communal built environment – think of undeveloped favelas and shantytowns which stud the outskirts of so many cities, depositories for the poor from which they are not expected or intended to climb. Think of the homeless within your own cities, people lying in doorways and camping on roadsides. Individually we give to charity or directly to the people we see on the streets – perhaps we sometimes give them food rather than money so we can be convinced that our good deeds won't go towards drink or drugs or things which we do not approve of homeless people consuming.

But think more deeply on how the structures of our society allow people to live in these deplorable conditions, and the mind recoils. To live without walls or ceiling, to live without the promise of food or the means to get it. To live in such hopelessness and emptiness, or to be one of the hundreds of thousands of people in Britain alone only a single missed payday or sudden fine from finding themselves there too. In countries with a history of established and widespread racially based legal and physical segregation, such as South Africa or the United States, these physical divisions are still largely based on the race of the inhabitants; in others it's their class background which sees them hived off into communities with fewer resources and opportunities; and in others still it is our acquiescence in the inadequacy of our social safety nets which permits this state of affairs to continue.

Chapter Ten

GENDER OPPRESSION: WOMEN AS GHARBZADEGHI

I have a hesitancy in writing this chapter around the ancient and perhaps inherent oppression of gender. The debate over what constitutes a woman and what she is or isn't permitted to do has flared up again in recent years amid arguments over whether trans women, people born with male sexual characteristics who identify as female, should really be considered women or not by society at large. This situation, a modern rectification of historic European social restrictions which have insisted that the genders were inviolable and unchangeable, has led to heated argument over who can and cannot claim womanhood, particularly on social media, where every word spoken on the subject is examined, parsed and debated for content that becomes bewildering for those not aware of the specific meanings of terms in this context.

And yet, by shying away from the conversation, I would be

unable to directly tackle a prominent form of contemporary prejudice and on a broader note, examine why the arguments around trans women have been so heated, for which the inevitable answer is that in Europe and North America women have only very recently gained the most basic rights to describe themselves in most theatres of public life, and in many countries in the world they still do not have that right. It is no surprise therefore that arguments abound when meaningful, self-described womanhood is in social terms such a new phenomenon and still so unsettled.

Oppression of women by men, though not exactly a human constant, is widespread throughout the world, and has been throughout human history – Judeo-Christian theology teaches after all that the first man and woman were cast out of the garden of Eden, stripped of their innocence, because of the naive greed of Eve, the first woman, and women have been paying for this ever since. The core of the issue comes down, as always, to a cynical assessment of power – men are physically stronger than women and many men, far too many men, have and are willing to use that strength against them violently. Somewhere, far back in the earliest parts of human history, that physical power seems to have become entrenched almost everywhere in political, economic and social power, the maintenance of this order backed up by the ever-present threat of physical and psychological violence enacted by men against women.

The feminist author Laura Bates has written eloquently on this subject, noting that 'Men hurt women. It is a fact. It is an

epidemic. It is a public health catastrophe. It is normal.'* That
not all men participate in this epidemic is, beyond the individual
level, irrelevant – that some do it is enough to create sufficient
fear to colour all male/female relationships with the lurking
threat of violent oppression. There is an expression, commonly
attributed to Margaret Atwood, that in a dating scenario men
are afraid women will laugh at them (or in some misogynistic
iterations, be overweight), while women are afraid that men will
kill them.

And men do kill women with a hideous regularity. According
to the United Nations, 87,000 women were murdered worldwide
in 2019, with nearly two-thirds killed by members of their own
family – usually their husbands, brothers, sons or fathers.† That
is six women are killed by family every hour, 137 every day. Statistics for how many of the remaining 30,000 or so were killed by
men are not certain, but I think we can all acknowledge that the
number is terrifyingly high. Nearly 40,000 of these murders took
place in Asia and Africa, but it is by no means a problem confined
to these parts of the world. In the UK alone at least two women
are murdered by a man every week – that is significantly more
than a hundred since I started writing this book. And that is just
murder. In June 2020 it was revealed that rape convictions in the
UK had plummeted to new lows, with fewer than one in sixty

---

* Bates, Laura, 2020. *Men Who Hate Women.* Simon & Schuster, London, p. 181.
† UNODC, 2019. *Global Study on Homicide: Gender-Related Killing of Women
and Girls.* United Nations Office on Drugs and Crime, Vienna, Accessed online via
https://www.unodc.org/documents/data-and-analysis/gsh/Booklet_5.pdf

reported rapes going to court, and estimates suggesting that as many as two-thirds of rapes go unreported.* Bates has tied these statistics to a burgeoning 'manosphere', a culture on- and offline which normalizes, revels in and encourages a violent hatred of women and which justifies and drives some men to commit violence and sexual assault and relies on police apathy to survive and grow. The problems with addressing crimes against women in the UK alone – in the legal system and society at large – are clearly endemic and deeply ingrained in the institutions responsible for preventing these crimes from taking place.

Though this is undoubtedly horrifying, it perhaps shouldn't be surprising. This book has sought over and again to demonstrate that change is slow, incremental and often fraught with opposition and resistance. It is perhaps easy to forget on a day-to-day basis in supposedly modern Britain – which has had two female prime ministers, and a female head of state since 1952 – that within recent memory women in Europe or North America had quite literally only those rights the men in their life permitted them to have – the same men who could, and as the statistics show frequently did, kill or assault them. It is only in the last few generations that the right to full personhood for women, to have complete control over their own destinies, has been established.

---

* Barr, Caelinn & Topping, Alexandra. *Fewers than one in 60 rape cases lead to charge in England and Wales, Guardian*, 23 May 2021. Accessed online via https://www.theguardian.com/society/2021/may/23/fewer-than-one-in-60-cases-lead-to-charge-in-england-and-wales; BBC News, 2021. *Priti Patel and Robert Buckland 'deeply ashamed' of rape conviction rates*. CNN, 18 June 2021. Accessed online via https://www.bbc.co.uk/news/uk-politics-57511425

It is in many places barely four decades old, and often is still stymied and hampered in situation after situation by cultural and religious barriers. The debate about abortion rights in the United States, for example, is driven by religious groups that exclude women from their upper echelons and actively preach inequality of the sexes. These groups include men such as former Vice-President Mike Pence, who seek to enact controls over women's rights over their own bodies.

There are though many places on earth where even these closely bounded and hard-fought rights – the ones some women believe are under threat from the language around trans people – are alien and seemingly impossible. These are places in which the UN report identified women dying in vast numbers, places where the second-class status of women is not only culturally established, but enthusiastically enshrined in law. These places highlight very clearly for those of us in the freer and supposedly fully emancipated nations of Europe and North America that the battle for women's rights is so often between women and the establishments who permit them to be fully human within the limits imposed by – largely male – political bodies. To illustrate this situation, it's useful to look at a nation in which women's rights made an enormous retrograde step in recent decades, and where female individual personhood has only begun to emerge again as a significant political issue in recent years and remains subject to very strict controls: Iran.

In June 2009, as protests surged across Iran during the generally chaotic Iranian presidential election of that year, a young woman stepped out of a car on a Tehran street. Her name was Neda Agha-Soltan, she was twenty-six years old, and she embodied many of the contradictions of modern Iran. She was from a middle-class metropolitan family, well educated and intelligent. She'd studied philosophy but struggled in the male-dominated environment of the Islamic Azad University and dropped out. She had married young, fallen out with her husband over their interpretations of Islamic faith and its strictures on the role of women in Iranian society, and they divorced.

On 20 June 2009, she travelled to a protest in order that her voice be heard in the company of a friend, Hamid Panashi, dressed modestly in accordance with Iranian law and tradition. Stepping from her vehicle in the heat of late afternoon, Agha-Soltan stood observing the protests from the pavement when suddenly a single shot rang out. She collapsed before horrified onlookers, blood pouring from a wound in her chest. She died right there on the street, filmed, as George Floyd later was, on the cameraphones of bystanders. She was a woman killed by a man, a figure in a sea of statistics – but one remembered more widely than most, as her alleged killer, who is reported to have opened fire from a nearby rooftop, was a member of the Basij militia, a government-led paramilitary group attached to the Revolutionary Guards, the principal enforcement unit of the Iranian state.

The Basij are a powerful political faction in Iran, devoted to the preservation of their own power and that of the Iranian state which pays and arms them. Their purpose is to afford deniability to the more organized arms of Iranian state control, infiltrating and watching protests, armed but ununiformed. Their presence is intended to intimidate – shadowing unarmed protestors menacingly, theoretically there as auxiliaries of the police, but in reality tasked with the constant threat of violence and the role of breaking up protests through arbitrary arrests, provoking physical encounters and random violence such as, for example, the indiscriminate shooting of a young woman standing nearby. These are acts which force those wishing to protest against the state to think again before attending, lest they too take a bullet to the chest.

The alleged shooter was apprehended by the crowd but later released. No one involved was under any illusions that he would face even minor sanction for committing an act of violence on behalf of the state, whether under direct orders to do so, or, more likely, with the impunity to make whatever decision he chose, safe in the belief that any violence would go unpunished. State TV in Iran later accused Agha-Soltan of faking her own death. Meanwhile eyewitness accounts reported members of the Basij torturing and murdering abducted political protestors by burning them alive and driving over them with a truck.

Ten years later, when fresh protests broke out against the Iranian government, the Basij were there again, this time more ruthless and efficient, combat-trained and experienced from their large-scale volunteer service in the brutal Syrian Civil War, during which Iranian irregular forces joined the army of dictator Bashar al-Assad in conducting military operations and terror campaigns against his domestic opponents. After nine days the Basij were again able to crush the protest, arresting nearly 5,000 and killing twenty-eight in indiscriminate violence across the country, working in co-ordination with Iranian police and soldiers to eliminate resistance or dissent.* Agha-Soltan, the dead of 2019 and so many others have suffered and died so that a government which actively defines what constitutes a woman and what a woman may do within very restrictive parameters is preserved in power.

Iran is an ancient nation. Its precursor, the Persian Empire, fought Alexander the Great and battled the Roman Empire for centuries. In the nineteenth century, however, Persia became squeezed between the expanding European empires. Old friends and rivals disappeared, subsumed into the growing Russian Empire to the north, with the British advancing west from India. Sandwiched between these rivals and the crumbling edifice of the Ottomans to the west, Iran saw its borders shrink and its influence wane. As empires crashed into one another in the First World War, British, Russian and Ottoman armies criss-crossed northern Persia with little reference to the Persian government, radically destabilizing the patchwork of alliances which held the country's disparate minority groups together. In the Second World War, the British and Russians

---

* Amnesty International, 2020. *Iran: Details released of 304 deaths during protests six months after armed forces' killing spree.* 20 May 2020. Accessed online via https://www.amnesty.org/en/latest/news/2020/05/iran-details-released-of-304-deaths-during-protests-six-months-after-security-forces-killing-spree

went further, invading and capturing Persia (now known as Iran) to better exploit the independent nation's oil wealth during the conflict.

In the aftermath of this conflict the Allied armies withdrew, but their companies did not. Power was held by the Shah, Mohammad Reza Pahlavi, who governed Iran as a secular kleptocratic dictator from 1941 to 1979, maintained in post by British and American military and security support which ensured that threats to his authority and in particular to the dominance of British and American industrial and commercial concerns were swiftly eliminated. Most notably this occurred in 1953, when a modernizing and redistributive prime minister, Mohammad Mosaddegh, was overthrown by a CIA- and MI6-backed coup to prevent the loss of lucrative oil contracts. The shah then led an authoritarian crackdown which struck at both democratic opponents and advocates of traditional Iranian fundamentalist Islamic culture. It was during his reign, and in response to the brutality of his regime, that the notion of Gharbzadeghi became popular in Iran.

Developed in the 1940s and expanded in the 1960s by Jalal Al-e-Ahmad, Gharbzadeghi is a political philosophy which disdains Western culture as alien to Iran. It effectively classifies the commercial, secular and political structures of Europe and the Western world as akin to a disease or pollution which over time will corrupt Iran, destroy the structures which hold it together as a nation and lead to the enslavement of its people by the 'machines' of capitalist industry. To the shah, a devotee of opulence and client of Western oil companies, Gharbzadeghi was an intolerable threat to his authority.

At the same time as Gharbzadeghi was rising to prominence, and in response to it, the shah instituted the White Revolution, a top-down reorganization of the social and economic structures of Iran designed to modernize industry and strengthen the wealth and power of the shah and his supporters by forming alliances with sections of society capable of preserving the shah's power base. One of these groups were women, who were now freed from many social and religious restrictions, particularly among the urban middle classes.

Before the shah's father took power in 1925, women in Iran were largely restricted to a second-class status as chattels of their family or husband. Though women had rights, they were curtailed in accordance with social custom, family stricture and religious doctrine, a situation not unlike that in much of Europe of the time, the principal difference being the nature of the faith which asserted their inequality, rather than much greater freedom or autonomy.

During the White Revolution Iranian women, so long held in subservient positions and subject to widespread social control, were suddenly able to take educational and employment opportunities, to act how they wished and wear what they wished, or at least to do so on legally equal footing with men for the first time. It was by no means a complete overthrow of the patriarchy, but it was a substantial increase in the autonomy and political engagement of Iranian women.

By the 1960s and 1970s, middle-class metropolitan Iranian woman were able to access educational and professional opportunities similar to those of women in Western democracies. This was part of the shah's cultural alignment with those democracies who backed his autocratic regime, and part of his modernist approach, but it was also a pointed and deliberate snub to Islamic hardliners preaching a version of Islam that not only explicitly relegated women to permanent second-class status, but went so far as to strictly mandate what they were permitted to wear and with whom they were permitted to associate.

This was hardly an altruistic act in itself, because the White Revolution offered a conspicuous alternative to Garbzadeghi and the religious fundamentalism which accompanied it. The shah could brook no opposition, because his regime was thoroughly dedicated to the systematic looting of Iran, and he pursued his aggressive modernization campaign based on the secular economics and cultural mores of Europe and the United States because it directly enriched him, not for the people of Iran; his regime notably lacked the freedom of the press or representative democracy maintained in the West. He amassed hundreds of millions of dollars in personal wealth and controlled huge swathes of Iran as a personal fiefdom in addition to his political dominance. His secret police, the SAVAK, operated with impunity against enemies of the regime, employing torture and extrajudicial murder to intimidate and threaten those who would oppose or resist.

In 1979, the shah was driven from power in a revolution

launched by fundamentalist theocratic organizations, in the wake of an increasing cycle of violence between Iranian religious protestors and the shah's military forces. Large-scale protests – some violent, but not military or paramilitary in nature – were met with brutality and violence by state security forces who left hundreds dead. Vacillating and anxious, unwilling either to grant freedom or unleash his armies on the protestors, the shah wavered for too long, allowing the protests to gain momentum so that by the time he finally caved and began reforms to the security services, they were far too little, far too late. On 8 September 1978, responding incoherently, the shah's forces massacred protestors on Black Friday, even as his government accelerated reforms to end the protests.

The revolutionary leaders, driven by firebrand clergy, sensed the shah's weakness and pressed their advantage, leading to a general strike even as the religious groups, loosely led by Ayatollah Khomeini, formed an alliance with the secular opposition led by Mehdi Bazargan. Facing united opposition, and still unsure what action to take, the shah allowed the revolutionaries to organize, resulting in armed militias forming. The shah's forces began to lose control of whole areas of the country. Millions of Iranians joined street protests and in January 1979 the shah fled, taking vast amounts of cash and leaving the revolutionaries in charge of Iran.

In the power vacuum which he left behind, the alliance against him fractured and two rival governments sprang up, a liberal government under Bazargan and an Islamic government under

Khomeini. Undermined by internal divisions, military defections and a swell of popular support for Khomeini, the liberal government lasted just ten days. By mid-February Iran belonged to the Islamic fundamentalists and their Revolutionary Guard militia.

Over the next year the Islamic Republic of Iran launched a campaign of authoritarian terror, purging not only agents of the departed shah, but also their liberal and communist allies. A significant part of this process sought to reshape Iranian society by combining strict Islamic teaching with Gharbzadeghi. Women were progressively excluded from a range of professions, from educational institutions, and from many spheres of public life, and they rapidly became subject to a series of increasingly discriminatory laws. Women had been at the forefront of the revolution, Khomeini himself praised the women's organizers within his own group, but the system's authoritarianism, allied to the purge of Western influence, led to female autonomy and Western feminism being seen as imposed external aspects of the shah's regime. His effort to gain female support had rebounded on the women it was intended to benefit.

Most specifically, women were subject to laws about where they could and couldn't go, with whom they could associate, especially without supervision from male relatives, and what they could wear. The hijab became mandatory where once it had been uncommon, and restrictions were laid down on how and when women could assemble: leisure activities, such as sports, were entirely forbidden, and thus it was that Iranian women lost the opportunity to enter stadia. Though there have been ebbs and

flows in how strict Iranian laws on women are, and how rigor-
ously they have been enforced, women in Iran remain restricted
in all kinds of ways fundamental to their personhood. They are
not the property of their male relations, nor are they forbidden
education and employment, as is the case in other parts of the
Middle East, but where and how they can participate in these
opportunities is closely restricted and monitored. Their roles in
Iranian society are limited and constrained by systemic legal and
political oppression which deliberately relegates them to second-
class citizens in the name of religious teachings on feminine
modesty and decency. This prohibits women from many everyday
pursuits which we take for granted, such as publicly dancing or
singing, wearing whatever clothes they wish and attending sports
matches. Many of these restrictions apply to men too – in 2014
three young women and three young men were sentenced to
a year in prison and ninety-one lashes each for appearing in a
video dancing to the Pharrell Williams song 'Happy'* – but it is
women on whom they fall disproportionately, and who hold no
meaningful power in Iranian political structures.

In October 2019, an Iranian law was changed which allowed,
for the first time since the Revolution of 1979, Iranian women
to watch the national football team compete while seated in a
stadium. It was a relaxation of Gharbzadeghi which might seem
like a step towards greater freedom for Iranian women, and to

---

* BBC News, 2014. *Iran: Happy video dancers sentenced to 91 lashes and jail.* 19
September 2014. Accessed online via https://www.bbc.co.uk/news/world-middle-
east-29272732

indicate new opportunities, the kind desired by the protestors on the day Agha-Soltan was murdered. But this is probably not so, for this was not an organic development from within Iran, but an imposed law from without which was designed to satisfy not women, but men; the law was changed not through an overwhelming pressure within Iran by female sports fans demanding entry to stadia, although ever since the Revolution Iran has had a persistent women's movement which seeks to gently force change on the country's strictly misogynist governance. Instead the pressure came from outside, from FIFA and the Asian Football Federation, who threatened sanctions against the popular Iranian national team unless women were permitted entry to watch Iran's World Cup qualifying game against Cambodia in Tehran. Threats from a male-dominated, Swiss-based international sporting body and its regional equivalent to eliminate something predominantly important to Iran's male population resulted in a small change to the laws governing the control of women in Iran, granting them a modicum of extra freedom and equality, but only so long as it was convenient to men.

The legal change in itself means little, but it demonstrates quite strongly the cynicism and transactionalism of the laws governing what women can and cannot do in Iran, and indeed almost everywhere women are relegated below men by custom or law. While it suits the male rulers of Iran to impose, under threats of violence and in the guise of religion, a specific, restrictive way of life for Iranian woman, and while the regime acts at times to kill them with impunity as an example to other women not to publicly oppose the government, it is willing to toss these rules aside in the face of opposition from a supernational organizing body whose sanctions will create unpopularity and unrest among the Iranian male population.

Iran has not mellowed. Homosexuality is illegal and gay people are routinely persecuted and murdered without government response or interference. Teenagers can still be locked up and whipped for dancing to music. Iran has not become a liberal country because a few women are now allowed to sit in a stadium, and restrictions on personal freedoms still abound in a nation which hosts frequent elections but not for those – the religious leaders – who control the levers of power. All that has happened here is that women were granted a tiny portion of freedom to enable men to continue a male-dominated hobby without external threat.

The new law has provided Iranian women with some minor freedoms they previously lacked as a token in their cultural battles with the West, and clarifies mostly how certain freedoms can be issued or withdrawn at a government's whim. In the aftermath of the coronavirus pandemic, it is important for all of us to consider by whose consent and in what jeopardy we have our freedoms, and who benefits from their existence and disappearance, and who controls the levers of power by which those laws are made. We must be on our guard that the subjective oppression of lockdowns does not become the arbitrary objective oppression of a government determined to impose its will on how people think and feel and live.

Gharbzadeghi has oppressed the women of Iran by encasing them in a cultural system backed by political and legal structures, which has sought to use them as pawns in broader political games, fuelled by fundamentalist interpretations of an ancient religion which is itself being used as a political structure. Under the shah the freedom of women was ensured, even mandated, as a monarchist structure designed to solidify masculine power. Under the revolutionary government, this was stripped away for the same reasons. It is in this way that systems of oppression in Iran have led to the restriction of female opportunity for oppressive governmental ambition, and change is generally forced on the country from outside rather than developed from within.

I began this chapter discussing the debates, largely among women, about whether trans women should be allowed to claim and inhabit womanhood. As a man I appreciate that my opinions are not necessarily welcomed in this debate, and that any statement for or against either side will attract both approbation and reasoned argument. Nevertheless, I believe that ultimately self-expression is a freedom that is already denied to too many around the world, particularly women, and to deny it further to a group already struggling with so much intersectional oppression seems an unnecessary cruelty. Gatekeeping who can and cannot self-identify, especially if you do so out of fear of whether male predators might abuse the privilege to hurt women, is an unjust hardship inflicted on people born with more than their share of hardships already.

It is understandable too that the title of woman – the right to define yourself as a woman – is something precious and worth defending. Because to define oneself as a woman is to accept the reality that the world in which we all live was designed by men for men – that the struggles women have faced in the last century or so in Europe and North America aimed to achieve a parity which still seems far away at times and is nothing but a dream for women in much of the rest of the world. We imagine ourselves modern and enlightened. We imagine ourselves egalitarian and deny that we are sexist, and most of us strive to treat others equally, regardless of gender. And yet within the very systems of the workplace, the school and the societies in which we live, women often are forced to struggle against a history which insists on a position allotted or permitted by the men who still so often retain and jealously guard control.

Chapter Eleven

EDUCATIONAL OPPRESSION AND THE BRITISH ESTABLISHMENT

I went to private school. I grew up in leafy suburban Chiswick in West London, the son of an accountant and a teacher, and my parents were determined to give me as strong a start in life as they could. For many middle-class British kids that means, or at that time meant, where possible, private school. About 7 per cent of British children are educated at private schools, which run the gamut from the major boarding schools like Eton and Harrow, to a broader range of 'minor' public schools, to more modern bespoke and experimental schools. They are all expensive, with the average cost today running somewhere above £17,000 a year per pupil, though bursaries and scholarships are often available.

The school to which my parents sent me, a parochial single-sex environment, badly run, where bullying, racism and homophobia ran rampant and unchecked, made my every day a misery and I do not look back on it with fondness – and yet even in this environment the quality of education it provided gave me a foundation in life I would otherwise have struggled to achieve. It conspicuously and deliberately prepared me for university, for the world of white-collar employment, and laid the ground-work for networks which in certain professions are gateways to bright career prospects. I write this chapter acknowledging this privilege and the reality that I – always an indifferent student up to postgraduate level – may never have been in a position to write this book had I not had an educational leg up in early life denied to 93 per cent of my peers in an environment which, poorly run though it was, still taught its pupils relentlessly that they deserve and are expected to achieve success.

This chapter both is and isn't about education – it's mostly about social class, and doesn't focus too strongly on schooling or the school system, but it cannot escape the reality that the class system in Britain, and the Establishment with a capital E, rely almost totally on a two-tier school system which creates and perpetuates privilege right through British society. And it is this establishment, its control on the levers of power, and what this means for modern British citizens in the twentieth century which is the subject of this chapter.

There have been fifty-five prime ministers of Great Britain or the United Kingdom since the first, Robert Walpole, assumed the position in 1721. Walpole attended Eton College, one of the oldest and probably the most prominent private school in Britain. Since then, a further nineteen prime ministers are alumni of the school, another nine attended Harrow and most of the others were privately educated. Only nine attended state or church schools. These statistics perhaps sound shocking – that one school (and one small group of schools) should have produced so many leaders of the country. If you understand the intersection of class and education, they should not be.

For one thing, there has only been reliable non-private education in Britain for little over a century – certainly the type of education which could lead to eligibility for high office. For most of this country's modern history, access to education of almost any kind was a mark of privilege. My own grandfather on my mother's side was sent down the mines in South Yorkshire at the age of twelve. The very notion of any meaningful schooling was absurdly beyond the means of a working-class family of that time and place. The first non-privately educated prime minister didn't take office until 1916: David Lloyd George, who attended a Welsh church school, nearly 200 years after Robert Walpole's ascension as the first modern holder of the office. For most of modern British history, politics was a strictly reserved profession for those who could, by birth or wealth, buy their way into the Houses of Parliament or inherit a position there.

But even after that glass ceiling was broken, there have still been more privately educated prime ministers than state, by a considerable margin: after Lloyd George the next was Ramsay MacDonald, also the first Labour prime minister, who attended a church school until he was fifteen, before an unbroken string of privately educated prime ministers until Harold Wilson (also Labour), some thirty years later. Wilson was a grammar school pupil, as were his contemporaries Ted Heath (Con.), Jim Callaghan (Lab) and Margaret Thatcher (Con.). John Major (Con.), Gordon Brown (Lab.) and Theresa May (Con.) were all educated at comprehensive schools. Interspersed among these leaders were students of Rugby (Neville Chamberlain, Con.), Haileybury (Clement Attlee, Lab.), Fettes (Tony Blair, Lab.), two from Harrow (Stanley Baldwin and Winston Churchill, both Con.) and no fewer than five from Eton (Anthony Eden, Harold Macmillan, Alec Douglas-Home, David Cameron and Boris Johnson, all Con.).

The office of prime minister, by dint of its authority, is perhaps the starkest illustration of the power still reserved to pupils from the private sector, but in almost any elite arena of British public life (except perhaps the national football team), there will be a leavening of privately educated men and women out of all proportion to their numbers in the general population; across law, business, the arts and sciences, and indeed many sports, private school pupils do better, and the more prestigious the school, the better they seem to do.

The reasons seem perhaps obvious, and are not solely rooted in their education alone. They come from families who are on the whole wealthier and better connected; they have relatives and family friends able to give them a head start in their chosen field, and are far less likely to have their health and emotional wellbeing impacted by poverty and income insecurity. All of these things grant an advantage, and the state-educated children of wealthier parents also have significant advantages over their peers. But it is in private education that so many skills are nurtured and networks built which maintain membership of and access to the higher echelons of British society, and the opportunities and protections that it brings.

Not least of this is greater access to elite universities. Compared to secondary education, universities in the UK are somewhat more even-handed in that any child attaining good qualifications, no matter their schooling or parental wealth, can theoretically gain access in a way which is only occasionally possible within the private school system, where it requires a much greater element of luck to access far fewer places. Yet again, though, the advantage which the high quality and greater investment of the private schools grant to their pupils translates into advantage in university access, aided often by old boy networks and familial connections, as well as the simple training in how to apply and what is expected of an applicant – skills which are less readily available in schools with smaller university intakes.*

As a result, the proportion of private school pupils attending elite universities is once again out of all proportion to their numbers in the general population, and the effect is a further narrowing of access to the highest levels of British professional society. This narrowing has profound effects – principally that it

---

* Herrmann, Joshi. *Britain's best universities are dominated by private schools. Could I help level the playing field?* 10 October 2020. Accessed online via https://www.theguardian.com/education/2020/oct/10/britains-best-universities-are-dominated-by-private-schools-could-i-help-level-the-playing-field

limits the priorities and preoccupations of those in power. There are always those in both parties of middle- and working-class backgrounds, and both main parties are slowly but surely becoming more diverse in a reflection of modern British society, and yet it is that privileged axis through which the world view of British politics and law is set.

It is, and to an extent always has, been possible to climb these ranks. Indeed it is notable that unlike most other European countries, where the old feudal and post-feudal aristocracies fell in the eighteenth, nineteenth and twentieth centuries, often in murderous coups and civil wars, the British version has remained stable and retained, albeit quietly, much of its political power. Britain is led by an hereditary monarch with real, if carefully limited, political authority, and there are still ninety-two hereditary peers in the House of Lords, people granted a right to vote on and debate legislation based on nothing more than who their father (and still very specifically their father) was.

This is fairly astonishing in the abstract, and only unremarkable in Britain because it is better than the old system, abolished in 1999, which reserved hundreds of seats in the House of Lords for unelected aristocrats – a complex and largely unaccountable oligarchy which did its best to hold the country preserved rather than to advance its political or social interests. By contrast, the French slaughtered many of their aristocrats in 1793–4 and removed most of the remainder from power in a series of often violent political revolutions in the nineteenth century. The

Russians did likewise in their Revolution and Civil War between 1917 and 1921. Though Spain still has a king, it didn't for much of the twentieth century: the monarchy was replaced with a dictatorship which eroded the power of the aristocracy and church even as it lauded those institutions, and the German aristocracy was destroyed in blood and fire twice in three decades. Outside vestigial microstates, nowhere in Europe is such political weight still retained by so few, for so few.

The system survives, in part, by a willingness to admit new members, particularly those who bring wealth with them. Using the private school escalator and the universities, the upper echelons of British society absorb valuable parts of the middle classes – those ambitious and successful enough to connect with the networks their schools afford them to make money and in turn send their children to these same schools. This process has only accelerated since the demise of the grammar school system in the 1970s, which left private education – including funded places at private schools for less affluent pupils, which were on offer until 1997 – as the most effective means to secure university places and educational advantage.

Often mere attendance at the school, and in some cases not for very long, is sufficient to achieve the desired effect, an ability to convince others that you belong in this tier by virtue of educational association and the accompanying understanding of the mores and customs of the privately educated network. No one exemplifies this principle as effectively as the story of Brendan Bracken, latterly the Right Honourable Viscount Bracken.

Bracken was born in 1901 in Templemore, Tipperary, a tiny rural Irish town. His father, J.K. Bracken, was a local politician, sports administrator and professional builder with strong republican leanings. J.K. died when Bracken was just three, and the family relocated to Dublin, where young Brendan struggled to fit in and developed a reputation as a troublemaker. Sent away first to a Catholic boarding school, and then to Australia to live with a relation in the town of Echuca, Victoria, Brendan refused to settle, travelling the country, before returning to Ireland at age eighteen. Quite where he had picked up the notion isn't clear, but Brendan Bracken learned on his travels that the way to get ahead in British society – Ireland at the time was of course a part of the British state – was through private school.

Showing up unannounced at Sedbergh School, a three-century-old boarding school in Cumbria, Bracken spun a fantastical tale about his past as a young Australian boy orphaned in a bush fire, and called on an entirely fictitious relationship with the headmaster of Harrow to secure himself a place at the school in the coming year. In all honesty I think it is highly unlikely that this bizarre account was believed, but somehow through dint of persuasion and bare-faced lies, the adult Bracken did convince the headmaster William Nassau Weech to accept him as a fifteen-year-old pupil. Bracken was at the school for less than a year, but in that time developed all the skills and contacts he would need in later life, building a network of privileged access and the manners and language required to activate it in a remarkably short space of time. Based on nothing more than a quick tongue and a flair for invention, Bracken had seized a place, or at least the potential for a place, at the top table of British society.

He did not let it go to waste, exploiting school contacts to first become a teacher, then a successful magazine editor and then a political consultant, forming an attachment to Winston Churchill, already a political star. Advising and supporting Churchill in his efforts to regain a seat in the House of Commons, Bracken proved his loyalty when he took a knife wound in a street brawl following a political rally in Westminster, though Churchill lost that election by a mere forty-three votes. Having seen his boss restored to Parliament later that year, Bracken himself became an MP in 1929, at just twenty-eight years old. He remained an MP almost continuously for the next twenty-two years, and was a lifelong close friend and confidant of Churchill, as devoted to his boss as he was to relentlessly hiding his modest Irish origins.

When Churchill became prime minister at the height of the Second World War, Bracken was by his side and was elevated to minister of information, using his publishing expertise to direct government propaganda from Senate House, the looming headquarters of the University of London in Bloomsbury. An imperialist and capitalist, Bracken was a thoroughgoing Conservative who, in 1945, still an MP, took over and revitalized the *Financial Times* and operated it from Bracken House in central London, replete with a large clock featuring Churchill's face. In 1952 his war and political service was rewarded with the title of Viscount Bracken, and he died six years later of cancer, a very wealthy and firmly respected member of the British establishment. Late in life he was even appointed to the Board of Governors of Sedbergh School.*

The ability of a half-schooled Irish son of a widowed mother to rise to the top of British society and achieve important things in doing so, particularly during the Second World War, marks a rare achievement in its day and age. That Bracken was able to do so was in no small part due to the way in which he was able to access the old boy networks of Sedbergh, tapping into broader public school society in a way almost impossible without that experience. However, it was not just his attendance at the school which propelled him forwards, but also what he learned there: Bracken was able to move in British society by studying and practising the customs and foibles, the ethos and language of the public school-educated men who ran (and still run) the country.

There is a common joke, repeated whenever class encounters appear in literature or on screen, of outsiders not knowing which fork to use with which dish. It is a seemingly absurd issue – something as simple as a piece of cutlery should not be causing anxiety in any rational society. Yet it does, precisely because not knowing marks you out as someone improperly raised and schooled, someone who does not belong. By attending Sedbergh, by observing his fellow pupils and their behaviour,

---

* Lysaght, Charles & White, Trevor. *Churchill and the Irishman: The Unbelievable Life of Brendan Bracken*. The Little Museum of Dublin, p. 14.

Bracken, clearly possessed of a superlative understanding of human interactions, was able to learn what was necessary to disguise the fact that he did not belong, to convince others that he did, and thereby seize a slice of access and power for himself. It is a remarkable testament to the ability of a private school education to provide even a brief attendee with the veneer of class respectability.

The story of Brendan Bracken reveals something else, though, about the British establishment. Founded though it largely is on hereditary privilege, it has survived so long when so many of its European counterparts have fallen by its willingness to adapt not just to new members, but also new ideas. Even as the left wing of British politics has struggled generation after generation with the philosophical underpinning of its cause and organizations, the British right, manifested in the Conservative Party, whose very name exudes a desire to slow the pace of change, has adapted wildly to circumstances. While one half of the British political settlement has repeatedly deteriorated into a never-ending argument about core principles, the other has shown again and again that it is willing to adapt its principles as long as they lead to electoral victory and the broad maintenance of British social hierarchy.

When the Conservative leader of the opposition Margaret Thatcher saw disunity and dysfunction spreading through the Labour party in the late 1970s, she responded by tightening discipline on her own ranks and turning their full force on those she saw as disruptive elements in British society. The primary target of her ire were old Tory foes in the form of the trade union movement, but many others were swept up and targeted as socially undesirable, including homosexuals, immigrants, ethnic minorities and those with disabilities, all subject to oppression through aggressive policing, propaganda campaigns and the withdrawal of essential funding for public services. As Theresa May, later prime minister herself, noted when she served as shadow home secretary, the Conservatives gained a reputation during this period as 'the Nasty Party'.

And yet while this scattergun series of oppressive campaigns was likely heartfelt by many in the party, they were also cynical operations to scapegoat and attack those seen as responsible for the rapidly changing face of British society, allied to a media campaign through compliant press who victimized these groups for the same reasons. Small-scale persecutions of this kind were popular among the British public as long as economic prosperity was delivered simultaneously. And it was – for much of Thatcher's tenure the economy boomed and enough engaged voters were happy enough with the results to hand her three landslide election victories, making her one of the most popular prime ministers of the twentieth century where it really counted, at the ballot box.

Some fifteen years after Thatcher left office, the Conservatives were in opposition; politics was dominated by a Labour leader (and private school alumnus), Tony Blair, who had learned from Thatcher that in Britain victory was located on the centre of the political spectrum and had dragged Labour rightwards to meet it. Blair knew that popularity in this arena relied on sufficient individual prosperity among key demographics, principally the political alert middle classes. So the Conservatives and much of the establishment changed tack.

They had watched Labour in their turn, and a new Conservative Party was born from a leadership election which saw a wealthy Old Etonian, David Cameron, take the helm and promote a new conservatism, rooted in social justice and compassion while advocating, after a time, strident fiscal restraint. That these two things were largely antithetical to one another was irrelevant – by being seen to be compassionate the Conservatives could secure the vote from a fracturing Labour Party, and then enact whatever policies they wished. A hung parliament in the 2010 election afforded an even more effective smoke screen via a coalition with the Liberal Democrats, ushering in a wave of progressive social policies while Cameron and his chancellor, George Osborne, set about effectively demolishing a number of organs of state via a programme of severe austerity, ostensibly a response to the 2008 financial crash, but in reality an ideological rebalancing of the role of the state as a giant and poorly planned experiment.

The Conservatives had adapted, reading the mood of the country and responding accordingly, choosing to leave certain groups behind in their efforts to build a winning coalition of voters attracted by moderate and socially liberal policies and economic restraint which saw more people taking home more of their wages through tax cuts. It was not to last, though.

Enthused by victories in referenda on the voting system in 2011 and Scottish independence in 2014, Cameron was determined to use this tool to put to bed the Conservative Party's internal obsession, one which had riven the party for decades: the debate over membership of the European Union.

The outcome of this campaign is well known. Cameron gambled his own and the nation's futures on an outcome which would allow him to silence his critics on the right of the Conservative Party for a generation. He lost, and plunged the country into a division so severe that a Labour MP was murdered as a direct result, her killer shouting 'Britain first' as he shot and stabbed her, as convinced of his righteousness as Eric Rudolph (see chapter six) ever was. Having created this upheaval, Cameron then just resigned and walked away, literally singing to himself, leaving the stage for new Conservative leaders. And, in response, the Conservative Party changed once more, realigning with the voters who supported the Brexit campaign most vociferously. It took two changes of leader, an unsuccessful election and the possibly illegal proroguing of Parliament, but three and a half years later the Conservatives had swung, dramatically, remorselessly and rapidly from a centre-right liberal conservative position on social issues and immigration, to an increasingly hard right party, focused on the traditional fallbacks of such political movements: an increasingly empty populism, demonizing of immigrants and an authoritarian isolationist stance. When Boris Johnson, newly prime minister, was invited to tone down his rhetoric against fellow MPs from fear that extremists might attack them, he dismissed such concerns as 'humbug'.* The nasty party had returned with force.

These changes are, I believe, driven less by ideology, and more by a determination to preserve the privilege and power of the elites in British society, and to weaponize nationalism to that end. it has proved effective. In the run-up to the 2019 elections, new Johnson, an Old Etonian compatriot of David Cameron, systematically purged Conservative moderates such as Philip Hammond, chancellor under Theresa May, Sir Nicholas Soames, Churchill's grandson, and Kenneth Clarke, a minister under Thatcher and Major who first sat in Parliament when Johnson was just six years old. These moderates were stripped of the whip – effectively renounced by their parliamentary party for opposing the hard Brexit Johnson demanded and his increasingly outlandish efforts to force it through Parliament. Some were later restored after making suitable apologies; others, including Clarke, ended their parliamentary careers orphaned. Johnson was rewarded at the ensuing election with a hugely increased majority.

The about face in response to the public mood, from Cameron's modern centrist Conservatism to Johnson's rapidly advancing culture wars over immigration, education and foreign affairs, is indicative of the willingness of the British establishment, as embodied by the Conservative Party and well documented over recent centuries, to bend to the prevailing winds to harness

---

* Bates, Laura, 2020. *Men Who Hate Women*. Simon & Schuster, London, p. 218.

popular opinion and weather periodic public storms. The ability to do so is fostered in the private school background of so many, which inculcates an ambition to make an impression on the world, a depth of privilege worth preserving, and the education, networks and resources required to retain it.

Conclusion

AMERICAN CARNAGE

When I first wrote the outline for these chapters in early 2020, I was hopeful that we would see a watershed in the creeping oppression which has gradually emerged within democratic governments all over the world. This was perhaps more in hope than good judgement, with unabashed state control continuing in China, an established authoritarian kleptocracy in Russia, theocracy thriving in Iran and the privilege-defending and increasing populism of the British government ironically matched, even as Britain distances itself from them, by some of its European neighbours. But there was one place where there was an opportunity to start turning the tide.

I have already talked at some length about the inherent structural problems within the United States – its bloody history of genocide and cultural appropriation, the enduring legacy of the slave state and its ongoing oppression of citizens of colour, and the role of religious fundamentalism and the rise of politically driven violence. Yet there is something worth admiring in a nation which historically and traditionally takes such pride in its civic institutions and its national desire and dream to promote and provide equality for its citizens (however unsuccessfully this may turn out in practice). It has also long seemed a nation if not immune then at least protected from the bursts of authoritarianism and populism which have sparked such upheaval elsewhere in the two and a half centuries since it was founded. It is, in part at least, this security which permits the regular conceit that the United States is the greatest country on earth and thus an exceptional place to which the regular rules of diplomacy and discourse need not apply, a canard responsible for real suffering when taken as a justification for straightforward might justifying right, whether militarily or economically. It is an attitude often called American exceptionalism: that there is something so fundamentally different about the United States from other countries that it is immune to the dysfunction and violence of civil insurrection and responsible enough to set its own rules and agenda.

Though it was never really true in practice, this has been retained as a belief in many quarters to this day, but it's a rationale that nearly fell apart in practice in 2016. The inherent security of American institutions was exposed as crumbling in the face of the election of a man who held them not only in contempt, but also, astoundingly, in almost total ignorance. Donald Trump wasn't meant to be elected president. A TV personally known for crudity and public embarrassment, hailing from inherited wealth and with a personal record of unethical activity stretching back at least four decades, he seemed an unlikely choice. Polls and pundits said that he would be beaten (or at least many did – there were those sounding notes of caution), and it always seemed that the latest crude outburst would finish him off – whether it was mocking the disabled, picking fights with the parents of a deceased war hero, or ultimately being caught on camera boasting of sexual assault. It seemed to so many that Hillary Clinton, the veteran political operator he faced, would sweep to power, and yet at the 2017 inauguration it was Donald Trump, a repeatedly bankrupt corrupt property mogul, credibly accused rapist and serial liar, who took the oath and announced that he would bring about the end of what he called 'American Carnage'. His exact words were:

> Americans want great schools for their children, safe neighbour-
> hoods for their families, and good jobs for themselves. These are
> just and reasonable demands of righteous people and a right-
> eous public, but for too many of our citizens a different reality
> exists. Mothers and children trapped in poverty in our inner
> cities, rusted-out factories, scattered like tombstones across the
> landscape of our nation, an education system flush with cash,
> but which leaves our young and beautiful students deprived
> of all knowledge, and the crime, and the gangs, and the drugs
> that have stolen too many lives and robbed our country of so
> much unrealized potential. This American carnage stops right
> here and stops right now.

The solution for these problems, exaggerated as generalities but in places very real blights on American life, was described a few paragraphs later:

> We assembled here today are issuing a new decree to be heard in every city, in every foreign capital, and in every hall of power, from this day forward: a new vision will govern our land. From this day forward, it's going to be only America first, America first.*

Donald Trump's vision was clear. Using the 'America First' slogan first popularized by American fascist organizations in the 1930s, he was turning America inwards, away from allies and international organizations, and towards a protectionist and insular view of a great nation surrounded by untrustworthy allies and looming enemies. It was a paranoid and anxious vision of a nation not uneven but ambitious in hope, but in permanent, catastrophic decline, a decline only to be reversed by turning on enemies within and abroad, and mostly imagined.

Three and a half years after the American Carnage speech, Donald Trump stood clutching a Bible in a teargas-filled square as the American carnage he had wrought through incompetence, division and racial animus filled the streets of America's cities. The election of Donald Trump and its chaotic aftermath is the

---

* Politico. *Full text: 2017 Donald Trump inauguration speech transcript.* 1 January 2017. Accessed online at https://www.politico.com/story/2017/01/full-text-donald-trump-inauguration-speech-transcript-233907

perfect phenomenon for concluding this study of the ways in which systems of oppression develop, sustain themselves and draw whole nations into their web, whether in support or opposition, and through individual culpability in their perseverance and persecution. Crude and ungainly in its composition, the Trump presidency illustrates the ways in which creeping authoritarianism can invade even the strongest and longest-standing democracies. Trump's legacy continues to wreak havoc on American civic relations and institutions in a manner which makes it hard to see how an American recovery will even be possible – yet seventy-four million Americans looked at his divisive, destructive politics, and voted for four more years of it, a number that seems almost insurmountable when trying to reintroduce not only civility, but also maturity, into American politics and public life.

The election of Donald Trump in 2016 has fundamentally and probably permanently changed the United States. Not, or at least not just, because he pledged to 'drain the swamp' of corrupt interests in Washington, while simultaneously firmly entrenching them in every aspect of his administration, nor because he ran the first nakedly racist campaign and presidency since the early twentieth century, to the howling adoration of supporters at his rallies. Nor was it because he systematically and aggressively attacked American institutions, filling them with ignorant, nakedly criminal or brutally partisan followers, up to and including the placing of a credibly accused violent sexual offender on the supreme court.

Perhaps Trump's great change to the United States comes instead in that promise of the American Carnage speech: in what he has done to the US abroad, turning a sometimes overbearing but always staunch ally of key planks of modern pluralist society into a direct threat to democracies all over the world. Trump has coddled and fawningly praised dictators, even calling for their assistance against domestic opponents; he has defunded and attacked the international institutions which have held together peace since the end of the Second World War, and he has insulted and isolated key allies, even abandoning some, such as the Syrian Kurds, to destruction at the hands of authoritarian governments he favoured. Three days after Trump withdrew US troops from Kurdish territories in war-torn northern Syria in October 2019, Turkish troops crossed the border. Recep Tayyip Erdogan, the authoritarian president of Turkey, has a close relationship with Donald Trump, and was even allowed, during a state visit in May 2017, to order an attack on protestors in Washington which went entirely unpunished.

Most damningly of all, Trump unleashed this attack on America's allies and standing in the world under the blanket of thousands of lies, lies so deep and thick that he carelessly, recklessly and fundamentally changed the nature of truth in the Western world, introducing the idea not only that truth does not matter, but that information anywhere can no longer be trusted.

Such is the nature of American carnage. A nation richer and more successful than it has ever been is reshaped in imagination as a place of chaos and decay which can only be saved by the iron hand of an authoritarian and unchallenged leader. Since truth no longer matters, a man known for serial adultery, bankruptcy and corruption can be recast as a beacon of hope and idealism without ever changing anything about himself; the message itself alters to such a degree that what was once reprehensible is now laudable, and what would once have spelled political death is now popular. His enemies are no longer political opponents, but traitors for the sheer effrontery of refusing to acknowledge his greatness. It is in this situation that democracy dies, lost in a sea of lies. Voters believe what makes them feel better, unable any more to tell the difference between what is real and what is not and what will help them and what will not. They become lost, forced to react emotionally to what they can no longer logically determine.

When in early 2020 the coronavirus pandemic washed over the United States the country was woefully unprepared, fatally weakened by the political, ideological, religious, economic and racial divisions which had torn the country in half, and in particular by the total breakdown in trust between Americans and their elected government. Inadequate medical care, official disdain of expert advice, aggressive evangelical denialism, and corruption and incompetence at the apex of government cascading down into local municipalities left the United States exposed and vulnerable. The disaster that followed should have been avoidable but became inevitable in the face of a system of oppression which favoured carnage over restrictive, managed oppression to save lives. The cost will not just be the hundreds of thousands needlessly dead, nor the vast economic depression which Congress largely failed to mitigate; it risks also being the death of that flawed but hopeful American democracy and its replacement with something far more oppressive. When the Black Lives Matter protests began, the president cheered on the American carnage through the tear gas, as unidentified, heavily armed and armoured units patrolled Washington and other American cities.

The pattern which brought Trump to power and precipitated the disaster is being studied and copied, driven by ideological authoritarians across the political spectrum, who see it as an ideal process for driving through major social and political changes without mass support or even engagement. Even perhaps without realizing it, Donald Trump, a man possibly in the grip of dementia and widely acknowledged as suffering severe paranoid narcissism, fundamentally reshaped the world in oppressive and authoritarian ways during a grave international crisis that was hard to combat and harder to recover from. The message is stark. If America can become this then anywhere can, and though Trump lost the 2020 election, his legacy in American politics is poisonous and deep rooted. On 6 January, exhorted by the president and his media cheerleaders, Trump supporters stormed the Capitol, determined to disrupt the ceremonial transfer of power in the belief that they could force the retention of Trump's presidency amid a state of emergency. For the first time in American history the peaceful transfer of presidential power risked being broken. Five people were killed, including a police officer.

The attack on the Capitol was a watershed moment because it forced Americans, and particularly American politicians, to decide who and what ideology they supported – the violent illegitimacy of Donald Trump or the moderate consensus which recognized Joe Biden as the new president. But even as the Capitol still showed the scars of the insurrection, with offices and corridors shattered and smeared with the faeces of Donald Trump's supporters, nearly 150 Republican Congressmen and women sided with the attackers. Within weeks almost the entire party had followed them, determined to disperse blame and demand concessions from those who had been attacked. Efforts to establish bipartisan investigations into the causes of the attempted coup were stymied for lack of Republican support. All the while, Mitch McConnell, now Republican minority leader in the Senate, used the arcane magic of the filibuster to prevent the Democrats passing meaningful legislation to protect democracy from a repeat of the previous violence, even as ever more restrictive laws were passed in Republican-controlled states to limit access to the vote and introduce mechanisms to overturn unfavourable election results, just as Donald Trump had demanded in 2020.

While Donald Trump's election was an unexpected result which caused chaos at least as much through incompetence and negligence as it did through malevolence, his successors are and will be far more organized, driven by a desire to preserve the privilege of wealthy White Americans at the expense of others – just as the founding fathers for the most part practised, even if they did not preach it. America faces a perfect storm – just as Britain, its ally across the Atlantic, turns away from the world and diminishes. Crises, of race, of religion, of political expediency and populist ignorance are combining, their growth accelerated by the damage done by Trump's administration. Far from arresting and reversing so-called American carnage, the Trump administration hardly lifted a finger to help people, caused economic turbulence through his poorly planned America First policies, and opened the door to violent insurrection and authoritarian takeover. Where America has led, other liberal democracies are hastening to follow. Politicians are looking across the Atlantic at the successes of division, conflict and prejudice and experimenting with homegrown versions in their own countries. The legacy of American carnage has only just begun, and it promises to make life harder and angrier for millions more people.

This may well include you, directly or indirectly, in ways you may not be able to fathom, as the butterfly wingbeats of Washington politics or British club rooms fan out across the world. You may be insulated from most of it, able to continue living as you always have done, and if so you are not just lucky, you are privileged. Privilege is a term which makes people bridle – we do not like people to assume that it means that our lives haven't been hard or that we don't deserve the things we have.

But this is of course to misunderstand privilege. It is, for the most part, not about you, the reader of this book, who are more likely to have it. It is instead about those others who do suffer – those who, for personal, structural or unfortunate reasons, find things harder than you do. They deserve things as much as you do, as we all do, and yet they are denied them by the same social structures and networks which give them to you. And when institutions crumble, particularly political institutions designed (if not always successfully) to level privilege, huge numbers of people may suffer as a consequence. The field becomes unbalanced and people who thought themselves secure are at risk. We have all lived through just such an upheaval in the coronavirus pandemic, and witnessed first-hand just how fast privilege – in this case the privilege to meet your family, go to your workplace or participate in normal social life – can come undone. I hope that this alone, even if you were unaware previously, has opened your eyes to the reality of uncertainty and anxiety which the destabilization of privilege can bring. But perhaps not. So many have chosen to take the opposite perspective – to indulge in conspiracy theories and aggressive, selfish efforts to undermine international operations to bring the disease under control. So many saw their privilege not as a benefit to be appreciated and nurtured for others, but as an essential pillar of their identity to be protected at the expense of others.

This is the future of oppression, a world in which information and the processes of disseminating it become key only in that they can spread disinformation, create confusion, and make scapegoats for perceived injustices. In the process dividing, conquering and establishing a new order which may protect people from new Kings of Clipperton Island, but saps away at their other freedoms and certainties.

Understanding this is key to resisting it, to building awareness of the dangers of oppression and the maximization of freedoms which enable people to move, work, live and love how, where and in what way they choose. Vested interests have always abused these systems we build to protect ourselves from chaos, but it is up to us to decide to what degree we let them dictate and control our lives. This is the essence of oppression: to identify how much is healthy and how we as a society should moderate its effects while retaining its securities.

This book is therefore for people who want to understand their place in the world. Even if the specific examples here do not apply to you or your family or your nation, by following the case study accounts of how the modern world came to be the way it is, you can begin to get a sense of why things work the way they do, the histories which have led to them operating in this way, and acknowledge the myriad privileges and imbalances that contribute to global hierarchies of oppression.

For that is the nature of the oppressions I have described, the process whereby some groups attain exploitative advantage over others and abuse that advantage in ways reminiscent in some circumstances of the terrible King of Clipperton Island. Victoriano Álvarez was not a good man, and once authority was removed, he never pretended to be, violating the authority he had seized at the point of a gun to harm the other inhabitants of the island. Álvarez is thus a salient lesson in the type of threat that justice systems are designed to nullify, but as we've seen, his behaviour was only a small-scale version of the world in which he lived, a world in which global empires were free to act above or without the law, using their economic, legal and military systems to overwhelm and entrap other nations and peoples in the slavery of empire and the trap of debt and obligation. The Venezuelans of 1904, rich and poor, were mere cogs in this system. Some profited for a time, but most did not and a few were killed by the machinations of companies and governments thousands of miles away who cared nothing for them.

We in Europe and North America, none of whom were alive at the time of the bombardment of Fort San Carlos, and few of whom directly profited by descent in any way, share a collective responsibility for these actions because the institutions on which we rely – the governments and economic structures – did profit from them, did exploit them, and are built on these profits and still operate today. If we cannot acknowledge that – and under- stand the myriad ways that this book has illustrated collective culpability – then we cannot start to recognize our position as oppressors and the inheritors of oppressors. Growing up in systems which are or have been exploitative towards others does not make us bad people, but it does require a recognition of the harms done in our name, and that demands a reckoning with the realities of imperial history.

So it is with the Shuar, a people overwhelmed not by foreign armies but by the bow wave of capitalism, a force which assigns a value to everything on such a vast scale that there is almost nothing, up to and including human heads, which someone, somewhere won't buy. And when a market develops so does competition, and in an unregulated, unlegislated environment Clipperton Island rears its ugly head once more. Unregulated economic pressure destroyed the cohesion of the Shuar communities as surely as European armies or disease, demonstrating most clearly that sensible balancing of justice with freedom must require certain restrictions to apply. There are certain limits necessary to prevent entire communities turning in desperation not just to the hunting and selling of human heads, and to stop them building a society in which mass murder of that type was normalized not as ideology or prejudice, but as simple economics. These systems should not only apply within the narrow confines of our own borders, but recognize that harm deferred abroad is not less a harm than one at home. Such a reality is not as far-fetched as you might expect.

The Shuar are not, contrary to the opinion of Spanish explorers and rubber-tapping invaders, primitive savages. Their lives revolved around complex social and political structures centred on loving family bonds, and there was nothing in Shuar nature or culture which made them especially violent or murderous. Rather, the economic systems imposed upon them from outside, by empire and economics, created an environment in which thousands of Shuar men decided their only option for survival and prosperity was the mass murder of men, women and children; Shuar or non-Shuar, it didn't matter as long as they got the head. Thus it was that those long networks of trade stretched around the world. The seemingly harmless (if to modern eyes macabre) economic activity of buying curios and objects of horrified fascination made from human remains was in fact fuelling death and suffering on a grand scale among a people who had no concept of museums or Britain or ocean travel but what they heard at second or third hand, but who understood clearly that in a competitive, unregulated market you must do what it takes to win or you will die, for only the most ruthless will thrive on Clipperton Island.

As important as understanding the warping, destructive effect of European history, and the collective responsibility we bear for it, is to recognize that its legacies are not a forgotten ancient history which bears no effect on the world before us. They are current, active and devastating, and will inevitably continue to shape and warp the world for generations to come – the people of empire-building countries have not absolved ourselves as nations of the crimes committed in our collective names simply because we stopped committing the injustices. And we cannot hold up our hands and claim that we never personally owned a slave or never invaded another nation, because that is beside the point. Colston fell in Bristol not because he was a slave-owner, but because he was a slave-owner that Britain, as a nation, inexplicably chose to continue to celebrate in 2020. The ongoing harm to Britain of publicly lauding and commemorating such a man vastly outweighed any heritage or cultural value of the statue itself. And the harm was certainly to Britain collectively, not only to those descended from enslaved people or those for whom Colston's White supremacist ideology is a direct threat to their wellbeing, though they were understandably hurt by his presence. No, the harm was to Britain, a stain on our collective cultural memory, and one now deservedly erased, though many more still stand.

But erasure really isn't enough, for we have erased, in some cases quite literally, many of our colonial histories, considering countries such as Kenya or Uganda with a collective shrug, as if our presence there is something old and forgotten, not essential to the very shape and foundation of those nations. So buried are the histories of Britain's actions in these places, and so deep is the collective amnesia about them, that prominent political figures feel no shame in stating, in a public forum during the EU referendum in 2016, that 'The United Kingdom is one of the few countries in the European Union that does not need to bury its twentieth-century history.'* That figure was Liam Fox, then former defence secretary and later, during the reshuffle which followed the referendum, international trade secretary. Whether Fox was lying for political effect, truly ignorant of the history of twentieth-century Britain or feels that the violent execution of the campaign in Kenya and other countries was something of which to be justly proud is impossible to speculate.

But ignorance is perhaps not such a strange defence in this case – the British government systematically destroyed records of its campaigns of colonial violence in Malaya, Yemen and Kenya, as well as other places, specifically to prevent political opponents both within the former colonies and without from gaining access

---

* https://twitter.com/liamfox/status/705674061016387584?lang=en

312

to the records and revealing the truth of what was done in the name of controlling former colonies at one remove.* We are not bad people for not knowing, but to know and seek to ignore or downplay or excuse violence – murder, rape, terrorism and the systematic and racist bias in governance which allowed these crimes to thrive – or to turn away and pretend that these things done by the British government on behalf of the British people within living memory are nothing to do with us is to indulge in those racist hierarchies which led to this violence in the first place. It implies the suffering of non-White people at the hands of White authority is somehow a lesser crime, a natural phenomenon or can be justified by reasoning. If we accept that then we cheapen the notions of justice, fairness and honesty on which our nations are supposed to have been built.

We can choose to ignore these things in part because it's often what our neighbours, friends and families do. It is easier to ignore things which seem abstract and far away if noticing them is uncommon and popular – with the right encouragement and sufficient threat of violence, almost anything can seem reasonable. Which brings us to China and the Kill the Sparrows campaign. One might of course study it as a sort of mass psychosis or exceptional event, but it wasn't really. The people on the ground doing it knew it was stupid, they knew the risks, and they knew that not to do it meant that they might face punishment – even

---

* Cobain, Ian, Bowcott, Owen and Norton-Taylor, Richard. "Britain destroyed records of colonial crimes". *Guardian*, 18 April 2012. Accessed at https://www. theguardian.com/uk/2012/apr/18/britain-destroyed-records-colonialcrimes

a death sentence administered at gunpoint by their own friends and relatives. Better to turn that frustration and anger at the unfairness of the situation outwards against harmless little birds rather than potentially suffer the same fate.

The massacre of the Chinese sparrows and the human disaster for which it was partially responsible are a good example of what happens when an oppressive regime takes hold and attempts not only to foster power for themselves but also to sow as much confusion and chaos among their opponents as possible, and populations are faced with acquiescence or violent anarchy and choose the former. Mao's mission wasn't really to kill sparrows, it was to unify the Chinese people in a community-organized campaign around the newly formed farm collectives, foster a community spirit based on hatred and violence, disguise the failing impact of the new and unsuccessful farming techniques, and ultimately to sever the links with the past that he believed were holding China back from greatness. Manipulating the structures of a communist system which inherently lacks a process of meaningful checks and balances, Mao was able to create a devoted cult of personality even as he both deliberately and carelessly authorized the deaths of millions, perhaps tens of millions.

There was probably nothing those millions of Chinese peasants could have done to avoid the disaster coming for them – certainly not individually, and perhaps not collectively. They were out-organized and faced oppression on an industrial scale for minor infractions, let alone outright disobedience. That in itself is a harrowing lesson which we in modern Europe or the United States might struggle to acknowledge – that there are oppressions so great and so corrosive that there is nothing that can be done but endure them and try to survive as best you can – a Clipperton Island with tens of millions of people on it living in fear. We don't on the whole like to think about death or disaster, and when we do we rarely imagine that, caught up in one, we would be powerless to prevent it from destroying us, still less that we might find ourselves resorting to violence and cruelty to others in the name of survival. The starving Chinese farmers likely thought the same for the most part, and yet they died anyway, and the generation which followed them was more prepared than ever to ensure that it was others and not themselves who were destroyed in the ensuing Cultural Revolution.

But there is also a lesson here in vigilance. It is critical to be aware of the world around us and to try to live our lives with an awareness of the importance of the historical movements which sweep people up. To live within or alert to oppression is to take the time to assess the information in front of your eyes and draw conclusions about what is truth and what is truly motivating the people advising and informing you. The peasants could surely see that the new farming techniques and sparrow ecocide were harming their crops and risking famine. They just had no means of avoiding the impending calamity, as the state had progressively stripped away their systems of adaptation and survival.

Hundreds of millions of people all over the world live in systems which deny them the opportunity to escape such conditions. They lack the freedom of movement, or freedom to associate with and where they want, and to choose what kind of news they consume and from whom it comes. This is part of the manner in which oppression on that kind of scale operates – it denudes your ability to think for yourself, to act for yourself and to survive through your own ambitions and resources. It was this assurance we gave up more or less willingly during the COVID-19 pandemic, and it was this feeling of helplessness, that the tools of survival were being taken away, which in part prompted such angry responses from so many affected by it. Twenty-first-century Britain is not mid-twentieth-century China, and the freedoms we gave up were relinquished to save us and have been mostly returned, but the notion of individual survival was exploded. We had to work together as a nation and more broadly as a species to try to halt the spread of the disease, and thus it is that as peoples we live or die together.

Thus it was too for the Native American inhabitants of North America as colonialism swept over them in the seventeenth, eighteenth and nineteenth centuries. They were crushed one by one, their communities, united or otherwise, swept aside by the westward march of settlement, disease, almost continual betrayal by government decree and ultimately the murderous actions of the US Army. But their degradation did not end there. It was not enough that they were defeated and seen to be defeated, but that defeat had to become not just inevitable, but just and right and a matter of pride and celebration. Thus began one of the greatest and most sustained propaganda campaigns in human history, the Western. This one genre dominated decades of the greatest and most effective mass communication revolution in human history. Where film and television flourished, it was the Western that flourished with them, and intruded into the lives and homes of people worldwide. And the stories the Westerns told were of White heroes like John Wayne, crack shots with a rifle capable of knocking down dozens of 'Indians' while sitting on the top of a rattling stagecoach, or the dark and nefarious nature of the 'Indian' coming through via betrayal, backstabbing and the threat of sexual violence to innocent White women.

But what to expect from 'savages' who wore warpaint and feathered bonnets, what to imagine from those who are so different to be almost unimaginable? And so it was that the Native Americans on screen were not played by Native Americans, as they had been even under the watchful eye of the first such showman, Buffalo Bill. Instead they were White men, or Mexicans, or indeed anyone who could be relied upon not to point out the glaring inconsistencies, or comment on the brutality of the racism on display. And thus over time Native American culture became simultaneously a thing of the past, an historical relic to be parodied and appropriated; a savage and threatening monstrosity lurking at the limits of (White) American hegemony, and thus perfect as an allegory for communism or whatever was exercising people's anxieties at the time; and finally a joke, a punchline about being stupid, out of date, obsolete and imprisoned and locked away and turned into part of the founding myth of the nation which had deliberately destroyed them.

And so representation matters, stereotype matters. Think about what it is you see when other races or other peoples are portrayed on screen. Try to work out whether it is realistic, whether effort has been made to really tell other peoples' stories, and most importantly whether the people involved have been consulted or have any creative control. Who is telling this story, and their ambitions in doing so, become very important considerations, and never less so than when the subject is marginalized and invaded peoples.

There is no initial shame in ignorance or lack of awareness, in not knowing a thing is false or cruel. But if the means to learn are at your fingertips, if the people insulted or abused tell you that your ignorance, and the ignorance of others like you, causes them suffering and you do nothing to examine your behaviour, nothing to adjust to match their hopes and expectations, if you resort to defensive anger in an effort to maintain your prejudiced status quo out of fear that you will suffer or be expected to pay – then in that circumstance there is great shame indeed. Sometimes the things we cherish, or the world we know can be cruel, are rooted in violence, corruption and oppression. We must have nothing that cannot be re-examined, explored for hurts past and new and addressed and adapted and if necessary abandoned in the face of new, more inclusive and supportive understandings.

Much is said these days of cancel culture, the idea that something harmful or dishonest must be eliminated so its voice or image can no longer spread pain. Yet that term does not adequately explain the reckoning that is taking place and must continue to take place. Cancel culture does not say that people may not speak, images may never be seen; rather, it insists that when those words are spoken, or those images portrayed, there are other voices explaining that there are entirely different worlds living in other viewpoints, worlds that demand an understanding that, for example, what happened in the American West was nothing less than a genocide which remains unaccounted and unacknowledged, and will and probably can never be put right. And that the films which portray the noble myth of American heroism in the face of savagery, the Great Sioux Massacres and their counterparts, are as much a part of that genocide as the murders along the Wounded Knee Creek. There is no need to 'cancel' Westerns, as long as these basic parts of its history are properly understood. Truth and conversation, proper acknowledgement, mitigation and ultimately repatriation are the only routes to a mature reckoning with the ongoing harm of these histories.

The police are employed to enforce laws, and pursue those who refuse to follow them. Their role is to enforce limited and accountable government oppression for the major benefit of the majority of the law-abiding population. Sometimes these laws are unjust, and often they are unevenly applied, but the police's job remains the same, to enforce those laws, and we as a population accept this role – the ability and even the responsibility to enforce state-sanctioned violence and restraint on those who do not conform to our collective understanding of justice. And it is justice that this book considers – how we define justice, and what happens when a particular group, usually singled out for their race or religion or economic circumstances, always a disenfranchised one, is no longer afforded the respect and protection of the law. In such cases the police lose legitimacy, their authority is squandered, and violence becomes their remaining resort.

This is why Samuel Devenny died – because the RUC and their Loyalist allies in Derry were not interested in keeping the peace or enforcing the law, but in instilling in the Catholic population a fear that simply being near a protest was enough to incite extraordinary and extreme violence. The response was so outlandish and savage that ordinary citizens would shrink from attending protests or complaining of violations of their rights; their spouses or parents or children would warn them to stay away, to keep quiet, lest men with batons enter their house and kick and beat them to death. The sheer indiscriminate nature of the violence was the point – Devenny did nothing to draw it onto his family other than to be a Catholic in a Catholic neighbourhood, and could have done nothing to avoid it except perhaps to hide inside with the doors locked and curtains drawn when he saw police uniforms in the street. It was part of a campaign designed to terrorize the Catholic population and preserve the prejudiced status quo of Northern Ireland in favour of the Protestant majority who controlled all the levers of power. To take such an action in a nation with a history of violent armed uprisings can really only be seen as provocation and incitement to war. To such a crisis there are no easy solutions, but the American civil rights movement, and its modern descendants in the Black Lives Matter movement, have shown that peaceful protest, non-violent resistance and political, cultural and social change are capable of effecting changes in approach, albeit incremental and always vulnerable.

This was also the case following the murder of George Floyd, as it was determined a year later by a jury: it was a similar, if less focused, act of brutality on a minority community. Though it lacked the religious and ostensible party-political nuance of the murder of Devenny, it was nonetheless an act of extreme violence intended to subdue not just one man, but the entire community from which he came. The routine nature of the killings of Black citizens by law enforcement officers in the United States in these non-violent circumstances speaks to institutions who have lost all respect for Black lives, if they ever had it, and thus truly earn the opprobrium of those insisting that Black Lives should Matter. To Derek Chauvin, kneeling on the neck of an unarmed man accused of a petty crime as onlookers begged him to stop, Floyd was not a man but a representative of a problem community who had to witness what it meant to cross the Minneapolis Police Department. This message was one echoed right across the United States in the days and weeks to come, as police departments in cities and towns took deliberate, public and conspicuously violent action to intimidate and brutalize those calling for accountability in police action and acknowledgement of severe bias in policing – these people too, of all races but with a significant proportion of their make-up African American, had to be shown that to peacefully and legally stand up to police authority was to risk a beating or worse.

What I hope you will take from these encounters is the simple realization – obvious to people from certain communities and yet largely unknown to people from others – that the police forces in democracies are inherently oppressive by design. Their literal purpose is to oppress criminals, but the decision about what constitutes crime relies entirely on the institution policing it. If the police decide that certain speech is a crime or even a person's presence in proximity to that speech, or still a person's religion or skin colour in what they deem to be the wrong place or time, they can take violent action to quell it and, as in the case of the murder of Samuel Devenny and of so many Black men and women in the United States, they can evade responsibility for their actions and continue to perpetrate oppression through the generations. It is only by forcing, through whatever means are available, the democratic impetus to address police brutality that it can start to be addressed, violent actions can start to be punished with the severity they deserve and slowly, slowly, cultures can start to change.

Official and legal structures are not the only ones that have been changing and adapting in recent years. Organized religion is changing as well, to fit within the new nationalisms which are springing up. I focused on the rise of anti-abortion evangelism in the United States, and the way in which a relatively niche debate on the precise point during pregnancy at which life begins, according to church doctrines, has collided with public health and women's rights to create a political dispute which has led to murder and terrorism, all tied to a devoted ambition to create a nation supposedly perfect under God.

Anti-abortion activism is generally couched in language that deplores the violence, but understands the motive, and can and increasingly has been extrapolated to all sorts of other areas of American life – such that Republican identity politics is not only explicitly pro-life and anti-choice to the degree that judges are often chosen on this criterion alone, regardless of competence, but also anti other things this constituency can be relied upon to hate. This list includes but is not limited to immigrants, ethnic minorities, political leftists and those who would place limits on the right to own and operate heavy weaponry in domestic settings. These overlapping groups, loudly supported by major media infrastructures, build walls around certain issues and come to believe that others beyond these walls are not only wrong, but anti-American and therefore corrupt and dangerous. It is in this breeding ground that Rudolph emerged.

This is by no means an American phenomenon alone, though it manifests in the United States in a particular way not always copied elsewhere. In every country there are extremists within groups who hold specific issues so dear that they cannot conceive that fellow citizens might feel differently, and consequently come to believe that those citizens do not deserve the privilege of citizenship, or, often, of life. Such was the case during the Brexit campaign in Britain, for example, when an obsessed Brexiteer and racist murdered a politician supporting Remain while screaming racist slogans, or in the tragic horror of the 22 July 2011 attacks in Norway when a man killed seventy-seven of his fellow citizens as a protest against what he saw as the corruption of Norway by foreigners, particularly Muslims, choosing to live there. Such people are by nature maladjusted and incapable of living normally in society, but that does not make them mad – they are following the cold logic of prejudice and division, drawing on domestic and international networks which legitimize these extremist views for long-term political gain.

As responsible citizens it is the duty of all of us to recognize that the people around us, even when we disagree vehemently with them on basic and fundamental subjects, are people just like us, with loves and hopes and dreams just like us, and that our disagreement does not and should not invalidate their personhood and the rights and freedoms that that conveys. We do not have to agree with such people or respect their views – some views are cruel and exploitative and do not deserve respect – but we have to recognize their right to be held or the entire system will start to crumble, and violence will be legitimized based on religious belief or private conviction or political affiliation. Once this has become normalized in society, it is a mere matter of time before it appears in legislation, and the basic foundations of democracy and liberty are rent asunder. Those days are, in many countries, becoming uncomfortably close, or have already arrived. This does not mean that such violent views should ever be allowed to pass unchallenged or accepted. Those who aspire to a better, more cohesive world must stand up for their beliefs with as much peaceful intensity as our opponents, and speak to the majorities out there who deplore violence and hatred.

Earlier in this book I looked at this idea in relation to one of the most historically oppressed groups in American history, at how divisive and explicitly racist laws and social practices have combined to create conditions actually designed to keep large numbers of young Black Americans in circumstances of poverty, crime and incarceration, and at risk of violence not just from police, but from one another. Slavery is often called the original sin of the American nation, a brutal, degrading practice rooted in its very founding constitution, though the genocide of Native American sits alongside. Comparisons between these two monumentally cruel institutions are pointless and unhelpful, but while Native Americans were pushed to the margins of American society and driven towards extermination, African Americans were brought across the ocean in vast numbers and then kept in close proximity – not close enough to actually live side by side in anything approaching equality, but close enough that even after the end of slavery the exploitation of Black Americans was a fundamental part of much of American business and society, particularly in the old slave states of the South.

The result was a division which pushed a significant proportion of the American population into a trap of poverty, crime and violence which wrecked community relations and further generated a national obsession with the racist notion of the supposed inherent violence and criminality of African Americans. The lesson is that when considering why certain populations live in specific circumstances, are stereotyped in certain ways or have customs which seem alien or even threatening, there is always an explanation rooted in the historical circumstances in which that community was formed, and that by examining the institutions within which the community has been shaped, we can learn the circumstances through which these conditions have come about and understand that for many people the very streets they walk are a form of oppression, built up around them to limit their options and hold them in place. It is our responsibility to understand the ways that infrastructure – political, legal and physical – can act as an oppressive force on certain populations, and then hold those populations in place and in poverty for the convenience or carelessness of others. Instead of engaging in lazy stereotypes and casual dismissals of the hardships of others, remember that historical movements have conspired, as in the American city, to force entire populations into difficult and dangerous situations along racial lines, and that the lives of these people matter too – forget that, ignore it or dismiss it, and you oppress them as effectively and deliberately as those who would exploit them.

And we come then to the oldest oppression of all, that of women by men, an oppression so deep and abiding that it is rooted in the human origin story for many of the world's religions, demanding that women accept collective blame for introducing sin to humankind through their supposedly gentle trusting naivety, which requires both correction and guidance from the stronger men. It is a foundation taken very seriously in many countries in which these religions have a strong and constitutional role in the development and enforcement of laws.

Women have to fight for space; they have had to claw holes in the institutions established by societies which have for centuries valued male expertise over female for no greater reason than the possession of a penis. It is still going on, and even in Europe and the United States there are still many spaces where women can only tread with an apprehension of violence and discrimination, walking hallways designed for men and still often unsympathetic to those barred for so long. The situation is much worse in a society governed in an explicitly misogynistic manner, one in which the roles for women are defined and designed by a literal priesthood of men from which women have always been explicitly excluded.

The result in Iran is the battle between modernization and Garbzadeghi, in which the theocratic authorities seek to oppress women as a form of protection by encasing them in layers of tradition, religious threats, social condemnation and legal requirement that deliberately stifles individuality and independence except in ways which reinforce male domination and, effectively, ownership. Here is a timely reminder that for all the freedoms we hotly debate in Britain or the United States and for all the performative mask refusal and vaccine refusal we've seen over the last couple of years, the right to do and say these things in defiance of government policy is actually quite rare in the wider world. Billions live in nations in which claims of freedom are met with police brutality and legal sanction. Indeed, as the chapter on the police showed, there are plenty of subsets in European countries and North America for whom that kind of freedom is already limited and subject to oppression. But this is nothing compared with those nations in which stepping out of line in ways we generally think of as simple and non-controversial – dancing to a popular song, for example, or joining a mass peaceful protest, might have violent, life-changing or even fatal consequences, and never more so than if you are a woman.

It is also an effort to explain that many of the victories women justly celebrate the struggles to gain are made not by reforming misogynistic institutions, but by simply shuffling them aside to make room for women within the existing structure. This fails, or perhaps refuses, to address the fundamental chauvinism with which the system is constructed. This is how you end up with gender pay gaps, with unfair promotion opportunities and the massive gaping disparity between maternity and paternity leave and the effect that these disparities have on future career prospects.

There is little that can be done to change the situation for women in Iran or elsewhere from the comfortable confines of British or American suburbia – the Iranian government will brook no interference on a subject like this, and certainly not from long-standing enemies. There are very limited options for Western governments to have an effect, though supporting refugees and immigrants seeking a more equitable life seems a valuable contribution as a minimum. But we all owe it to ourselves and each other to understand how these systems were created, the way that sexist institutions in our countries have still only at best adapted, not – for the most part – substantially reformed themselves, and that the deep-seated structural imbalances often remain and play out in subtle but devastating ways. Women and men need to understand it, and men in particular need to learn to recognize when they are profiting from systems which oppress women (or actively engaging in them) and which keep women from competing on a level playing field. In such circumstances it is incumbent on all of us to work to make the changes necessary for a more mutually supportive, coherent and fairer life.

Key to this is the idea that these Western nations are places without oppression – that people are free to say what they like, live how they like, and vote in accordance with their wishes. Laws are, in principle, constructed to place comparatively few legal restrictions on activity and association, and police and security monitoring is, in theory if not always in practice, dedicated to the pursuit of serious crime, rather than social or political crimes. As previous chapters have shown, this has not always been true, and remains inaccurate for many – particularly those in ethnic minorities.

As we have seen through the prism of education, if you scratch the surface of these nations you will find inbuilt structural oppressions which define the country, and dictate how it will operate. In Britain in the twenty-first century this manifests as class privilege conferred through education and in no small part funded by hereditary wealth. The rich and well connected in Britain are thus able to wall themselves off from less wealthy and less well-connected people and secure advancement and promotion via the contacts, skills and modes of behaviour which enable them to reach the highest levels of government, business and society, preserving and bequeathing wealth and education in turn.

In the United States there is also a conservative status quo determined to maintain itself for its own profit, and education there plays an important part too, but much more significant there is the raw power of money, and the control of government for relatively small sums by a body of billionaire oligarchs determined to untether themselves from the oversight, administration and legal niceties of the federal government. It is a project which has been largely successful, supported by a cheerleading media infrastructure, highly organized grassroots political structures and oceans of campaign money now elevated to the same status as speech by a compliant Supreme Court. Underlying it all is a fervent opposition to immigrants, minorities and even (or perhaps especially) the poor, who can be relied upon, year on year, to vote for them.

The final lessons of this book are relatively simple – you are not a bad person. You do not, on the whole, seek to do bad things; and neither for the most part did your ancestors, whether they participated in colonial systems or fought against them. Some were bad, some were desperate and many were convinced by deliberate propaganda campaigns, lasting generations, that what they did was the right thing. For the most part this question is academic anyway. They are dead, and there is no reason their personal sins should be imposed onto their children or grandchildren like a sort of hereditary curse. Far more important is that we interrogate the systemic and institutional causes of these past horrors – the capitalist and imperialist mindsets that structured the world and whose legacies remain strong and for which we can contemplate restitution or recompense. It is only by acknowledging and confronting these histories, not hiding from them or pretending that they do not matter, that we as a society can mature and progress and begin to mitigate the lasting harm that they caused.

We all bear an individual responsibility to understand how these movements have shaped the world around us, and to look closely at the institutions which individually and collectively rely upon that history for their prosperity and longevity, starting of course with governments themselves. This is not a clarion call for reparations, though recompense of some sort must inevitably be part of a mitigation process, because reparations assumes that by paying off survivors and their descendants you can assuage yourself of the guilt for these past collective crimes. You cannot. These terrible things were done in the names of our ancestors, and the harm they have caused has trickled down the generations right across the world. That harm is active, it is real and though it can be mitigated, it is itself a critical part of the national make-up. It cannot be bought off or waved away; it can only, finally and tragically, be confronted, accepted and understood. In understanding it, we have to understand the difference between subjective oppression, our own personal emotional responses to circumstances, and the objective oppression of systems, cultures and societies imposed upon us by decree, and learn to question the justice that objective oppression enacts.

Only then can we have mature discussions about culpability, about institutional toxicity, and about the most fundamental basics of how racism and sexism operate in structural ways in society, and how oppression is enacted and inflicted within our own communities. We have, by and large, accepted the oppression of COVID-19 lockdowns and masks as a public health necessity for a limited period. We have though also accepted as a society, over a far longer period and seemingly permanently, that some groups among us must suffer for the benefit of the majority. We do not put it in those terms, and such feelings are of course far from universal, but that is the bargain we have made to keep the Kings of Clipperton Island, literal and metaphorical, from our door.

So educate yourself on the ways in which democracy and freedom can die. Educate yourself on the corrosive histories of our cherished institutions and start to question how they came to be and whether they should continue in the same formats once their harm is exposed. Educate yourself about lies – institutional, governmental and personal – and learn to oppose them, to organize against them and to demand the truth as your right. Educate yourself about the suffering elsewhere in the world, and that beyond our own limited areas of freedom there are billions with fewer options and greater risks than we face. And use that education to do better, in your everyday lives among your fellow citizens, and, over the longer term, in how you approach institutions and institutional change. Always be listening to others, and heed those with experiences different from yours. Change your life where you find that guilt or compassion crimp at the edges and question why that is so. And don't look away. Don't say it is none of your business or not your problem. It is, and it always has been. Don't look away.

ACKNOWLEDGEMENTS

This book would not be happening without the dedicated support and advice at every stage of my agent, Nelle Andrew, and her colleagues at RML. If a book is a collaboration, and they always are, she has been my chief and most important collaborator.

Likewise, I owe an enormous debt of gratitude to Katy Follain and her team at Quercus, whose professional dedication has been a huge privilege to experience. Working with people of their calibre means that writing a book is not such a lonely experience after all.

I also want to thank more broadly the scholars, activists and researchers who have worked on all the subjects discussed in this book – their work over decades on decades is what builds a historical record, the legacy which allows us as humans to, hopefully, learn from our mistakes. I hope I have done justice to that legacy.

Finally, and most personally, I would like thank my friends, my colleagues, my family and all the vital relationships that have shaped my life and viewpoints and hopefully enabled me to see the world empathetically. And to my wife and son, who make all of this work very real and worthwhile everyday, this is for you.